'Joseph Aguayo has emerged in recent years as [...]
lars of W. R. Bion's psychoanalysis. Among ol [...]
with curating the valuable *Los Angeles Seminai* [...]
greatly appreciated his extraordinary ability to ε [...]
lucidity and a clear and communicative writing ε ι .-. ι ιυw ocseph Aguayo gives
us the gift of an entire volume of his writings in which these qualities shine to the
fullest. For this very reason, *Introducing the Clinical Work of Wilfred Bion*
stands as an ideal and enjoyable introduction to a thought that often discourages
readers because of its inherent difficulties. Not so this book, which instead stands
as a fascinating exploration into the geography of Bion's thought, from Kleinian
studies to the great books of his mature period, but without neglecting essential
references to biography and clinical seminars. I can only recommend *Introducing
the Clinical Work of Wilfred Bion* to all psychoanalysts and psychotherapists. It
is easy to predict that this brilliant text will be very well received within the psychoanalytic community. It will become an essential reference not only for Bion
specialists or those who are most interested in the clinical use of his concepts, but
for *all* analysts. It is no longer a mystery to anyone that Bion is one of the
authors who brought to psychoanalysis a completely unprecedented sensibility, a
new and more "humane" way of dealing with psychic suffering.'

Giuseppe Civitarese, *author of* Sublime Subjects: Aesthetic Experience and
Intersubjectivity in Psychoanalysis (*Routledge, 2017*)

'Here is a beautifully clear and incisive introduction to an aspect of Bion's
work which has tended to lie hidden behind grand theories. This is Bion at
work in various clinical settings—psychotherapy, group work, psychoanalysis
of psychotic states, and then of the depth of personalities. It is not only a
sensitive account of his clinical approach but it is set clearly, though painfully,
against the background of the traumas of Bion's life experiences. And thus,
the book comes alive as an enquiry of Bion's inspiring professional career.'

Bob Hinshelwood

'Joseph Aguayo, a psychoanalyst and historian, has garnered his extensive knowledge of Wilfred Bion's life and the milieu in which he grew from childhood into the
most influential psychoanalyst of our day. Aguayo acquaints us with Bion as an 8
year old in Colonial India; the "undeserving" World War I hero; "the reluctant
Kleinian"; and the internationally venerated psychoanalyst. Aguayo notes that
most writing about Bion has addressed his theoretical concepts, leaving a gap in
Bionian studies about the important and unappreciated clinical applications of his
work. Aguayo's writing is exceptionally clear and conveys the intertwining of Bion's
life with his analytic theories and his unique "method of clinical inquiry". This is a
book that beginning and seasoned psychoanalysts can appreciate because of the
clarity of Aguayo's discussions of many complex concepts.'

Lawrence J. Brown, *Faculty and Supervising Child Analyst, Boston
Psychoanalytic Institute, USA and author of* Transformational
Processes in Clinical Psychoanalysis (*Routledge, 2019*)

Introducing the Clinical Work of Wilfred Bion

Introducing the Clinical Work of Wilfred Bion takes a fresh approach to this much revered analyst, focusing on the unique contributions to be found in his analytical and supervisorial work and developing of received Kleinian theory.

Starting from his childhood in India and his schooldays, through his experience in the Great War and later life, this book considers the way in which Bion's personal experience informed his later work as an analyst. Aguayo looks at how Bion's loyalty to Kleinian theory, especially in his work on psychosis, and how the subsequent in-fighting rife within the psychoanalytic community impacted his approach. Aguayo also considers the epistemological work done by Bion in the early 1960s while President of the British Psychoanalytical Society, as well as his seminars from Los Angeles and Buenos Aires. The book concludes by proposing that the spate of recently published Clinical Seminars, fresh with new clinical examples from Bion's analytic and supervisory work, now represent a potential for a 'new wave' of interest among analysts and scholars alike. Aguayo also engages the work of important contemporary specialists in Bion studies, such as: Ron Britton, Giuseppe Civitarese, James Grotstein, Robert Hinshelwood, Betty Joseph, John Steiner and Rudi Vermote.

As Bion's clinical work continues to inform contemporary psychoanalysts, this book will be essential reading to all analysts interested in Bion's work and ˙ legacy it holds in contemporary psychoanalysis.

ᵒᵘayo is a Training and Supervising Analyst at the Psychoanalytic
ᴸifornia in West Los Angeles, USA. He is a Guest Member of the
ᵃlytical Society in London and holds UCLA doctorates in both
and Modern European History. His many contributions have
ᵃational *Journal of Psychoanalysis* and *Psychoanalytic*
translated into French, German, Hebrew, Portuguese,

Tradition,

The Routledge Wilfred R. Bion Studies Book Series
Series Editor
Howard B. Levine, MD

Editorial Advisory Board
Nicola Abel-Hirsch, Joseph Aguayo, Avner Bergstein, Lawrence J. Brown, Judith Eekhoff, Claudio Laks Eizerik, Robert D. Hinshelwood, Chris Mawson, James Ogilvie, Elias M. da Rocha Barros, Jani Santamaria, Rudi Vermote

The contributions of Wilfred Bion are among the most cited in the analytic literature. Their appeal lies not only in their content and explanatory value, but in their generative potential. Although Bion's training and many of his clinical instincts were deeply rooted in the classical tradition of Melanie Klein, his ideas have a potentially universal appeal. Rather than emphasizing a particular psychic content (e.g., Oedipal conflicts in need of resolution; splits that needed to be healed; preconceived transferences that must be allowed to form and flourish, etc.), he tried to help open and prepare the mind of the analyst (without memory, desire or theoretical preconception) for the encounter with the patient.

Bion's formulations of group mentality and the psychotic and non-psychotic portions of the mind, his theory of thinking and emphasis on facing and articulating the truth of one's existence so that one might truly learn first hand from one's own experience, his description of psychic development (alpha function and container/contained) and his exploration of **O** are "non-denominational" concepts that defy relegation to a particular school or orientation of psychoanalysis. Consequently, his ideas have taken root in many places…. and those ideas continue to inform many different branches of psychoanalytic inquiry and interest.[1]

It is with this heritage and its promise for the future developments of psychoanalysis in mind that we present *The Routledge Wilfred Bion Studies Book Series*. This series gathers together under newly emerging and continually evolving contributions to psychoanalytic thinking that rest upon Bion's foundational texts and explore and extend the implications of his thought. For a full list of titles in the series, please visit the Routledge website at: https://www.routledge.com/The-Routledge-Wilfred-Bion-Studies-Book-Series/book-series/RWBSBS

Howard B. Levine, MD
Series Editor

---

[1] Levine, H.B. and Civitarese, G. (2016). Editors' Preface, *The W.R. Bion* Levine and Civitarese, eds., London: Karnac 2016, p. xxi.

Introducing the Clinical Work of Wilfred Bion

Joseph Aguayo

Routledge
Taylor & Francis Group

LONDON AND NEW YORK

Designed cover image: "Sky Field" by Cheryl Yaney, 1995. Oil on Paper, 48" x 32". Private collection.

First published 2023
by Routledge
4 Park Square, Milton Park, Abingdon, Oxon OX14 4RN

and by Routledge
605 Third Avenue, New York, NY 10158

Routledge is an imprint of the Taylor & Francis Group, an informa business

British Library Cataloguing-in-Publication Data
A catalogue record for this book is available from the British Library

ISBN: 978-1-032-42895-6 (hbk)
ISBN: 978-1-032-42885-7 (pbk)
ISBN: 978-1-003-36479-5 (ebk)

DOI: 10.4324/9781003364795

Typeset in Times New Roman
by Taylor & Francis Books

Contents

PART III
The Distillation of Clinical Experience and Everyday
Practices   121

Figures

Acknowledgments

Once again, I acknowledge and thank Nicola Bion, who kindly granted us permission to publish Bion's Clinical Seminars from his visits to Los Angeles and Buenos Aires in 1967 and 1968. Both sets of seminars had been preserved for years, in Los Angeles, by Arthur Malin, who recorded Bion's lecture visit to Los Angeles in April, 1967, and by Lia Pistener de Cortinas, who preserved Elizabeth Bianchedi's Spanish translation of Bion's visit to Buenos Aires in July/August 1968. Both sets of seminars have made possible a different interpretative reading of Bion's clinical work.

I remain warmly appreciative of Jim Grotstein, now and for many years a continuously inspiring source for my work in Bion studies. He alone was the pioneering American source that launched Bion's work in the United States in the 1980s, and until his death in 2014, remained steadfast in bringing Bion's work to the attention of scores of analysts and students. Over the years that I had the pleasure of knowing him and consulting with him and discussing ideas regarding clinical research in our field, I usually left Jim's house feeling uplifted, and feeling that I could breathe the fresh air of new ideas and concepts, as if for the first time. Jim truly had and never lost the beginner's attitude: he felt fascinated by what he was privileged to hear, see and think in relation to others. *Amicitia nostra sempiterna fore!*

Special thanks also to my dear friend and historian colleague, Robert Westman, Professor Emeritus of the University of California, San Diego History Department—someone who has seen me through so many interweaving intellectual and analytic adventures in history and psychoanalysis. And of course, thanks to Peter Loewenberg, who embodies the interdisciplinary ideal of the historian as psychoanalyst.

Many thanks also to so many colleagues and friends that can be counted as avid Bionistas—Larry Brown, Bob Hinshelwood, Sira Dermen, Nicola Abel-Hirsch, Howard Bacal, John Lundgren, Giuseppe Civitarese, Jack Foehl, Howard Levine, Avner Bergstein and Barnet Malin. Thanks also to the many colleagues with whom I had had the pleasure of learning with in many Bion seminars over the years: Afsaneh Alishobani, Charles Ashbach, Debbie Bilder, Lesley Caldwell, Evelyn Pye, Lyn Yonack, Bruce Reis and Judy Eekhoff. Special thanks also to a small seminar group, affectionately known as the 'Little Bion Group'—friends and colleagues such as: Susan Finkelstein, Marie Murphy, Maxine Nelson, Caron Harrang, Dana Blue, Debbie Sandy, Ingrid Newstadt and Jeannie Newstadt.

Lastly, but most importantly, heartfelt thanks and appreciation to my wife, Marina—and our two adult children, Siena and Morgan—for their unwavering support and tolerance, love and sustenance of belief in my analytic endeavors.

Introduction
Orienting Towards Bion's Clinical Work

Any analyst who considers writing a book on Bion's clinical ideas must first ask himself: why contribute another book to a field in which many introductions to Bion's thought already exist? While there are important works, such as the serviceable intellectual biography by Gerard Bléandonu (1994), *Wilfred Bion: His Life and Works (1897–1979)*, and more recently, Rudi Vermote's (2019) *Reading Bion*, an extensive review of the various phases of Bion's theorizing, I maintain that the field of Bion studies is on the cusp of a new development, a 'new wave' of studies based also on his actual clinical work. Until recently, we have only had limited access to Bion's actual analytic and supervisorial work, but within the last ten years, there have been a spate of publications from his 'late' period: the *Clinical Seminars* that he conducted in Los Angeles in 1967, Buenos Aires in 1968, and two volumes of *Bion in Brazil* in the 1970s. A great deal of new clinical and supervisorial material has surfaced, something that gives analysts and scholars interested in his actual clinical method new material for study (Bion, 2013, 2017, 2018).

In pulling together the various strands of the clinical work of Wilfred Bion, we have a new opportunity to take a fresh and less trodden path, one that can integrate his developments in theory with his actual analytic work itself. The clinical emphasis in this book thus stands as a meaningful counterpart to the existing theory-laden books on his work. It is also a shorter read than either Bléandonu or Vermote's important volumes, no doubt a function of spending less time on Bion's extensive theorizing and more on his now extant clinical work.

Doubling back to the groups and individual patients—psychotic, borderline and narcissistic—treated by Bion helps us to appreciate the breadth and scope of his technical endeavors, especially since these particular areas were less explored by both Freud and Klein when they treated or wrote about quite disturbed patients. To be clear, while there is clearly a clinical emphasis to this current work, it does include some, but does not overdevelop the theme of Bion's theorizing.

Chapters 1 and 2 briefly review Bion's childhood in colonial India, schooldays in England, his participation as a young tank commander in the killing fields of France during the Great War, and subsequent university days at

DOI: 10.4324/9781003364795-1

Oxford. I quickly traverse Bion's medical/psychiatric training, his days at the Tavistock Clinic in London in the 1930s, his first marriage and initial group work with men at war associated with the outbreak of World War II. These chapters culminate with his training analysis with Melanie Klein (1945–1953).

An incessant questioner of himself and others—young Bion annoyed his parents by insisting on being both seen as well as heard—rugged in his adolescent physical frame, playing rugby and on the swimming team at Bishops Stortford College (where he went to public school), he would later recount that his physical size and strength saved him. His exploits and bravery in the Great War were honored in his time, having received the Distinguished Service Order for valor in combat. Yet his bravery had a very dark side: the trauma of seeing men under his command die alongside him left him with horrific and lifelong feelings of responsibility, which in turn became a lifetime of work dealing with psychic wounds and traumatic residuals.

Perhaps, as Nicola Abel-Hirsch has suggested, Bion dealt with a sense of profound survivor's guilt by working with the most disturbed patients of his time. He took up Klein's (1946) program to analyze psychosis, certainly a bold move insofar as she disagreed with Freud (1914) in believing that the psychoanalytic treatment of psychosis was possible. Along with fellow analysands, Herbert Rosenfeld and Hanna Segal, Bion enthusiastically took up Klein's ideas, and those of his first analyst, John Rickman in the early 1950s, such as role-assignment, the understanding of countertransference, projective identification and the paranoid/schizoid and depressive positions.

Chapter 3 extensively details Bion's (1950) first psychoanalytic case study, 'The Imaginary Twin,' which served many functions, among them, a portal into the experience of psychosis. He struggled hard and long to understand a state of mind that eluded him: the Twin lived inside a protective imaginary enclave, appeasing the analyst while keeping him at bay and off balance. The analyst's eventual contact with this interior enclave revealed someone living in a severe dissociation from reality. By the time he concluded the case, Bion had demonstrated that he had learned his analytic craft as he then sailed directly into the foreboding realm of the psychoanalytic treatment of psychosis. He further explored the idea first broached by Freud (1900) in the Dream book: if it is true that there is a 'psychotic island' within all of us—after all, Freud wrote that at some point during the day (usually in our sleep when we are dreaming) we are all profoundly irrational and sometimes mad, Bion began to suspect that there must be a neurotic island within psychotically disturbed patients.

In Chapter 4, we find Bion, already well acquainted with the grueling hardships of warfare encountering a different kind of civilian war in the form of the three mutually antagonistic training groups—the Freudian, Kleinian and Independent—coexisting rather uncomfortably with one another at the British Psychoanalytical Society in London. Amidst all the in-fighting, Bion demonstrated his loyalty to the Klein group by supporting her views on psychoses in the 1950s. While this intense acrimony may sound strange to us so many decades later, we must not forget that Klein herself believed strongly that her own theoretical perspective was greatly endangered when it faced the challenge of Anna and Sigmund Freud coming to live and practice in London in 1938. The animosity between Anna Freud and Melanie Klein groups, which had for years been at a great distance, was now unavoidable as they were all members of the same analytic society. The battles that occurred during the time of the Controversial Discussions (1941–44) cast a long shadow over the subsequent development of the British Society.

Yet, despite his loyalty, all the in-fighting left Bion a bit uneasy as he was too familiar with how groups could easily be at war with each other. Along with colleagues Herbert Rosenfeld and Hanna Segal, Bion maintained a strongly Kleinian 'internal line' in understanding psychosis—their abiding aim was to elucidate the primary psychological mindset of the psychotic patient, which, among other things, excluded a consideration of environmental factors. In the cloistered atmosphere existing in the small Klein group in London, there were also antagonists within the group—at least Mrs. Klein thought so. This suspiciousness resulted in her expelling former collaborators and talented analysts, such as D.W. Winnicott and Paula Heimann. While Heimann (1950) had made a compelling case for unconscious-to-unconscious communication in the countertransference, Klein officially disavowed these views, all of which underscored her followers treading lightly on this subject (Spillius, 2007).

Retaining his independence of spirit, Bion slowly interrogated both Freud and Klein's ideas about psychosis, making fresh observations, such as drawing attention to the internal experience suffered by psychotics when they attacked their own minds—and the minds of their analysts. This was an important variation of Klein's (1957) notion of the infant attacking a both needed but frustrating breast. Bion also increasingly questioned and expanded Freud's ideas about psychosis. From the vertex of psychotic functioning, Freud's theories of neurosis appeared somewhat different: since Freud assumed his subjects were capable of representation, making it possible for them to report night dreams, Bion extended our awareness by discussing the psychotic's non-representational states, pockets of sensory emotional experiences that needed to be understood.

When Bion drew attention to the internal experience suffered by psychotics, as when they attack their own minds—and the minds of their analysts—he began increasingly to encounter Freud's rudimentary writings on psychosis. He especially dialogued with Freud's (1911) 'Two Principles of Mental Functioning,' focusing his attention on the psychotic's enduring *internal* experience in real time in the transference to the analyst.

Chapter 5 grapples with the emergence of Bion's distinctive views about psychosis, something my colleague Sira Dermen has encapsulated by terming it his 'method of clinical inquiry.' This idea stretched in two directions:

towards an implicit clinical technique deployed in the consulting room—and here, I term it 'implicit' because, aside from the famous 'Notes on Memory and Desire' paper, Bion (1967a) was disinclined to write about technique. It was also a method of questioning existing clinical theories as he made his own conceptual generalizations. His 'method of clinical inquiry' now established a means for differentiating his views on psychosis from those of Freud and Klein. This was a genuine paradox insofar as Bion was a core member of the 'all-in' Kleinian group while simultaneously beginning to differentiate his work from it. He was increasingly an uneasy Kleinian, feeling that he was of the group, but distant from it at the same time.

Here, as an example of how his method of clinical inquiry stretched in both the technical as well as theoretical directions, I highlight one of Bion's (1958a) extraordinary intuitive conceptual leaps made in his 'On Arrogance' paper: the patient's experience of the analyst as an ingress-denying or obstructive object underscored Bion's incisive re-reading of Freud's Oedipus myth. Bion regarded the analyst's role as the bearer of the 'truth-drive,' and as such, could appear obstructively to the patient's preferred mode of defensive evasion. This is not to say that Freud's version of the sexual Oedipus no longer had any purchase. Far from it: Bion was merely saying that it was secondary or existed in the neurotic layer, and the psychic reality that informed the psychotic layer exerted a pre-potent and dominating influence over the personality—and as a result, it needed to be analyzed first.

In Chapter 6, we see further examples of Bion's (1959) distinctive style, where his notion of the psychotic's 'attacks on linking' served as a Janus-faced concept that stretched to the clinical situation, where the patient levied defensive attacks on his own mind or on the meaning provided by the analyst, an experience that usually led to the patient's continued instability. Yet by being able to push the experience towards the conceptual as well, Bion now moved towards evolving a truly interactional psychoanalysis based in the notion of analytic containment, all calibrated in the real 'here and now' experience *between* patient and analyst. Attacks on one's own mind deepened the Kleinian discourse, which had anchored itself in part-object work, such as attacks on the providing breast. Bion accessed core experiences of psychotic patients, all of which led to new concepts and treatment strategies with both borderline and narcissistic personality disorders.

Also, since there was not a clearly set out Kleinian technique in the 1950s, as Klein's lectures were privately circulated among her students, Bion extended his analysis of psychosis by now including work with 'borderline psychosis' (Klein, 2017). He shaped his understanding of this new hybrid, a 'psychotically neurotic' patient who displayed episodic flashes of extremely primitive, irrational behavior. Bion here was extremely influential insofar as he generalized what has been termed by Kleinians as the 'psychotic core' of the experiences of patients in analysis, an idea that allowed for the supple understanding of psychotic mechanisms operating in the borderline and less disturbed neurotic personalities.

In Chapters 7 and 8, considerable time is spent on the epistemological work done by Bion (1962a, 1962b) just after Melanie Klein's death in 1960. While he preserved the essence of the Klein group's findings on psychosis, he simultaneously expanded their conceptual reach by now also theorizing about the evolution of normal thinking in the context of a ministering maternal figure. Perhaps D.W. Winnicott's epistolary entreaties urging Bion to take up the 'environmental factor' finally took some root (Aguayo, 2018a). Through a creative misreading of Freud's 'Two Principles' paper, Bion thought he could now account in a more all-encompassing way for the development of normal, neurotic as well as psychotic forms of thinking. He widened the psychoanalyst's scope by specifically including the psychotic patient's *internal* psychic experience of the maelstrom to which he was subjected—and in turn subjected others to.

Bion's new model of mother and infant, which he termed 'container/contained,' conceived of the patient-as-infant (i.e. in his most infantile or primitive state) as a set of 'thoughts without a thinker,' who needed a ministering and receptive figure who could help him grow his mind. Bion's model drew upon both Klein and Abraham's view of the infant as 'suckling,' born instinctually rooting for the breast (R. Steiner, 1989). Grounding himself in British Object Relations theory, particularly that of Melanie Klein, Bion was well accustomed to discussions of a hypothetical or virtual infant governed by internal object relations.

Chapter 9 further delineates Bion's new epistemological style as reflecting a form of cross-modal, interdisciplinary thinking, where he borrowed ideas from other disciplines—philosophy, mathematics, history and literature—and pressed them at times violently into the service of fashioning a meta-theory that was essentially a thinking man's guide to how to reason about the psychoanalytic situation and its theoretical underpinnings. In setting out what he considered an objective model that might be inclusive of the most enduring findings of both Freud and Klein, Bion abstracted from these two systems of thought, attempting to both transform and learn from his psychoanalytic experience to that point. From the outset, however, Bion's preference was for concepts that could be loosely defined, 'unsaturated' to use his term—neither being too specific nor too general. Bion preferred these types of terms because they lent themselves to a 'penumbra of associations' (Aguayo, 2018a).

With now familiar concepts such as container/contained (originally a term purloined by Bion from Jung's 1925 essay on marriage), the bi-directionality of the paranoid/schizoid and depressive positions (P/S and D) communicative and pathological projective identification, alpha and beta-elements, Bion rendered explicit the implicit two-bodied (or multi-bodied) nature of the Kleinian model. He welded this Kleinian theory with his group theory, effecting a two-person theory of interacting subjectivities. Britton (2008) has termed this conceptual transformation of a small field of two interacting and processing subjectivities as the 'variable infant' and the 'variable mother'—with clear exponential implications for the psychoanalytic couple as well.

Chapter 10 represents a gloss on both *Elements of Psychoanalysis* and *Transformations*, where Bion (1963, 1965) attempted to provide a theoretical structure for analytic theories that could be drawn upon by the everyday analyst. It was intended to be a theory of theories. He further elaborated theoretical ideas that were at the same time both specific and vague, yet general enough to encompass normal, neurotic and psychotic forms of thinking. They were specific enough to be relatable to the immediate clinical situation, and yet be sufficiently general to be an 'element' that could be compared with other theories. Here Bion drew upon the analogy of the alphabet, where just a few characters could be combined in an almost infinite number of ways to make millions of words. Just as there was a 'table of the periodic elements' or Euclid's 'elements of geometry,' Bion posited basic elements that can be combined to produce many variations of ideas that were applicable to the analytic situation—and he wrote: "Similarly the elements I seek are to be such that relatively few are required to express, by changes in combination, nearly all the theories essential to the working psychoanalyst."

When paired with the administrative fact that Bion was President of the British Psychoanalytical Society during this time (1962–65) and therefore presided at all scientific paper presentations given at the Society's meetings, he was also immersed in a still highly contentious institute atmosphere. In the aftermath of the Controversial Discussions, when three rival schools of psychoanalytic thought were in disdainfully close and often antagonistic contact, Bion constructed what he thought of as scientific models and tables, such as the Grid, in which the 'elements of psychoanalysis' might be thought about in an objective way. The epistemology monographs simultaneously represented Bion's attempts to systematize what he called the 'invariants' of the psychoanalytic situation, so that amidst this 'war of schools,' the everyday analyst might be able to ascertain objectively the subjective psychic reality lived by his patients. By the time *Transformations* appeared in 1965, Bion had also set aside attempts to 'scientize' psychoanalysis through the use of deductive methods gleaned from his reading of historians of science, such as Richard Braithwaite (Malin, 2021).

Chapter 10 also signals Bion's return to clinical matters, the treatment side of his 'method of clinical inquiry.' His mode here was to form direct impressions of how he worked in the analytic situation (e.g., keeping a fresh mind, one that is not over-dominated by too much memory of previous sessions) as he searched for the 'invariant' or 'truthfulness' in the descriptions made by his patients. Put differently, it was a search for sets of constant conjunctions, whose form remained constant even though their phenomenological descriptions varied with situation and person. Put forward in his aphoristic form, the analyst remained mindful of 'memory and desire' as obstructive factors, focusing instead on relating to the 'unknown' in the session. He urged the analyst who attempts to cling to what he knows to resist doing so for the sake of achieving a state of mind analogous to the P/S position. In short, the analyst is patient and suffers, tolerating frustration and waiting—and in a nod to Keats (1817)—he advocated 'patience' without 'irritable reaching after fact and reason' until a pattern evolves. Then he will attain 'security' of the depressive position, a resting point of integration.

Chapter 11 now actively plays in Bion's clinical as well as supervisory examples, once he decided to leave London and move himself and his wife to live and practice in Los Angeles in 1968. By this point, his years of writing theory-laden monographs was largely behind him, and he had grown weary of analytic institute strife, having been stretched thin by his numerous administrative responsibilities as both President of the British Psychoanalytical Society and Chair of the Melanie Klein Trust. Bion decided to uproot himself and practice from what his wife termed the 'cozy domesticity' of London. Many analysts have speculated on why he made such a move so relatively late in life.

In Bion's (1966) 'Catastrophic Change,' a paper which was one of his last given in London, he made an ironic statement about the mystic and the envy-ridden Establishment, perhaps a reference to his own problematic relationship wh members of his own Society, one that promoted (and here a quotation from its 1970 text) "the individual to a position in the Establishment where his energies are deflected from his creative-destructive role and absorbed in administrative functions. His epitaph might be: 'He was loaded up with honors and sank without a trace'" (Bion, 1970, p. 78). In the late autumn of his life, he privileged his work and family life, allowing his leadership and administrative responsibilities to fall by the wayside.

Put differently, Bion (1967a) now began to distill the clinical essence of his epistemological research. His energy now turned in a technical direction, quintessentially expressed in his remarkably short paper, 'Notes on Memory and Desire,' merely thinking that he was crystallizing what many British Object Relations analysts had been practicing for years, namely that all analytic sessions needed to be conducted in the present moment. When Bion stated that analysis need not be overly concerned with what *had* happened any more than what *would* happen, it might have appeared to be another way of saying what Melanie Klein's work with young children had demonstrated for decades—and James Strachey's (1934) paper had implied: all analysis occurred in the present moment, as the analyst simultaneously uncovered the unconscious mental processes dominating the patient's conflictual life, while simultaneously being the object of those very primitive psychic processes.

Yet when he reprised 'Notes on Memory and Desire' in Los Angeles in 1967, this paper that had appeared rather commonplace in London now created intense controversy in a foreign analytic culture that was the Los Angeles Freudian community. Bion also instigated a radical departure from years of theory-laden work when he made his ideas on technique and clinical work accessible to a new audience of American analysts, many of whom were incredulous that Bion could so seemingly and easily dismiss the staples of

Freudian work: transference as a displacement from past to present; psycho-sexual stages of development and genetic reconstruction. To their ears, it was at the heart of the analytic endeavor! Nonetheless, the reception Bion (2013) received in Los Angeles at his initial set of lectures in April 1967 proved to be enough to his liking to cause him to abandon the Old World for the New one (Aguayo, 2014).

Chapter 12 continues the presentation of one of Bion's (2013, pp. 81–82) own cases from the *Clinical Seminars* period, that of a young borderline woman (first presented in Chapter 11) who began verbally attacking and reviling the analyst the moment he opened the door to the waiting room—and he literally could not get a word in edgewise. He finally confessed that he simply could not hear himself think, as it seemed that she had destroyed the communicative link with her analyst, so that no interpretation was possible.

The analyst felt at a profound loss, despairing that he could make no satisfactory interpretation let alone think of an explanatory theory after the patient left the session. At this juncture, Bion invoked his newer ideas about memory and desire—if he approached such intensely grueling experiences, having exposed himself fully to the emotional and sensory onslaught pre-sented by the patient, how was he to make sense out of such sheer cacoph-ony? Some audience members, like Ralph Greenson, stated that perhaps such disturbed patients were untreatable by psychoanalytic methods.

But here Bion disagreed, subtly stating that his young analysand was untreatable *at that moment*, viewing the analyst's task to withstand such emotional assaults, as the patient actually relied on the analyst's capacity to make sense eventually of what was bothering her. So, with the patients beta-screen attack in mind, Bion thought after the session about what might be the invariant here, the unalterable something that remained undetectable in a variety of different situations.

In this example, Bion drew upon a notion of disciplined receptivity, where he exposed himself to the full onslaught of the patient's violent projective evacuations, causing him to momentarily 'lose his mind' before he was able to recover it and make a pertinent interpretation.

In the Buenos Aires *Clinical Seminars*, Bion continued the case presentation of his stormy borderline patient, only in 1968, he presented even more disturbing aspects of his experience with this patient. Right from the beginning, there were profound difficulties: two previous failed analyses that left the patient feeling quite despondent. In hindsight, Bion confessed that perhaps he had made some technical errors (e.g., talking with a member of her family). This is an important point because in the 'Commentary,' Bion (1967b) discussed the potentially harmful impact of the analyst's listening to 'hearsay' evidence about patients who consult with us. There is always the question of how much we want to hear what our colleagues tell us about the patient they are referring.

The issues in the analyst's management of a situation that soon reached an impasse, when the viability of continuing the analysis was questioned, are taken up in terms of John Steiner's (1994) ideas about the types of interpretations that are tolerable to borderline states of mind. The complementarity of Bion's own notions of the analyst's model of the patient's mind, the patient's model of her own mind is filled out by discussing Steiner's idea of the patient's model of the analyst's mind as represented by what he termed the 'analyst-centered interpretation.' These comments are also understood in a historical context insofar as analysts in the 1960s were seeing a new type of patient in their practices, the borderline patient—and like many others, Bion initially felt baffled as many other analysts did in terms of how to handle the stormy unruly borderline patient.

Chapter 13 continues the presentation of Bion's own case, demonstrating in detail how he approached the analysis of an overly agreeable young male analysand, who annoyed his analyst by incessantly agreeing with every inter-pretation. The interpretative law of averages simply didn't apply to this ana-lysand, any more than it did with patients who constantly quarreled with the analyst. By taking up the patient's dream material, we were able to examine how Bion understood its communicative function in terms of how his image was shaped in the transference. The case also offered Bion the opportunity to revisit his earlier formulations regarding the countertransference. In this instance, how could he account for his annoyance? From his early group period through the period of the psychosis papers—and now in the late *Clinical Seminars* period, Bion was remarkably consistent in his position: the analysis must start with a disturbance of feeling, which must be 'sustained and subordinated' so that the unconscious meaning of the countertransference can be deciphered.

A contemporary and uncannily similar example of an overly agreeable patient is described in the work of Betty Joseph (2000). In my view, her 'here and now' technique stands as a meaningful extension of Bion's own theore-tical and clinical work, gaining traction after his death in 1979. Such mean-ingful 'post-Bionian' extrapolations provide further proof of how his work has endured. Betty Joseph (who incidentally was a candidate classmate of Bion) represents the initial generation that worked to distill his and other Kleinian ideas into a systematic technique beginning in the 1970s.

Bion and Joseph's separate cases are examples of what the historian of science Thomas Kuhn would term 'spontaneous discovery,' where workers in two separate countries (and in this instance, different points in time) make a similar discovery independently of one another. In this instance, Bion's work in 1968 remained unknown to Joseph when she published her own paper in 2000, 'Agreeableness as an Obstacle.'

Chapter 14 serves as a final conceptual review of the most enduring clinical concepts evolved by Bion in the 1960s. In *Attention and Interpretation*, Bion (1970) distilled what I think of as his 'method of clinical inquiry' for the last time. Since this work was contemporaneous with the *Clinical Seminars*, we can examine how the clinical situation and its underlying conceptual structures, such as the model of 'container/contained' interpenetrate one another. Bion made it clear that his ultimate audience was the workaday psychoanalyst who needed to constantly vary the ways in which he approached the understanding of his analytic task. A veritable and whirling Catherine wheel, one that was never at rest, Bion rotated his listening vertices, for instance deploying the Grid as a way to examine if either the patient or analyst's communications opened up or foreclosed further inquiry. He differentiated those patients who could and could not suffer or bear their own psychic experience. In a memorable psychological aphorism: could the patient modify their frustration or did they feel forced to evacuate it?

He extended the frontiers of Freud and Klein's explorations by conceptualizing the sensory, affective and non-representational states, what he at one point termed the 'infrared part of the spectrum.' Reconceptualizing the beta-element as O, which now signified infinity or the vast potential of meanings associated with ultimate truth, Bion left behind a legacy of concepts with which analysts still grapple to elucidate and define afresh today (Vermote, 2019). I give an extensive comment of Vermote's efforts to conceptually encapsulate Bion's major theoretical innovations by describing the differences in transformations in knowledge to transformations from what he terms the 'infinite undifferentiated zone.' Lastly, he affirmed the optimal listening receptivity of the analyst, one minimally encumbered by the need for memory and desire. This disciplinary ideal operated in spite of the fact that as analysts, all of us are to a certain extent saddled with our preconceptions.

Finally, in Chapter 15, the book concludes by proposing that the spate of recently published *Clinical Seminars*, fresh with new clinical examples from Bion's analytic and supervisory work, now represent a potential for a 'new wave' of interest among analysts and scholars alike. The field of Bion studies is now in a position to learn in more detail just exactly how he went about the process of clinical inquiry. I give two additional clinical examples from Bion's supervisory work in Los Angeles in 1967 and Brasilia in 1974. I especially focus on the ways in which Bion listened to clinical material—and offer a grid of my own to plot what kinds of interventions he made vis-à-vis either the clinical material presented or the assumptions of the analyst presenting it.

In ending my work here on Bion's clinical methods and findings, I hope to have remained faithful to the spirit of his work, leaving space open, unsaturated to use his term, so that something generative and new can evolve from what hasn't been known.

Joseph Aguayo
Los Angeles
California
June 2022

Part I

Beginnings: Forays into Groups and Psychoanalysis of Psychosis

Chapter 1

Bion's Early Life

India, Schooling in England, Soldiering in World War I and II, and Life as a Psychiatrist and Innovator of Group Methods of Psychotherapy

In this chapter on Wilfred Bion's life and work, my overview follows Gerard Bléandonu's (1994) timeline, dividing Bion's clinical work in three parts— group (1940s), psychosis (1950s) and epistemology (1960s). In addition, I add a fourth period, namely his international clinical seminars (1967–78), focusing more attention on his considerable analytic and supervisorial work rather than explicate his late, less clinical, literary/aesthetic works (e.g., *A Memoir of the Future*, Bion, 1977a).

I begin with some introductory comments about Bion studies before turning to his early life in India. It is a regrettable truism that Bion works his reader quite hard—and even the secondary sources on his work can also be difficult reads; excellent as they are, they are also lengthy expositions (e.g. Bléandonu, 1994; Vermote, 2019). My aim here is to provide a concise and short introduction to Bion's main clinical ideas and theories, setting out the clear themes in his clinical, analytic odyssey, as he effected a transformation of the London Kleinian development as well as provided a new reading and understanding of undeveloped aspects of Sigmund Freud and Melanie Klein's work.

Clinicians who read Bion hope to gain something from his work so that they can apply it to their practices with patients. Fair enough, but Bion until recently has not lent himself to such easy extrapolation. Some of his most well-known published work, especially from the epistemology period (1962– 70) is theory-driven, often pitched in a dense and opaque manner, and rather sparse in terms of clinical examples. I hope to rectify this situation by concentrating whenever I can by drawing upon clinical examples from his published works. Rather than focus too much attention on the well-trod road of explicating his clinical theories, I think the time has come to understand Bion's work by focusing on his clinical examples as another starting point for understanding his theoretical development.

There is another difficulty in reading Bion's work. He tended to present his ideas as if they were isolated from their informing contexts—and was often rather sparse in citing the work of others. In his later career, this gave rise to the sense that he spontaneously generated his own ideas—and his reticence to

DOI: 10.4324/9781003364795-3

cite his sources also helped give rise to a feeling that one was in the midst of a 'guru,' who in Hinshelwood's (1994, p. xi) terms was "linked in with 'truth' in a way that ordinary mortals were not." Yet turn we must to Bion as a primary source because nothing can substitute for reading the thing-in-itself, his oftentimes bewildering yet illuminating texts.

Early Life through World War I (1897–1918)

Bion was born in 1897 to a British Empire middle-class family in late Imperial/ Victorian period (father was a civil engineer, mother a homemaker in the Punjab, Muttra, India). In terms of his childhood, by the standards of an English family living in India, his family was well to do, but Bion would remain somewhat an outsider back in an England when he came to live there at the age of 8. Middle-class empire families like the Bions had a more comfortable existence in the colonies than they would have back in England. As a child, he felt emotionally distant from his mother, comparing her to a cold breeze blowing inside the family home. He had a younger sister that he tolerated and with whom he played, but felt emotionally closer to his Ayah, his Indian nanny.

As a boy, Bion was an incessant questioner and a bit of a provocateur: he annoyed his parents with his disruptive questions to the point of exasperation. One example of Bion's childhood accidental humor was directed against his father: when as a boy, he tried to learn the Lord's Prayer, or the Our Father, he transformed it into the 'Arf Arfer.' God's name was made to sound like a barking dog! His parents seemed to be somewhat strict but erratic disciplinarians—children were better 'seen but not heard' and corporal punishment was not unknown in their upbringing. Perceived infractions and naughtiness would be met with spankings.

Like the boys of his social class, Bion was sent from Colonial India (at age 8) to public (i.e. boarding) school in England. He made the long voyage with his mother and would never return to India. His mother simply left Bion at school and he slowly watched her walk away, with only the top of her hat bobbing up and down just above a hedge. He was now alone, crying in his bed at bedtime at Bishop's Stortford College (84 miles from Oxford) known as a nonconformist school with some Christian overtones. He cried himself to sleep, felt especially homesick on weekends and felt isolated and abandoned to a bleak austerity. The other boys knew well enough to leave any 'new boy' alone, as he would cry himself to sleep for the first few days at the new school. The ceremonial Christian religiosity at school instilled both a sense of guilt and rebellion in boys like Bion. They went along and sang the hymns but scoffed at them once outside the chapel. One mate, Freddie, made fun of the rituals, but then died of an undiagnosed appendicitis—was this his punishment for his blasphemy? Young Bion took note.

By the time he was a senior, he was one of the 'big boys,' someone whose large physical frame and ruggedness was desirable as a teammate for swimming and rugby. He had also been invited to the proper homes of some schoolmates, being reminded of the family he had lost. He was enough of an insider to be invited, but remained an outsider, always feeling a bit different. Sexuality was simultaneously desired, loathed and hated by Bion; it wasn't 'proper,' and more the domain of the vulgar, lower classes. He had been punished earlier by his father for what he called 'wriggling' (or masturbating). The residual effect of(religious superstition was enough to instill a fearful guilt) in boys like Bion, so he dampened and sublimated his inhibitions and excelled at sports.

The socialization objective of schools like Bishops Stortford was the preparation of young men to become part of the Establishment, the ruling elite, a minority who would run the country and the Empire. It controlled the future of the nation. If one conformed to the school's strict discipline, cultivated well-placed connections with prominent families, and 'played the game' so to speak, one could hope to join the ruling elite, as Great Britain imposed its will on the Empire. Young 17-year-old Bion was in the last year of his studies when World War I broke out—at last, he could play his childhood games on a much vaster field; and like the boys of his class, he was absolutely thrilled to go to war, little realizing what it would mean. Like his schoolmates, he was expected to enlist and serve as an officer; it was a firm expectation of the boys of the university class. His heart was set on joining the Army. He felt humiliated to be rejected when attempting to enlist at first, but his father's social connections soon corrected the situation. The boy who pretended to play locomotive and fly airplanes was soon in the Tank Corps, the leader of men driving a massive but newly invented armored vehicle. Recall that the tank was a recent and top-secret invention of the British army in World War I, designed to repel machine gun fire, while rolling over the barbed wire that had become a staple of trench warfare in France after the first year of the war. Soon, Bion was off to the Front, aware of the class distinctions that(separated the officers from the enlisted men)—they rode in separate cars on the train and were stationed in separate quarters in the trenches.

The horrors of the Great War and the direct experience of men being killed under his command made an indelible lifetime impression on 18-year-old Bion. Many officers like Bion would suffer from incessant feelings of guilt and responsibility for the men who died under their command (Showalter, 1985). One only has to think of Bion's repeated depiction in his war diaries of the death of his runner Sweeting, who had half of his lung blown away while in the same trench with his young commander. One young person consoled another, as Bion offered illusory hope to a dying boy who asked him to contact his mother. Bion never fully recovered from these kinds of cataclysmic trauma, always suffering on behalf of the men who died under his command. Although he never used the word 'trauma' in his published work, he suffered grievously, and World War I gave him the raw materials for the work of a lifetime on the behavior of men in profoundly extreme situations. The war shaped his analytic sensibilities and "offered a template for the psychotic states he later described in his analytic patients" (a quotation from Mary Jacobus, cited in Roper, 2012, p. 130). In the last analysis, he subscribed, as so many did, to a fading chivalric ideal of heroic gallantry—only a coward and a 'shirker' or 'shell-shocked' would not remain at the front and do their duty. Lord Tennyson's (1854) riveting poem, 'The Charge of the Light Brigade' now seemed like a thing of a dusty past when soldiers and cavalrymen fought in hand-to-hand combat. The Great War now ushered in efficient methods of killing at long distances.

When he became a psychoanalyst, decades later in the 1940s, he could finally render his wartime experiences into words and feelings—and in a reciprocal fashion, the Kleinian emphasis on extreme mental and emotional disturbance gave Bion a language onto which he could graft and thereby comprehend undigested experiences from the Great War. Bion would return to his war remembrances time and time again, attempting to work through what could never be definitively finished and emotionally digested (Brown, 2012). As it is, Bion later wrote three different versions of his World War I diaries at different points in his life—a war diary written just after the World War I (as a way to compensate by providing his parents with a memoir for all the letters he never wrote to them during the war); and later versions written in old age. In spite of these attempts, somewhat successful in helping to mend his shattered psyche, there were some aspects he would never distill. To capture the feeling of British soldiers in a time of 'total war,' I recommend a recent documentary film on World War I—*They Shall Not Grow Old* (2018) which vividly portrays the horrors of a Europe at cataclysmic war, one which for the first time, the technological inventions (machine guns, tanks, airplanes) made murder at a catastrophic level an inevitable reality. These undigested aspects of the horrible carnage Bion was subjected to, no doubt discussed in his analysis with Melanie Klein (1945–53), are also paradoxical reminders of the residuals of what was *not* worked through in his analysis with her (James Grotstein, personal communication).

Just as men like Bion faced the possibility of daily death by any number of means, like bombardment, he also thought psychotically disturbed patients faced an internal bombardment from which they could not defend themselves. The soldier felt attacked from the outside, the psychotic patient from the inside. In my view, this is another aspect of what makes Bion's psychosis papers of the 1950s so profound in their significance. It is one of the main reasons I spend so much time attempting to understand Bion's work with extremely disturbed patients, as there was something deeply personal with which he struggled for most of his life. Yet at the same time, Bion's psychosis papers are so difficult and confounding to read: they compressed the experiences of the psychotics he treated, so ordinarily distant from our own experience, since most of us will have not faced either a descent into psychosis or service in armed military conflict, especially in extreme life-and-death situations. Yet as extreme as these situations were, they informed Bion about the less profound psychological suffering incurred by other types of experiences.

Years at Oxford, Medical Training and Tavistock Clinic (1919–39)

After the war ended in 1919, Bion went on to university, and took a degree in history at Oxford, (again feeling out of place)next to boys who came from privileged families with university traditions and social connections. He felt especially estranged from boys who had not been involved in the Great War. There is also much to be learned about researching Bion's life at Queen's College, Oxford. For instance, the Archivist at Queen's College, where Bion studied, relayed to me information on the entry card he filled out when he first arrived. When asked what occupation he wanted to pursue, Bion answered 'Schoolteacher.' While his teaching career after Oxford did not in fact last very long, he did go on to study medicine at University College London. After that, he worked as a psychiatrist at the Tavistock Clinic in the 1930s, where he met and was influenced by the psychodynamic view of J.A. Hadfield. Hadfield's therapy focused on making links between a symptom and its origins in the past. Bléandonu (1994, p. 41) surmises that Bion's initial psychotherapy was with Hadfield for 7–8 years; and judges that the results were not to Bion's liking. Bion later nicknamed Hadfield, 'Mr. Feel-it-in-the-Past,' as he frequently asked Bion to put unpleasant experiences off into the past! This no doubt included Bion's war trauma, but the idea that it all referred to the past that he shouldn't feel with his therapist, not the present being lived, was a piece of 'mad logic' that Bion did appreciate.

During 1934/35, Bion also saw Samuel Beckett (before he became a famous playwright) in three times a week dynamic psychotherapy. Now that we have Beckett's actual diaries—with some entries describing his work with Bion—we hear of his gastro-intestinal difficulties, problems in sleeping and feeling enslaved to his Irish mother. Beckett's (2009) remembrances also now serve as definitive proof that Beckett could not have been, as some analysts have maintained, the patient described in Bion's (1950) first psychoanalytic paper, 'The Imaginary Twin.' This was Bion's graduation paper for the British Psychoanalytical Society that we will discuss later. But here, just a short word: to think that Beckett was the patient described in the 'Imaginary Twin' paper is a dubious claim, one still advanced recently by Miller (2013), after Anzieu (1989). Bion simply would not have been allowed to submit for graduation a 'control case' treated years before his formal training at the British Psychoanalytical Society began in 1945 (R.D. Hinshelwood, personal communication).

One quick aside about how informal Bion's work with Beckett was: during the time of their work, Bion actually invited Beckett to dinner at his club and they both went along on 2 October 1935 to hear Jung's *Tavistock Lectures* at the Clinic! (Beckett, 2009, p. 238). It seemed that Bion thought little of inviting his patient out for dinner and a lecture. But these sorts of informal social practices were not unusual in the 1930s, as many analysands continued their work with their analysts (even traveling with their analysts on the analyst's summer holidays).

Bion had a more substantial analysis from 1937–39 with John Rickman, who had been analyzed by Freud and Klein and had also worked with Ferenczi. Rickman was a Quaker with solid moral values that had led to his psychiatric work with agricultural workers in Soviet Russia. Bion much admired his analyst, especially his open and inquisitive attitude. The outbreak of World War II in 1939 soon disrupted the analysis, but primarily because Bion wrote to Rickman and proposed a change in their relationship—from analyst and patient to collaborators! Both men accommodated to the new, wartime emergency situation by partnering up as British army psychiatrists in the War Officer Selection Board in 1942 and the Northfield Experiment later that year. The change in Bion's relationship to Rickman again shows us the difference in therapeutic mores in the 1930s, where analyst and patient could and did become colleagues and collaborators—with no one objecting, and no disastrous consequences from what we today would consider a 'boundary violation.' Far from it—theirs was a fruitful and rich collaboration.

Bion's Period of Group Work in War and Peacetime (1943–55)

In 1942, Bion and Rickman worked collaboratively as psychiatrists with the 'leaderless group' experiments for officer selection at the War Officer Selection Board. These were all very practical problems with which Bion and Rickman became concerned: the selection of suitable military officers. Rather than involve themselves in one-on-one interviews for selecting suitable candidates for officer training, the duo had small teams of men do practical tasks, e.g. getting a heavy gun over some obstacle; they then watched to see who facilitated communication and cooperation, who evinced the capacity to think of the overall well-being of the group in terms of completing the task. So in working with groups as a 'living organism,' their focus was away from the purely individual. In working with small groups, Bion again concerned himself with trying to observe qualities of leadership, in effect, qualities that would make it possible to select and train efficient military officers. As commonsensical as these ideas might sound today, this way of working also implicitly questioned an age-old British custom: that officers should only come from the university-educated class.

In late 1942, Bion and Rickman turned their attention to soldiers in need of psychological rehabilitation, victims of 'combat-fatigue,' experimenting with group processes at Northfield Hospital in Birmingham. They did so again because it would have been inefficient and impossible to treat the war veterans on an individual basis. Bion and Rickman tested the assumption that to rehabilitate soldiers, attention had to be paid to group morale as much as their individual symptoms. The rehabilitation group needed an 'enemy' just as soldiers did in combat. Bion and Rickman made the idea of 'neurosis' the 'common enemy' to be combated, subjecting their patients to 'thoughtful observations instead of taking disciplinary action against particular individuals.' An unmistakable *esprit de corps* developed at Northfield Hospital. Bion was successful there, then transferred elsewhere, much to his disgust and dismay. Hardly one to 'play the game' and curry favor with those in power, Bion would later relate somewhat bitterly that he entered and left World War II at the same army rank: Major.

After World War II ended in 1945, he continued his group work, only now in peacetime at the Tavistock Clinic in London, leading groups to study their own tensions in the here and now while they struggled with their work task. From the time of Freud's (1921) study of groups, it was well-known that there are always sub-groups within any given group. For instance, with the emotionally disabled soldiers at Northfield Hospital, some worked hard to improve, while others did not. Bion called these two groups, 'workers' and 'shirkers,' men who took up their daily responsibilities and those who sought to evade them. After the war ended, Bion in effect applied the method developed in wartime to now study 'intra-group' tensions in peacetime.

When working with a group, Bion introduced brilliant psychoanalytic innovations that in one sense went mainly unnoticed at the time. For example, after briefly introducing himself to the group, he remained silent much the same as a psychoanalyst would at the beginning of an analytic session. In other words, he gave no instruction as to how the group was to conduct itself. Eventually, the group began to free associate in various ways; Bion would make interpretations about the group process and the confusion that the civilian patients might be feeling, such as: "There are two anxieties here—that you will be treated like patients; and that you will not be treated as patients." It would sometimes quickly develop that the group members wanted to be led; and had to find out that they were expected to work as a group.

Bion's interest here was to examine and understand what he called the groups members' 'anonymous contributions' that helped to form the 'group mentality' in order to promote self-reflection amongst the membership. Of course, there would be tensions in the group, but the real point was: could these tensions be constructively thought about or reflected upon by the group members? Bion's idea here was that the 'group mentality' existed in counterpoint to the purported conscious aims of the group. The group leader attempts to shed light on what obstructs the group from realizing its aims. To explain this further, let us borrow an analogy from psychoanalytic treatment: just as the patient comes for analysis to understand the causes for his problems in living, he is also prepared to resist knowing more in depth about these underlying states. The same is true in groups: they can both work at understanding their underlying tensions, while at the same time moving against understanding by all sorts of defensive evasions.

In post-war civilian group work at Tavistock, a method of 'thoughtful observation' resulted in the study of intra-group tensions, a frustrating and hard to attain objective. Group members projectively shaped the image of the group leader, who was both the object of their projections as well as their interpreter. The group's view of the 'leader' resulted from their collected projections that reflected their anxiety about survival. The tension between the individual members and 'group mentality' produced the 'group culture.' One clear clinical example: Bion appeared with a group at the Tavistock: he came into the room, sat down and said nothing. After a while, a group member spoke and asked, "What does Dr. Bion want us to do?" Bion gave no answer. Someone else said: "Well, after all, this is Dr. Bion's group, so surely he will tell us.' Bion then interpreted: 'It is *wished* that this be Dr. Bion's therapy group instead of therapy by the group" (Bion, 1955b). The point here was that Bion interpreted the group's anxiety that was pressuring him into becoming their 'leader,' surely another way to evade the responsibility for attempting their own understanding of what was happening. It was a way to rely on the established authority rather than leaning into the authority of their own direct emotional experience.

For Bion, there were three Basic Assumption Groups that reflected an unconscious 'group mentality.' One way was 'pairing,' when two group members engaged in a 'public' private conversation in the group, acting as if the rest of the group did not exist; the other members were complicit in allowing this two-person conversation to happen. This phenomenon was analogous to two parents in intercourse being 'watched' by the other group members. The 'dependent' group was a second style and these groups were easier to spot, such as when members insisted on following the 'doctorly'/authoritative lead of a psychoanalyst. The example just given is a good example of a Basic Dependency group, where the members wanted Dr. Bion to be their leader and tell them what to do and how to conduct themselves. 'Fight/flight' is a third type, and occurred when there were intra-group tensions regarding the perceived status of the leader; was he to be joined up with or opposed and fought?

Postscript: Bion's (1952/1955) Paper, 'On Group Dynamics'

We end by discussing Bion's mature work on groups as reflected in his well-known (1952) paper, 'Group Dynamics,' one that he subsequently revised and republished again in 1955. This paper overlaps themes covered in Chapter 2, namely how Bion was influenced by his personal training analysis with Melanie Klein during this time. In one sense, we do not see Klein's influence in the 1952 paper, but it comes through quite strongly in the revised 1955 version. Let me illustrate.

I would say that the 1952 version was 'pre-psychoanalytic' or 'pre-Kleinian,' and reflected his group work in the 1940s, whereas the 1955 version now employed Kleinian mechanisms to illustrate how irrational (and even psychotic) group functioning could become. In 1952, Bion critiqued Freud's 'strange' descriptions and compared them to 'actual' experiences in groups (Sanfuentes, 2003). (It was a small irony that Freud (1921) wrote his work, 'On Group Psychology' while on a summer holiday in the Alps) (Gay, 1988, p. 403). Bion derived his experience from his war-time combat experiences and those when he worked as a psychiatrist treating combat neuroses. Naturally, Bion's understanding of group would differ from Freud's.

Yet as he trained to now become a psychoanalyst after World War II ended, Bion also applied findings about the group's unconscious mind to individual psychoanalysis: the unconscious could be a timeless void ((where past was confused with present),) so that the patient felt that he worked against an internally generated conflict-making enemy. Analysis went on in the presence of the resistance to change and new ideas. The neurotic struggled with the internal residues of his own experience with his primary family, just as group struggled with its own irrational, sometimes psychotic 'group' mind. Bion's ideas resonated deeply with the struggle for survival in the extreme context of total war when he wrote: "The individual is a group animal at war, both with the group and with those aspects of his personality that constitutes his 'groupishness'." Freud's emphasis on group as a family applied to the civilized niceties of peacetime living, something that Bion returned to once the shooting had finally stopped.

Bion could now apply some of his group postulations to illuminate individual psychoanalysis, particularly with psychotic patients who were at almost permanent war with their own minds. Likewise, the group could be at war with its own irrational 'group mind.' For example, John Rickman had impressed upon Bion the field theory work of Kurt Lewin, extrapolating from this work how the group facilitator is often 'pressured' into certain roles by various group members. As a result, the group facilitator had to pay attention to how his role was being projectively shaped by the group membership. Within a few years of his group work, Bion would then focus on how individual patients in psychoanalysis often ('pressured' him to take up one kind of a role-relationship,) something else that he had to be first subjected to before he could in turn stand outside and interpret its meaning both to himself as well as to his patient (Hinshelwood, 2019).

In the 1955 revision of the 'Group Dynamics' paper, Bion (1955b) thought that explanations of the group's functioning were to be sought in its matrix. But now he wrote with his analysis with Melanie Klein in mind: the mutually enriching analysis of both individual and group psychology would not occur until "there has been sufficient understanding of Melanie Klein's work on the psychoses." But what had changed in this uncustomary revision of an earlier paper? Bion now toned down the critique of Freud's work on groups, saying instead that Klein's work on psychotic mechanisms gave us a fuller picture of individual psychoanalysis, family and group life—and augmented Freud's findings. Bion now gave clinical examples of group work, taking up an individual's statement and re-casting it as reflecting an uncon-scious group tension about encountering distressful feelings.

He also now privileged countertransference as a way to orient towards the understanding of the group (as well as the individual) mind. The group analyst received the group's projective identifications—and here, (Bion relied on his own direct emotional experience to help him sort out what kind of a group 'projec-tive' figure he was for the group.)The countertransference became a different kind of 'receiving set,' almost like radar, one in which the aggregated projections of the group reflected a collectively determined image of the group leader. In his paper on 'Group Methods,' Bion (1948, CW, IV, 65) wrote: "In psychoanalysis a means of investigation is at hand in the transference, but in the group situation I do not feel quite as happy about postulating a transference situation as I do about postulating a counter-transference."

To summarize Chapter 1, Bion spent his early years in India, born to a civil service family, at times tormenting his parents by asking questions incessantly. Like other boys of his class, he was sent off to boarding school—and would never see his beloved India again. Overcoming his shyness and social inhibi-tion, he excelled at swimming and rugby, and soon went into World War I as a young officer in charge of small groups of men in the tank corps; the trauma of seeing so many men die left him with a lifetime of work dealing with its undigested and horrific residuals. He went to Oxford University and studied history after the war ended. After graduation, he found out that he was not suited to be a schoolteacher, but then studied medicine at University College London. He then became a psychiatrist at the Tavistock Clinic, and drew upon his World War II experiences in the study and treatment of war veterans to now study 'intra-group tensions' in civilian, out-patient groups at the London Tavi-stock Clinic during the 1940s. He wrote papers on group process and his book, *Experiences in Groups* (Bion, 1961) was the most well-known and popular of his many writings during his lifetime.

Chapter 2

Prelude to Bion's Papers on Psychosis, Melanie Klein's Work on Psychosis and an Overview of his Papers on 'Psychosis' (1950–59)

Melanie Klein's Innovations as a Child Psychoanalyst

In order to understand Bion's beginnings as a psychoanalyst, particularly his work with psychosis, we must first familiarize ourselves with the work of his training analyst, Melanie Klein. While she had worked in the early years of her career as a child psychoanalyst in the 1920s and 1930s, Klein took for granted a fundamental familiarity with Freud's work, so she accepted the existence of a dynamic unconscious as well as the operation of defenses against the awareness of pain, loss and absence. She accepted the adult patient's need for multiple times a week analysis, free association, laying on the couch and meeting for long stretches of time.

Fundamental to Freudian psychoanalysis at that time was a highly verbal, free associating neurotic adult or older child (at least of latency age). Excited by Freud's theories, Klein set about to work with younger children after being encouraged to do so by her first two analysts, Sandor Ferenczi and Karl Abraham. She became fascinated by her own children's play with toys. Just as the adult free associated with words, she began to see the child as 'free associating' with toys and small figures, all as a way of showing in what sort of internal world he lived. She thought that children expressed their conflicts through the way in which they played with toys (e.g., male and female figures in toy houses), being less capable of verbalization at ages 2 and 3. Klein innovated and revolutionized child analysis, as she developed a 'verbal/play-association' method. She now was able to mine a new kind of clinical data with children who were barely verbal and under the age of 3. The child's play with toys, both physical and verbal, provided a new kind of evidence for the existence of early psychical processes. Early on, it was her way of testing out some of Freud's assumptions about early mental development; only later did she start questioning some of his assumptions. Along the way, she also encountered opposition to her theories from Anna Freud, who developed her own perspectives on child analysis in Vienna in the 1920s and 1930s.

What Klein (1932) also found fascinating was the child's enactment of primally important phantasies, where the child could assert its freedom to enact

DOI: 10.4324/9781003364795-4

roles in analysis, all as a way to communicate its state of mind, such as power and size reversals. A brief example: when the child assumes the parental position and puts the analyst in the child position, the analyst gains direct access to the inner, subjective experience of the child *as it was occurring*, not as it was retrospectively reconstructed in the Freudian view of childhood. Klein initially regarded herself as a loyal Freudian. Wasn't it logical to see the child's play behavior as an exteriorization of mental phantasy? And since Freud extracted a conflictual early history from his adult case of the Wolf Man, going back to the primal scene he witnessed as a boy of three and a half, why couldn't Klein do the same by drawing upon the work with very young children? If the understanding of dreams was Freud's royal road to the adult unconscious, then interpreting toy play became Klein's direct route to the child's unconscious. Unlike Freud, who primarily viewed the infant's mother as the object of the child's Oedipal desires, Klein emphasized the earlier years of the infant's relationship to the maternal body. Using this template, the analyst analyzed the child's primal anxieties, not to cajole, reassure or prepare it for analysis. Positive and negative reactions to the analyst, present from the very first session, were grist for the analytic mill, with Klein easing the child's way by allowing for meaningful play with little toy figures, pencil and paper, and water.

Klein's overall organizing trope for understanding the child's communications was the mother–infant relationship—and she set about to see how the child's primal phantasies could make meaningful sense of how it negotiated its internal, phantasmic, subjective relationship with mother and other family figures. Klein in effect said that infants had a mental life which could now be accessed. Put in a clinical manner, she could and did begin to look at the phantasies that the child projected or split off *into the analyst* in the present situation. There was a new focus on the immediacy of the analytic situation, a concern with making the child's conflicts come to life in the present situation, an emphasis as fresh then as it remains today.

Klein's Analysis of Psychosis

To how Klein's work influenced the work of Bion and other members of her group after the end of World War II: having survived a massive struggle against the Anna Freud group at the British Psychoanalytical Society, a period of time called the Controversial Discussions (1941–44), in which there were heated debates about the origins of the infant's psychological life, she emerged with her own training group and attracted the likes of psychiatrists such as Wilfred Bion, Herbert Rosenfeld and Hanna Segal, who became her analysands and supporters. The Klein group existed as a legitimate training track along with the Anna Freud group and the so-called 'Independents' (i.e., primarily British analysts who retained a right to 'pick and choose' the theories they favored). Klein (1946) refined her views on what she termed the 'positions' (i.e., the Paranoid/Schizoid and Depressive Positions) which she discussed in her most famous paper, 'Notes on Some Schizoid Mechanisms.' By this point, Klein had reached her bedrock assumptions about how to analyze the infantile conflicts—both in her child and adult patients—and from these positions she would not waver for the rest of her life. The positions reflected the individual's enduring psychic structures through which their communications took on emotional significance.

In different terms, Klein placed relatively less emphasis on reconstructing the past in the sense of how the child was affected by either or both of its parents and siblings, but more on what her patients *psychically made of their real experiences. For Klein, the psychoanalyst herself incarnated the facilitating or change-making aspect of the environment through the use of direct transference interpretations.* It was in this fashion that Klein sought to bring about psychic and structural change. Elucidating the significance of environmental influence, both with past and present objects outside of analysis, remained an issue of secondary and lesser importance to Klein—what was of primary importance was effecting structural change in her patients.

Fundamental to Klein's approach is the direct and immediate analysis of negative transference, something that she felt a strong conviction about because aggression had been undervalued in psychoanalytic discussions of technique until the late 1920s (Glover, 1927). Klein was certainly alert to the possibility of the analyst being perceived as a bad mother, bad father, or a hostile parental couple (or combined parental figure) against which the patient must defend himself. Since she assumed that the infant had no way to mentalize the fact that the maternal breast that pleasured and fed it was also the same breast that frustrated the infant in its absence, a psychological template was set for frustration and resentful responses. From this, a Kleinian aphorism arose: the present good maternal breast that nurtures and feeds the infant is the same breast that becomes psychically 'bad' and frustrating in its absence. Hence, the infant's attacks on the breast it cannot completely possess. Applying this sort of template to more primitively disturbed patients, the pleasuring and understanding provided by the analyst became a source of frustration in his or her absence, say on the weekend breaks. The weekend could be experienced as the analyst preferring his own mate, or preferring an intercourse with his own mind, something which the patient could and did feel threatened about. In more Oedipally savvy patients, this sense of exclusion could be experienced as what occurred during either the weekend break or vacations, when the patient felt deprived while the analyst is off presumably enjoying the company of people close to him. Frustration and envious attacks could surface in relationship to the analyst's separateness, something which could represent how excluded the patient feels.

As Bion became familiarized with Klein's work and ideas through many years of five times a week analysis with her, he witnessed her expanding the meaning of her (1946) understanding of 'paranoid/schizoid' states to now include the analytic treatment of psychotics, as their problems were conceptualized as originating from the outset of life. Klein had long subscribed to Karl Abraham's idea, one that postulated that while psychotic patients were the most primitively regressed to earlier oral and anal infantile fixation points, they were nevertheless analyzable. This was an idea that parted company with Freud's (1914) well-known paper, 'On Narcissism,' where he essentially opined that the analysis of psychotics, whom he termed sufferers of 'narcissistic neuroses,' was impossible. Psychoanalysis as a treatment modality was restricted to the 'walking well,' the so-called neurotic patients. According to Klein, these types of patients garnered good experiences over bad experiences of the breast. On the other hand, Klein thought that psychotic patients garnered and hoarded bad experiences over and above those safeguarding the good ones. Klein thought that psychotics could and did project their better, saner qualities into the analyst, all of which left them feeling extremely internally persecuted and tormented.

More importantly, since Klein (1946) also hypothesized that even disturbed individuals maintained some sort of object link to their caregivers, she thought that they could be successfully psychoanalyzed. Schizophrenics, paranoids and schizoids could now be analyzed, an important point because, here, Klein disagreed and took issue with Freud's view that the analysis of psychosis was impossible: he assumed that psychotics were incapable of forming a connecting, bonding relationship with the analyst, and thus remained unanalyzable. No transference, no psychoanalysis. In her 'Schizoid Mechanisms' paper, Klein's (1946) fundamental point was that she believed that psychotics *were* analyzable, and emphasized instinct over nurture, destructive impulses rather than the failure of maternal provision (a factor crucial to Winnicott's (1953) different theory). Bion loyally took up along with others Klein's (1946) programmatic agenda of analyzing psychotic 'states of mind.'

More importantly, projective identification, a psychological mechanism of crucial importance was definitively described in Klein's (1952) revised version of the 'Schizoid Mechanisms' paper. Projective identification consisted of a complex set of interlocking ideas: the child projected harmful excrements into the mother, so that they could then be disowned by the subject and felt to be a part of the mother as a 'bad self.' A prototype of aggressive object relations ensued—and the child could in this instance fear persecution or retaliation from a vengeful mother. In simple words, the subject spitefully said, 'I am not bad and dirty—you are! And so, I must be on my guard whenever I am around you lest you retaliate!'

Prelude to Bion's Contributions to the Understanding and Treatment of Psychosis: 'The Imaginary Twin,' 1950

I now give an overarching view of a series of papers written by Bion in the 1950s, more of a prelude to material covered more extensively in the next chapters. Bion as a loyal Kleinian not only advocated for her understanding of psychosis, but also extended these aims with his own unique understanding. Looking ahead to subsequent chapters, it is important to say that the psychosis papers were also the basis of how Bion both incorporated the Kleinian paradigm while at the same time extended it with a new theory of psychoanalytic thinking that he would elaborate in the 1960s.

We, however, start with an anomaly: in the write up of his first psycho-analytic case, 'The Imaginary Twin,' Bion never once mentions the term 'psychosis' or 'psychotic' in reference to the patient. Yet he chose to include this case as the first of his series of papers on psychosis, which he republished in *Second Thoughts* (Bion, 1967b). The 'Twin' is best seen as a prelude to his work on psychosis. In learning how to work in a Kleinian fashion—and here, Bion was well served insofar as Paula Heimann, one of Klein's most articulate supporters (also a former analysand), served as Bion's supervisor on the case (Willoughby, 2006; personal communication).

One startling and organizing fact about the 'Twin' case: this adult male patient for months talked about relationships outside his analysis, purported to be real, when in fact they were figments of his imagination. Yet neither he nor the analyst was aware of it! Bion courageously wrote of his error in believing the patient's account when in fact, it turned out that the patient was adhered to an imaginary psychic realm of existence from which both he and his analyst were barred. The story of the 'Twin' revolved around how Bion tunneled his way out of this treatment impasse—and here, he relied on ideas learned from both his first analyst, John Rickman, and his current supervisor, Paula Heimann. From Rickman, there was the crucial idea of role assignment and its analysis: since the patient was bonded internally in a psychic world that excluded the analyst, there appeared in analysis a form of counterfeit exchange—a pseudo-patient with a pseudo-analyst. This was one part of the impasse from which the analyst had to emerge. From Heimann, Bion would have been encouraged to continue trusting his own direct emotional experi-ence with his patient. This was wise counsel insofar as Bion repeatedly returned to the point that there was something 'stale' and 'fetid' in the ana-lytic atmosphere, one that was so stultifying that he questioned whether he was the right analyst to be working with this very problematic patient. The deceived analyst had to get at the truth of the patient's disturbed state of mind in order to make any emotional contact. It would only be later on that he encountered the 'Twin's fear of psychotic decompensation, all of which interested Bion in articulating how psychotic and neurotic experiences seemed to interpenetrate one other. But here, Bion, like Freud and Klein, began to formulate far-reaching clinical generalizations from a small body of patients (near-psychotic and psychotic).

Fundamental to Bion's way of learning how to analyze his patients was a reliance on an introspective method. He questioned the validity of the patient's report as much as he did the soundness of his own understanding and interpretations made to the patient. It is important to note here that the Klein group in the 1950s had no identifiable method—at least from the perspective of analysts practicing outside their group—but were familiar with her institute and private lectures on technique (J. Steiner, 2017). In the 1950s, Kleinian ideas about technique were a loose set of practices based on a psycho-analytic understanding of patients in analysis. As noted by Elizabeth Spillius (2007), it would not be until the 1960s that the Klein group realized in a way recognizable by the wider psychoanalytic community that the 'novelty of con-tent' that they had analyzed in psychotics now represented a 'novelty of method,' a new psychoanalytic technique.

In the case of the 'Twin,' Bion ultimately overcame a countertransference impasse, perhaps a sign that he drew upon Heimann's (1950) work on its poten-tially informing nature. Heimann extended Freud's older idea of transference: if the transference was the analyst's greatest obstacle and ally, so was the counter-transference. Like Heimann, Bion regarded countertransference as potentially informing, one of the analyst's main 'instruments of research,' a sort of uncon-scious radar system that could detect unseen unconscious forces as they appeared. Like Bion, Freud (1905) earlier on had overcome his own resistance to realizing he had failed to take into sufficient transferential account that his young patient, Dora, had expected him to betray her trust, just as every other adult in her life. While this error had cost Freud his patient, understanding his error then led to the radical new idea of the transference.

Bion's Other Psychosis Papers (1954–59)

Again, we remain in a mode of overview. With Bion's (1954) 'Notes on a Theory of Schizophrenia,' he appeared as a Kleinian analyst in earnest, inte-grating Klein's (1952) new ideas about psychosis. There was a fundamental adherence to the idea that no matter how primitive the patient might appear, there was a rudimentary external object relationship that existed even in the most disordered minds. Think here of Klein's own analyst, Karl Abraham, who maintained that the infant (or 'suckling') is born instinctually rooting for the mother's breast. The newborn does not have to be taught how to suck at the nipple; it just does so.

But we also must bear in mind that the 'Kleinian infant' was not an actual baby—it was more the hypothesized or 'virtual infant,' the remnant of infantile conflicts that had been carried forward into the subject's later years. In this respect, Klein (and now Bion) regarded psychotic patients as treatable by means of a new understanding. Fundamental to that understanding was Klein's (1952) mature definition of projective identification, an idea that could include the subject's forceful psychic entry into the object, which could give rise to paranoia. The patient's forceful entry could lead to claustrophobic phantasies of imprisonment inside the mother's body (Aguayo, 2009).

Bion (1954) now produced clinical examples of psychotic patients who used splitting and projective identification and 'part-objects' in exhibiting schizo-phrenic thinking. In other words, rather than use their words as communications with the analyst, the schizophrenic used language as a form of action. Bion thought that the psychotic showed a preference for action on occasions when other patients would realize that what was required was thought. A dramatic example: one of Bion's (2013) patients missed his train stop on his way to his session and simply thought that he could get off at the next stop while the train was still in motion. He of course sustained injuries and contusions in doing so: he acted when he should have thought.

In 'Language and the Schizophrenic' and 'On Group Dynamics' (revised), Bion (1955a, 1955b) doubled back to familiar ideas, only now deploying them with a new kind of patient, the psychotic. Accustomed to drawing upon his direct emotional experience in dealing with civilian out-patients at the Tavistock Clinic, Bion used this 'instrument of research' as a way to further articulate his views on countertransference, using it in *both* individual and group treatment situations. In my estimation, this gave Bion a different perspective vis-à-vis his Kleinian colleagues who were not steeped in group work, as it made it easier for him to trust his own direct emotional experience. Yet Bion made sparse statements in 1955, especially with the psychotic cases on which he published. He contented himself with general theoretical statements, such as the use of countertransference as experiential evidence in tracking his patient's experience. One small example: one of Bion's (1959) psychotic patients, in session, talked while he clenched his fist. In drawing on a feeling of worry and dread, the analyst suspected a meditated physical attack on the analyst. Interpreting the patient's hostility led to a lessening of tensions. Here Bion I think linked Klein's projective identification with Heimann's wider and informing use of countertransference. It signaled a direction that generations of Kleinians would follow in the ensuing years.

Very much like Freud, who often in his papers would take up the charges and critiques he imagined the reader could take, Bion took up the countertransference. As an idea, it too was open to the charge that it merely represented the analyst's unwarranted projection into the patient's experience—and expecting him to line up with it. Just because the analyst has a subjective reaction does not make it a true reflection of the patient's unconscious state of mind. Here, we see something of Bion's method, as he became practiced in the art of posing questions that an analyst would want to take up, such as not coming to easy foreclosure in the clinical situation. Paula Heimann (1950) had cautioned that the analyst must 'sustain and subordinate' their own disturbed emotional reactions, so that they might discover their true origins—either in the patient, or in themselves or in their complex interaction.

Bion began to shift his epistemic ground here, by which I simply mean the posing of the question: how does the analyst *know* what he knows? It would leave some of his readers baffled, having more questions than answers. There was no short-cut or premature foreclosure to be had on the question of how the analyst knew what he knew; and this led to one of Bion's (1955a, p. 225) paradoxical conclusions: "I would not have it thought that I advocate the use of countertransference as a final solution; rather it is an expedient to which we must resort until something better presents itself." Bion put forward the view that, often, the analyst makes interpretations "on the strength of (his) own emotional reactions," precisely because he is on the receiving end of projective identifications. But these reactions had to be in turn subjected to further scrutiny. How does the analyst differentiate whether he has temporarily lost insight and thus has given incorrect interpretations? Failure to ask these searching questions could result in the analyst's feeling imprisoned in the patient's subjective phantasy. The countertransference could be a helpful ally or an imprisoning master.

Yet right alongside of Bion's interrogation of the analyst's own methods of knowing, he remained loyal during this time to the understanding and techniques practiced by his former analyst, Melanie Klein. For instance: in his 1957 paper, 'Differentiation of Psychotic from Non-Psychotic,' he made it explicitly known that his analytic task was the analysis of the psychotic's internal, phantasmic subjective state. There would be no consideration of the 'environmental factor,' something that Winnicott's (1953) analytic work especially had brought to light after the publication of his own groundbreaking paper on Transitional Objects. In different words, while being quite aware of environmental influences, Bion did not make that an explicit part of his analytic work at that time. Bion regarded the environment as a sort of constant but secondary factor and maintained the Klein line of internal state of mind practice during the 1950s.

A brief case example, Bion's psychotic patient, 'A,' talked in a fragmented and disconnected way, as if he was talking to himself in the analyst's presence. The Kleinian analyst here represented external reality, the meaning-maker, and structural change agent, who attributed psychological meaning then to 'A's' sensory/motoric activity in the non-representational realm. The patient twitched and turned on the couch, making elliptical statements, such as, 'I should have rung my mother.' The analyst's interventions were subject to 'A's' obstructive denials and rebuffs—dreams with no associations; no connection or interest in his physical movements on the couch.

Bion (1957, p. 54) linked 'A's' sensory experience, which existed in what psychoanalysts now call the 'non-representational realm,' to the world of psychological meaning. He hypothesized what he termed an "ideo-motoric activity, … a means of expressing an idea without naming it." In the statement of 'meaning to ring his mother,' it seemed that 'A' had attacked his mind, damaging the communicative apparatus, so that mutilated communication ensued. The link to both mother as well as the analyst had been ruptured. There was no connective link with the analyst. From my perspective, the irony in this case is that Bion mentioned but ultimately dismissed any interest in the patient's actual mother with her own attributes, past or present. He focused his interest instead with 'A's' internal experience of the analyst-as-mother in the here and now as a projection-denying object. Bion here marginalized what would have been the heart of the matter to Winnicott. Bion the Kleinian at this point refused Winnicott's entreaty to focus on the kind of actual mothering the patient might have experienced in childhood (Winnicott, 1955, 'Letter to W.R. Bion').

Bion adhered to a strict *internal* focus on analyzing 'A's' most disturbed aspects, which meant the meaningful analysis of the 'psychotic' aspect before the 'non-psychotic' states of mind. The damage to the patient's ego must be repaired if the patient was to have the chance to make communicative statements vis-à-vis those that obstructed or destroyed communication. Here, the analyst existed in a dual role: as objective meaning-maker or de-coder of the patient's fragmentary, mutilated attempts at co-operation in the analytic task, while at the same time remaining the object of the patient's attempts at communication. The therapeutic task here would be to facilitate 'A's' understanding that he had attacked his own mind, and thereby impaired his capacity for thought. This was the seedling of Bion's iconic (1959) paper, 'Attacks on Linking.' The analyst's efforts here, while helping 'A' to regain his sanity, elicited both the patient's admiration as well as his envy—another Kleinian idea to which Bion subscribed—insofar as the analyst's sanity reminded the patient what he himself was lacking.

Sparse though it may have been, there was still a rudimentary object relationship that 'A' was capable of, some reality sense left over, so that the analyst could facilitate a meaningful contact with the sane aspect of 'A's' non-psychotic mind. Bion here helped to establish Klein's idea that there are neurotic islands of functioning in psychotics just as there are psychotic islands in the neurotic. Bion portrayed the psychotic attack on the analyst-as-meaning-maker as a representation of how the patient also attacked his links and attachments.

In his paper, 'On Hallucination,' Bion (1958) further analyzed 'A,' focusing now on a clinically useful account of hallucination. Bion's method of inquiry now takes shape: the particular observational basis, the leap to an intuitive image, a hypothesis on the basis of repetition of a pattern, a hypothesis tested in an interpretation to the patient, and eventually generalizing his understanding of the psychotics he treated as a basis of broader generalizations. He also made the deft point that the analyst of psychotic patients—or to the psychotic aspect of neurotic patients—had to be willing to undergo being the object of (as well as identify with) hallucinatory attacks and invasions if he was to have a chance to be genuinely helpful to his patients. The analyst had to demonstrate that he could absorb or identify how internally bombarded his patients felt (Civitarese, 2015).

To summarize Chapter 2, we have presented Melanie Klein's program for the analysis of psychosis. She disagreed with Freud in believing that the psychoanalytic treatment of psychosis was possible. Here, she enlisted the support of bright psychiatric disciples like Wilfred Bion (1967), Herbert Rosenfeld (1965) and Hanna Segal (1964) who early on took up the call to analyze psychotic patients. The 'Imaginary Twin' was a prelude to this work but showed Bion's enthusiasm for ideas associated with the work of Klein and

Kleinians, such as role-assignment, the understanding of countertransference, projective identification and the paranoid/schizoid and depressive positions. In addition to these ideas, Bion added in his own distinctive contributions based on astute observations, ideas such as 'attacks on linking' and hallucinatory evasions of reality, a phenomenon he also linked to the idea he termed 'psychotic dreaming.'

Chapter 3

A Portal into Psychosis

'The Imaginary Twin' (1950) and 'Notes on the Theory of Schizophrenia' (1954)

Foray into Psychosis

It may strike the reader as a bit strange to return to the case of the 'Imaginary Twin' that was discussed in the last chapter. Yet the notion of doubling back or returning to previously analyzed material is very much at the heart of the analytic method. This is one meaning of what Freud termed *Nachträglichkeit*, or *après-coup*, a retrospective resignification of earlier material covered in anyone's personal analysis. It is an after the fact reordering of the potential meaning inscribed at one point from the perspective of a later one. It also opens up the possibility of the unknown, the unsignified, as well as alterity and new constructions. In this instance, one doesn't recover the past so much as one recovers how time is inscribed in the present.

So, to return to the case of the 'Imaginary Twin,' arguably the single longest case ever reported by Bion, other elements do stand out. He was courageous enough, especially in light of the 'Twin's lack of emotional responsiveness to conjecture openly that while perhaps this particular patient wasn't suitable for analysis, it was also possible that he himself might be a poor choice as the patient's analyst. Since Bion submitted this paper for membership in the British Psychoanalytical Society in 1950, it strikes one as a bit odd that a student could appear so confident, especially at the brink of what could have been a treatment failure. Yet Bion's incessant self-questioning appears unusual here, confident in the face of possible defeat.

The quality of relentless questioning now becomes part of Bion's enduring style as a clinician: to question himself as well as interrogate the patient's material; to maintain an openness to experience, allowing himself to be corrected by the surfacing of new material or new conjectures on his part on what he had failed to understand. Bion's introspective method implied a reluctance to easy foreclosure; and it made it possible to have a 'second look,' or as he entitled his book on the psychosis papers, 'second thoughts' about the analytic material under consideration (Bion, 1967b).

The historian of psychoanalysis similarly foots himself in the context of those few analytic references that Bion explicitly or implicitly made in the

DOI: 10.4324/9781003364795-5

published text of the 'Twin.' It is one way that one can measure the impact of analytic authors crucial to his development as a psychoanalyst. Unfortunately, there are very few references in the 'Twin' case, certainly a strange practice for someone trained in the humanistic study of history, as Bion was at Oxford University. So, in our own doubling back to the text of this case, I focus on one main inspiring influence that Bion had in mind (other than Paula Heimann, whose work on the countertransference and John Rickman on role-recruitment, which were discussed in Chapter 2): Melanie Klein.

This was a small, closely knit circle around Klein after World War II ended. Both Heimann and Rickman were former analysands of Klein, who during this time (1945–53) was Bion's own analyst. Bion cited the work of his training analyst in the 'Twin' paper, Klein's (1930) paper, 'The Importance of Symbol Formation in the Development of the Ego.' Likewise, Bion's repeated mention of the term 'personification' leads us to think that he had in mind, Klein's (1929) paper, 'Personification in the Play of Children.'

However, beyond these sources, we are in the realm of conjecture because Bion left us few clues about who his other sources might be. We have good reason, however, to think that Paula Heimann was Bion's supervisor on this case. Since all candidates at the British Society existed in one of three different training groups, each candidate had to choose their first supervisor from members of their own group. So, it appears that Paula Heimann was his first supervisor—and certainly his supervisor on the 'Twin' case (Grosskurth, 1986, p. 431; Willoughby, 2006). Bion's (1951) letter to his wife Francesca praised Heimann, saying she "was the best of the [Kleinian] lot." Bion's choice of Paula Heimann seems meaningful because he repeatedly mentioned the terms 'projection' and 'introjection' in his text, certainly crucial since Heimann (1943) had written an important paper on this same topic, 'Some Aspects of the Role of Projection and Introjection in Early Development'; projection and introjection modeled off of bodily experiences of taking in and expelling as the ego steadily builds up a selective sampling of external stimuli in its immediate familial environment. Just as important was the fact that Klein's (1946) notion of projective identification never appeared in the text of the 'Twin' case.

Lastly, John Rickman (2003) was mentioned in Chapter 2 as having written papers on role-assignment in analysis, something that derived from his experience of Kurt Lewin's Field Theory, where a social context like a psychoanalytic relationship underscored the various roles that patients can play (and enlist their analysts to go along with). It was the 'pressure' associated with these roles that represented Rickman's further elaboration of the importance of role-playing originally written about by Klein (1932) in her analysis of young children. Well, as it turned out, children could just as easily become involved in role-play as adults. But again, beyond role assignment was the analyst's task of examining critically his own subjective reactions as a response to emotionally intense patient feelings and projections directed at him.

So, to my organizing thesis for Chapter 3, Bion's (1950) 'Twin' paper derived from the analytic ideas of Klein, Heimann and Rickman. With these analytic references in mind, let us now take a more detailed look at Bion's 'Twin' paper. Doing so helps us build up a more complex picture of how Bion functioned as a practicing psychoanalyst. Bion's 'Twin' paper also serves a bridging paper, taking up as it does role-recruitment, an idea present in his groupwork with adults, now deployed in understanding the dyadic experience of transference and countertransference in the papers on psychosis. Just as group members recruited the leader into various role assignments based on the group's underlying anxieties and tensions, so did the individual patient in analysis in terms of transference configurations.

In Chapter 2, we saw that Bion belatedly realized that the 'Twin' lived in a counterfeit state, one that uncovered a maddening quadrille inside the analysis—pseudo-patient, pseudo-analyst, real patient and real analyst. The 'Twin' had created a stasis-making situation, an atmosphere of meaninglessness while appearing as a compliant false-self in analysis.

We now turn to the account of the emotionally fraudulent atmosphere itself. This *folie à deux*, where the analyst was recreated as an 'imaginary twin' of the patient, incorporated Klein's understanding of splitting, where the 'Twin's solipsism fashioned projectively an image of the analyst that reflected his own self-image. And here, we double back to some work done by other analysts who link the 'Twin's pathology to the work of Samuel Beckett (Anzieu, 1989; Vermote, 2019). There do appear to be some striking similarities between the 'Twin' and protagonists depicted in Beckett's plays. It is a bit ironic that Bion recognized the role of the patient as, in effect, that of an unreliable and self-subverting narrator. There is a post-modernist feel to Bion's 'Twin,' as if analyst and patient appeared as the two protagonists in Beckett's famous play, *Waiting for Godot*, where the pair talk past one another, giving rise to the impression that they remain, at their core, self-deceived and at best, existing emotionally in parallel universes.

So, while Samuel Beckett may not have been Bion's 'Twin' patient, there is something quite Beckettian about how the course of the analysis ran. The notion of two characters living in parallel universes is of course a post-modern idea, where truth appears elusive and unattainable; it was also encapsulated later by Bion (1970) with his notion of 'reversible perspective,' where it sounds like two people are talking directly to one another, yet in fact exist in parallel and non-intersecting dimensions of personal experience (Vermote, 2019, pp. 66–69).

Let's examine this post-modernist parallelism by further looking at how Bion went about inquiring about his own analytic method while he interrogated the 'Twin's own account. Bear in mind that the details matter here, as I think the 'Twin' case was one main gateway to Bion's later work with difficult-to-treat patients, those in the borderline and narcissistic spectrum.

The 'Twin' paper started in a rather standard way—the analyst charted the patient's early history. We hear about a tragic childhood filled with death and loss. The patient's sister, older by just a year, died very early in his childhood. Another profound tragedy was his mother's death when he was 17, experienced against a bleakness of an austere childhood. It all fell apart when he was 13 and had a breakdown himself (Bion, [1950] 1967b, p. 3). Yet in spite of these overwhelming and early losses, Bion didn't refer very much to them at all during the course of the case presentation. Now it was possible that these early losses were worked through and then not written about. However, more likely is that Bion, even at this early point in his career as an analyst, simply did not put much stock in reconstructing past neurotogenic experiences into active, present-tense work. Recall here his critique of J.R. Hadfield, his first therapist, as 'Mr. Feel-It-in-the-Past.'

Bion's listening to but not directly incorporating the 'Twin's early history might not have struck contemporaries as noteworthy—after all, Klein herself had written up so many child cases in which the analytic work occurred in real time, that of the present moment. But Bion took this point to an extreme—where he might have conjectured that the 'Twin' might have been a psychic manifestation of survivor guilt—he lived while his sister died, and hence an understanding of why he felt so persecuted. Yet there was no mention of it. Even more striking was the fact that there was next to no mention of the 'Twin's mother, so that we have little account of how he might have subjectively experienced her, surely a signal omission in a Kleinian case write-up. Bion depicted the bulk of the 'Twin's conflicts in real time in the 'here and now.'

In the course of the present moment, Bion was left stymied and wondering what in his interpretations might have felt valid to the 'Twin' patient. It was as if both men were playing at doing something serious, but it was all in vain—it seemed as if neither man had to take seriously what they were doing together. Bion interested himself in the stale emotional atmosphere, where stale associations invited uninspired interpretations. When this atmosphere was detected, the patient seemed to resent that usual rhythm being broken. Questioning this arrangement, Bion finally discovered the 'Twin' hiding in plain sight—as well as from himself—and in one sense, his condition matched Freud's (1914) description of a narcissistic, self-cathected individual who had no libidinal bond to others, least of all to his analyst. Yet to Klein's (1946) point, Bion assumed that there was some capacity for object relationship because the 'Twin' also was responsive to the analyst's efforts at emotional connection.

In this enlivened atmosphere, the patient reported a dream, *where he was driving in a car and about to overtake one in front of him; he pulled up abreast of the other car, but then the two slowed down in tandem; the other man got out—and now, the patient's way out was blocked. The other man came over and leaned on his door, leering menacingly at him through the window.* The patient awoke shaken from this dream and remained anxious throughout the next day. If we read this manifest dream in a line-by-line way, one possible rendition or understanding is that the 'Twin' depicted the analysis as some sort of competition, like a car race—who would overtake whom, and who would win? Yet the 'Twin' did not overtake the analyst, who is the man in the other car, but pulls up in tandem with him. I see this as a defensive reversal of what had just happened: in fact, it was the analyst who had just now emotionally calibrated and become attuned to the 'Twin's phantasied lair of mind.

Judging by the conclusion of the dream, the 'Twin' now emerged emotionally terrified. Now detected inside a secret enclave, the 'Twin' feared being subjected to reprisals, and exuded a sense of claustrophobically being 'pinned in' by a menacing, angry and threatening analyst. The price for direct emotional contact was terror and persecutory anxiety. Bion interpreted that he was the other driver, the 'Imaginary Twin' that the patient had spoken about in the last session. Just as the patient felt he had prevented the birth of his twin, perhaps his sister, his own twin now determined that the patient should not be born (i.e. have either freedom or independence). Bion (1950[1967b], p. 8) wrote: 'He was thus shut in, both by the twin and by his own act in parking his car so near the twin's car.'

To recapitulate: it was by way of defensive reversal that the analyst was depicted as trapped and not able to emerge as a real person to the patient. More importantly, the 'Twin' could not appear as real to himself. Yet at the same time, the fact that the analyst had made genuine emotional contact was experienced by the patient as blocking the patient's escape from analysis, a personification of the bad aspect of himself that had to be dissociated. Here, I think Bion employed Klein's (1929) idea of personification in the transference, where he appeared defensively depicted as 'leering and menacing,' in effect threatening the patient's enduring way of living inside a defensive fortress, where emotional contact was blunted off and evaded.

So, the 'Twin' *looked like and sounded like* a patient, but donned the role of 'pseudo-patient,' more adhered to a phantasied object relationship than a reality-relationship with his analyst. The deceived analyst had to get at the truth of the patient's disturbed state of mind in order to make any emotional contact. The analyst had been duped, taken in by responses that led him to believe that actual analytic work was being done. Not so, as the patient-as-'Twin' had made himself comfortable within the analysis so as not to be disturbed. He hadn't come to terms with reality, and the analyst had been led down a false trail—his linking interpretations hadn't touched the patient at all.

Put differently, it was as if patient and analyst were operating with two different models of the mind. The analyst's model of what was operative in the 'Twin's mind, while it purported to be *about* the patient's mind, ran in a parallel track to the patient's model of his own mind. The patient's own model of mind was premised on screening others out, all while appearing to be interested in emotional engagement. An *as-if* patient was in analysis, playing at having contact. Verbal communication was primarily a mode of action, more charade than realistic encounter. Bléandonu (1994, p. 110) has also brought this aspect of the case into greater direct light—Bion did in fact call upon a "range of subtle responses in order to find the meaning of his patient's ambiguous paradoxes." It amounted to Bion effecting a perspectival shift when he realized that his patient could not differentiate the real from the imaginary. This shift in perspective initially annoyed the patient, who in turn felt his analyst was not trying to work with him but doing something more like 'counter-complaining' against him.

But when real emotional contact was made, it turned out that the analyst had been depicted as having swallowed (or 'introjected') the patient-as-twin and the 'poisonous family' he felt *living inside himself.* In order to secure his otherwise tenuous emotional safety, Bion (1950, p. 19) concluded that the patient had to deny a reality different from his own. The poisonous family had been projected into the analyst. Bion thus located the 'origin of pathology,' in Bléandonu's words, "in an excess of aggression, resulting in the introjection of bad objects," "This aggression is a problem because it prevents reality-testing" (1994, p. 111). The problem posed to this patient resulted from the toxifying and endangering presence of a damaged internal object, which had been projected into the analyst, thus making him appear as such a potentially menacing and threatening figure. After the patient's acceptance of the imaginary twin, his analyst finally became a much more real person to him; and one would suspect, more importantly, the patient became more real to himself.

To conclude with some final words on this fascinating case: Bion added, at least to my reading, two additional case examples at the end of the 'Twin' paper, which strike me as extraneous, superfluous and in a real sense, unnecessary supplemental material to the case of the 'Twin.' So why include them? We can think here of putting the 'Twin's pathology in more disturbed terms: the patient was dissociated and secured his safety against psychotic decompensation by pretending to interact. Real emotional exchange might precipitate another breakdown like the one he experienced in adolescence. Bion adduced some important speculations here: one refers to the personification of splits. He wrote

> Is it possible that the capacity to personify splittings of the personality is in some way analogous to a capacity for symbol formation to which Mrs. Klein has drawn attention in her paper on 'The Importance of Symbol Formation in the Development of the Ego?'
>
> (Bion, 1950 [1967b], p. 20)

In other words, was the healthier part of the patient's personality at the cusp of the depressive position, which in Klein's understanding would entail a capacity for symbolization, which could potentially lead to alternative, fuller meanings? Perhaps. Yet the patient-as-twin didn't realize that his concretely evacuated projections required another mind to receive, distill and understand them.

It is in this way that I think the 'Twin's analysis was linked to a darker possibility, something else that would become a source of enduring interest to Bion in the 1950s—the understanding and analysis of psychosis. It is in this sense that the 'Twin' paper had its darker and more disturbed shadowy side and became a meaningful prelude to Bion's work on psychosis proper. In the last analysis, the 'Twin' feared having another nervous breakdown if direct emotional contact was made. Neurosis and psychosis appeared side by side here.

Bion's (1954) 'Notes on a Theory of Schizophrenia'

Bion delivered his first formal paper on psychosis at the International Psychoanalytic Congress (or IPA) in London, in July 1953, after he had been treating psychotic patients for a few years. He integrated the Kleinian work that explicated new ideas about psychosis. In Heimann's (1952) re-working of Freud, she maintained a primitive and rudimentary external object relationship obtained in even the most disordered minds (Klein et al., 1955). Thus, Freud's idea about 'primary narcissism,' or the infant's 'objectless' state vis-à-vis both auto-erotic and narcissistic phantasies was reconceptualized as a primitive object relationship existing in the paranoid/schizoid position. Psychotic patients were now treatable by means of psychoanalysis.

Klein (1952) formally and more completely defined projective identification, incorporating Rosenfeld's work of the patient's psychic and forceful entry *into* the object, which could give rise to paranoia (Aguayo, 2009). Forceful entry could lead to claustrophobic phantasies of imprisonment inside the mother's body. Heimann's (1952) work also came close to Klein's new definition when she discussed how the infant usurped the object's 'good,' i.e., pleasurable qualities, and treated them as if they belong to the self, and disowned his 'bad' painful qualities and treated them as belonging to the object. The hatred against parts of the self is now directed towards the mother. Heimann (1952) also used a more Freudian way of describing projective identification in terms of projective and introjective processes (akin to what Rosenfeld (1964) would later define as 'narcissistic object relations').

Bion (1954 [1967b], p. 24) now produced clinical examples of psychotic patients who deployed splitting and projective identification and 'part-objects' in exhibiting schizophrenic thinking. It entailed the first of three key characteristics that differentiated psychotic from non-psychotic:

> Language is employed in three ways: as a mode of action, as a method of communication, and a mode of thought. He will show a preference for action on occasions when other patients would realize that what was required was thought.

For the psychotic patient who claimed, "I am a prisoner of psychoanalysis …. I can't escape," the analyst had three interpretative options: the patient's own phenomenological description of his state of mind; or the psychoanalytic situation in which patient and analyst found themselves; and as a projective identification of a situation in which the patient experienced himself as being held captive *by* the analyst. But escape from the imprisonment offered no respite, as it also meant evacuating the capacity for thought into the analyst. This forceful evacuation left the patient depleted in a barren, dismantled state of freefall. Attacking the capacity for thought could result in fragmentation of experience to the level of minute particles of experience.

The patient felt assaulted internally by an introjected 'bad' and hostile object, concreteness and incapacity to form symbolic meaning. It left the analyst as the sole meaning-maker and bearer of sane thinking. Bion's work here adhered strictly to the Kleinian line of elucidating the patient's internal, phantasmic and subjective state of mind.

In terms of Bion's implicit model of analytic treatment, we can see that he began to elasticize the projection/introjection model, making mention of the countertransference as part of the analyst's armamentarium, another valuable 'instrument of research.' But he also did not elaborate on the counter-transference itself in print. There would have been a question of how aware he was of the growing divide between Klein and Heimann over the controversy about countertransference—Klein saw it as personal interference, where Heimann saw it as an instrument of research, an aspect Bion (1955a) would soon turn into the induced countertransference. In Klein's unpublished 'remarks' for this IPA London Congress of 1953, however, she acknowledged that psychotic patients *did* elicit sharp and intense reactions from their analysts, but she did not publish these thoughts (Hinshelwood, 2008; Spillius, 2007).

Bion (1954, p. 24) was also able to think about how the psychotic 'split' up his internal objects by a more elastic use of projective identification. He wrote:

> At the moment I want to consider only his use of it as a mode of action in the service either of splitting the object or projective identification. It will be noted that this is but one aspect of schizophrenic object relations in which he is either splitting or getting in and out of his objects. The first of these uses is in the service of projective identification.

In effect, Bion deployed Klein's formal definition of projective identification for the first time, when the patient forced himself hostilely into his objects, then felt trapped inside and then faced the problem of extrication. In this the patient used words as "things or as split-off parts of himself which he pushed forcibly into the analyst."

Bion's (1954, p. 25) clinical examples are hard to summarize because they contain wildly contradictory, quite irrational elements—as the patient is projecting split images, for example, the psychotic patient who stood bewildered before an elevator (or lift): "How does the lift know what to do when I press two buttons at once?" A psychotic patient could constantly maintain split images of the object—the object was both sides now—with the patient feeling hopelessly trapped in between. Put differently, if the patient was constantly disintegrating his objects, or splitting them up, he was mired in part-object thinking and unable to meaningfully deploy symbolic thinking. It would be more symbolic equations than anything else. Klein pointed out that verbal thought was an act of integration; and that the depressive position was one of active synthesis and integration. Analysis as a treatment employed verbal thought in the solution of mental problems.

Bion (1954, p. 27) gave a clinical example of a schizophrenic who showed splitting in the formation of symbols and the development of verbal thought. In the first session, the patient split the analyst's words up, so that the word 'penis,' so crucial to the analyst's interpretation, became fragmented into letters, contained no meaning for the patient and thus could not be thought about. The next day, there was no interesting food for the patient because as he interpreted, it had all been eaten up. The patient felt himself to be a 'mass of holes' (so badly injured that he is left empty). There had been his attacks on the penis (as a linking organ), leaving the patient with bizarre split objects (p. 28). More bizarre verbalizations ensued: he reported ten days later, "Tears come from my ears now." The patient, now in analysis for six years, was capable of a fair amount of identification with his analyst (p. 29). He deplored a blunder he had made, seeing it as another instance of an inability to put words together properly. Thus, to use the concept of symbolic equations, an idea coined by Hanna Segal, one of Bion's close Kleinian colleagues during this time, where a thing is inappropriately equated with a symbolic representation: tears from his ears = sweat from his skin, where he removed blackheads = urine that came from a hole where a penis had been but was now torn out; the bad urine still came. Bion took all this up in the transference, where he interpreted that the patient could not hear his interpretations well because his words were drowned by the tears in the patient's ears; he then made grunts and other unintelligible sounds; it seemed that there was no hope for effective communication. Was there some hostile object inside the patient that was attacking their verbal intercourse?

The internal attacks on the patient's capacity to communicate were then followed by his idea that "his verbal communication was extremely greedy." He had split himself into so many people, only to hear so many different interpretations from Bion, who concluded: "Clearly this patient felt that splitting had destroyed his ability to think." The loss of a capacity for thought is experienced by the patient as having felt left inside the analyst, or inside the analysis itself. If the patient had dislocated his mind, he feels himself to be 'insane.' If the analyst has effected his loss of mind, then the patient would be afraid of employing his new-found capacity for verbal thought lest it arouse the hatred of the analyst (Bion, 1954 [1967b], p. 31).

But the attainment of verbal thought could be felt as catastrophic by the patient, something so depressive that he resorted to projective identification, split it off and pushed it into the analyst. Without a mind, the patient felt insane; yet re-introjection of this capacity was felt to be overwhelmingly depressive because he would realize he had been acting insane. The patient dreaded the analysis now because he realized that it demanded of him the verbal thought that he dreaded. Violent disintegration could occur in the face of the depressive position.

To recapitulate Chapter 3, Bion's 'Imaginary Twin' patient fell between the poles of neurosis and psychosis. While his aching split was a delineated part of his self-experience, within the enclave itself, the patient appeared schizoid or dissociated from reality. Bion showed that he had learned his analytic craft by deploying key Kleinian ideas, such as splitting, projective identification, the narrow and wide use of countertransference, as he now sailed directly into the foreboding realm of the psychoanalytic treatment of psychosis. If it is true that there is a 'psychotic island' within all of us—usually in our sleep when we are dreaming—we can all appear as mad—so then Bion reasoned that there must be a neurotic island with the most disturbed psychotic patients. The neurotic island thus became a point of contact, where emotional meaning could be made.

Chapter 4

Bion as an Uneasy Kleinian Psychoanalyst

'Development of Schizophrenic Thought' (1956) and 'Differentiation of Psychotic from Non-Psychotic Personalities' (1957)

Further Work on the Psychoses

Before delving into Bion's later papers on psychosis, a brief word on his use of Kleinian terminology in his clinical method. We draw upon his clinical examples, which formulate in a loose way, how he conducted his psychoanalytic work in the 1950s. Recall that in the 'Imaginary Twin,' Bion (1950) used terms, such as 'projection,' 'introjection,' 'splitting' and 'personification,' where the analyst existed primarily as the interpretative de-coder of the patient's unconscious phantasies. After 1952, in 'Language and the Schizophrenic' and 'On Group Dynamics' (Bion, 1955a; 1955b) Bion adopted Klein's formal definition of projective identification—and after 1955, he then expanded its use in other generative directions.

One of the first areas of expansion occurred in the area of countertransference. Recall that besides Heimann, other Kleinians published very little about the countertransference between 1950 and 1955. A prominent Kleinian, Herbert Rosenfeld (1952), implicitly acknowledged the work of Paula Heimann (1950). He wrote:

> In my opinion the unconscious intuitive understanding by the psychoanalyst of what a patient is conveying to him is an essential factor in all analyses, and depends on the analyst's capacity to use his counter-transference as a kind of sensitive 'receiving set'.
>
> (Rosenfeld, 1952, p. 116)

Bion made a brief comment on countertransference at the International Psychoanalytic Congress (or IPA) in London in 1953:

> Evidence for interpretations has to be sought in the countertransference and in the actions and free associations of the patient. Countertransference has to play an important part in analysis of the schizophrenic, but I do not propose to discuss that today.
>
> (Bion, 1954, p. 113)

DOI: 10.4324/9781003364795-6

However sparse these comments, countertransference was also of interest to Melanie Klein at that time as well. Hinshelwood (2008) concurred with Spillius' (2007) view that Klein basically remained aligned with Freud's view of countertransference as personal interference when the analyst's unconscious complexes were activated by the patient's transference. (Think of Jung as the amorous object of desire for his patient Sabina Spielrein—he was unable to resist being the libidinal transference object). There is evidence however that Klein also had a more sophisticated view, written up as an 'intended contribution'—a comment on Bion's (1954) 'Notes on a Theory of Schizophrenia' for the 1953 IPA Congress in London. Klein was well aware of the impact that the psychotic's at times violent and hostile splitting had on the analyst. Klein wrote:

> In addition to all this, there is a point I wish to stress—the particular processes of the schizophrenic of splitting his own ego and of the analysis of projective identification, a term I coined to denote the tendency to split parts of the self and to put them into the other person, stir in the analyst very strong countertransference feelings of a negative kind. (Remarks on countertransference).
>
> (Hinshelwood, 2008, p. 102)

However, Klein never published these views and remained officially aligned with the Freudian understanding of personal interference.

In my view, one of the main reasons that so little was published on countertransference in the early 1950s was because of a personal antagonism that had developed between Klein and one of her leading disciples, Paula Heimann. As we just noted, there wasn't that much difference in Klein's unofficial view from that of Heimann. There were, however, other factors at play in Heimann and Klein's mutual distancing. I have maintained that from the perspective of having her group's theoretical and clinical contributions formally and institutionally recognized in the British Society's tri-partite training structure after 1945, Klein was also finally able to expect a more thoroughgoing allegiance to her theories than ever before. This new factor buttressed her increasing need to have 'all-in' Kleinian disciples who would take up her innovations in theory (Aguayo and Regeczkey, 2016). Makari (2008) described a similar phenomenon in noting that Freud turned his Viennese collaborators (e.g., Alfred Adler, Wilhelm Stekel) into adversaries after psychoanalysis gained international prominence in 1909. Freud could and did demand an 'all-in' allegiance to his libido theory, certainly one crucial factor that led to the eventual break with Carl Jung.

Likewise, Klein's popularity at the British Society grew post-World War II, also as a result of having three new promising psychiatrists-as-disciples and analysands. The trio of Rosenfeld, Segal and Bion exemplified the new, 'all-in' Kleinian. In her programmatic advocacy for the treatment of the psychoses, their loyalty to her theory was not compromised. Yet Klein's advocacy for this new group also put her at loggerheads with members of her old cohort from years past—and here, Heimann's (1950) work stood out. Long since aligned with Klein's work, Heimann's attempts at theoretical differentiation also ran afoul of an increasing intransigence on Klein's part. Heimann's emphasis on countertransference as an 'instrument of research' brought her conflict with Klein's newfound need for 'all-in' allegiance, especially pronounced in the early 1950s. A similar intransigence on Klein' s part also underscored Winnicott's (1953) departure, as he too was another long-term Klein collaborator, who also attempted to differentiate his own views on the importance of the maternal environment in his landmark paper on 'Transitional Objects.'

This emphasis threw a light on the strict focus that Klein and Kleinians like Bion maintained on the analysis of the patient's subjective, phantasmic internal world. Klein's increasingly strict emphasis on the child's phantasmic internal world as underlying its inherent psychological condition was now acquiring a defining prominence in her technique. Regardless of how evocative or truthful Winnicott's theory building might be about the infant's early psychological development as mediated by a maternal figure, it was in effect deemed less clinically relevant to the Kleinian analytic treatment of seriously disturbed patients (Aguayo and Regeczkey, 2016).

In light of the controversy over the countertransference, Bion took a measured path in putting forth his views during the mid-1950s. For example, by 1955, Bion now appeared more persuaded that the countertransference had to be considered more actively by the analyst—and he now wrote a bit more on the topic:

> The analyst who essays, in our present state of ignorance, the treatment of such patients, must be prepared to discover that for a considerable proportion of analytic time the only evidence on which an interpretation can be based is that which is afforded by the countertransference.

And a few sentences later, "I would not have it thought that I advocate this use of countertransference as a final solution; rather it is an expedient to which we must resort until something better presents itself" (Bion, 1955b, p. 225).

In other words, Bion now relied—in *both* the group and individual settings— on his direct emotional reactions as one way to assist him in the making of interpretations. He regarded the analyst as being on the receiving end of projective identifications and, with particularly disturbed patients, the issue of extricating oneself from such projective webs could be daunting. The possibilities multiplied with this expanded view of countertransference: there could be personal interference countertransference, where some personal complex obstructed the analyst clearly attuning to his patient's state of mind. There could also be unconscious-to-unconscious communications, where the patient unwittingly projected unmetabolized proto-mental systems (i.e., sensory experiences in the non-representational realm) into the analyst, leaving him confused and disorientated. These proto-mental systems could occur just as easily in work groups as they could with patients in individual analysis. The psychotic anxieties driving the subject in analysis were the same ones manifesting in Basic Assumption groups (dependency/flight–fight; pairing).

In 'Language and the Schizophrenic' Bion (1955b, p. 221) had previously described how the psychotic attacks his own mind by in effect attacking the ego functions associated with it. In effect, in his most regressed states, the psychotic patient attacked his ego functions in the form of "destructive attacks on all those aspects of his personality, his ego, that were concerned with establishing external contact and internal contact." Bion's phenomenological approach was in turn augmented in his 'Differentiation' paper when he proposed a different model for the psychotic's destructive attacks. Here Bion drew upon Klein's notion of the 'splitting of the self or ego' and the projective evacuation of the ensuing fragments. Not only could the psychotic split off despised affective states, but more importantly, he could attack, split off and project the mental functions Freud associated with the institution of the reality principle. It was clear in Bion's thinking that projective identification was the defining signature driving the psychotic's attacks on his own mind—and he had said so earlier in 1954:

> It is therefore to projective identification that I now turn, *but my examination of it is restricted to its deployment by the schizophrenic against all that apparatus of awareness that Freud described as being called into activity by the demands of the reality principle.*
>
> (Bion, 1954, p. 345; 1967b, p. 38; italics original)

Bion's Psychosis Papers of 1956/1957

To state in different terms the progression of Bion's thinking about psychosis at this crucial juncture: he had worked quite co-operatively with both Rosenfeld and Segal in the programmatic implementation of Klein's agenda that proposed the psychoanalytic treatability of psychotic patients. He had robustly expanded upon and demonstrated the fertility of concepts like projective identification in the understanding and treatment of psychosis. However, Bion also had a creative and fertile mind of his own. In 1945, when he started analysis with Klein, he even made it a condition of his treatment that he be able to retain his independence of mind as he underwent his analysis (Grosskurth, 1986, p. 427). It seems that he made good on this promise to himself because, at this precise juncture in the mid-1950s, he slowly began to make his own distinctive contributions, which simultaneously advanced the Kleinian program to analyze psychosis, while beginning to differentiate his own thinking from that of the Klein group.

To telescope my thesis: it was at this point that Bion began to engage what little Freud had written about psychosis in order to stretch his own conceptions about what lay at the heart of this puzzling disorder. Here, Bion focused and continued throughout the course of many years to return to one key paper Freud (1911) wrote on psychosis, 'Two Principles in Mental Functioning.' It is crucial to understand the argument put forth by Freud in this paper if we are to understand how Bion reread and revised it.

To Freud's argument in 'Two Principles,' the neurotic's 'flight into illness' forces the patient out of his real life and alienates him from reality. Reality is experienced as unbearable, so in neurotics it leads to repression; in the severely disturbed, the tendency towards 'hallucinatory psychosis,' an extreme turning away from reality that is often tied to a particular event that occasioned the outbreak of their insanity. The neurotic effects a less exaggerated version of what psychotics do with some fragment of reality. Contrasting these developmental derailments with those apparent at the outset of early mental life, the primary processes are governed by the pleasure–unpleasure principle (*Lust–Unlust*), which Freud now called the 'pleasure principle.' These processes strive towards pleasure and retreat from unpleasure. The infant's instinctual wishes appear gratified in some hallucinatory way (e.g., equating the thumb with the breast in imagined gratification) just as it occurs in the nightly dreams of adults. Yet the disappointment that ensues leads to the abandonment of this attempt at satisfaction by mean of hallucination. The psychical apparatus then decides on a different method when it forms a different conception of the real, external circumstances—and makes a suitable adjustment. A new principle of mental functioning emerges, one that is shaped by the reality principle.

The increasing importance of external reality heightens the importance of the "sense-organs that are directed towards the external world, and of the *consciousness* attached to them" (Freud, 1911, p. 220). Attention is developed to scan the external world to see how one's needs might be brought into alignment with it; 'notation' is developed, "whose task it was to lay down the results of this periodic activity of consciousness—a part of what we call *memory*" (p. 220). One compares experiences based on memory to see if some impartial passing of judgment can occur, one that supersedes judgments made previously based on the repression of unpleasurable ideas. Formerly under the domination of the primary processes, hallucinatory wish-fulfilment occurs in the form of motoric discharge of 'accretions of stimuli' by action. Now under the sway of the secondary process/reality principle, there is restraint instigated by the process of thinking. Thinking simultaneously allows the tolerance of increased tension while postponing the process of discharge. Freud wrote: "It is essentially an experimental kind of acting, accompanied by displacement of relatively small quantities of cathexis together with less expenditure (discharge) of them" (p. 221).

To clarify this somewhat dense language: there are always admixtures of the reality and pleasure principles, as older sources of pleasure are sometimes tenaciously held on to, so that split-off pockets could exist and remain immune to the reality principle. So, the ascendency of the reality principle does not therefore imply the complete eclipse of the pleasure principle, "but only a safeguarding of it" (p. 222). In sum, the reality principle never completely supersedes the pleasure principle. Think here of Freud's statement that in our nightly dreams, we briefly return to a pleasure oriented/narcissistic state of mind.

So, what about those instances where there is an entire disregard for the reality principle? Psychotic patients as we have seen can show a tendency to equate their thoughts with reality; and their wishes with fulfilment. Freud concluded his short paper by saying that his thoughts about psychosis were "preparatory, rather than expository" insofar as he had been looking at the "psychical consequences of adaptation to the reality principle and how it came into being" (p. 226).

Aside from his analysis of the Schreber memoir, Freud's project on psychotic disorders by and large fell by the wayside. Among the legacies of this fall-out, very few analysts expressed interest in taking up the arduous task of explicating the psychoses in a thoroughly systematic and psychoanalytic manner. Of the few that did, gifted analysts, such as Karl Abraham, died at an early age in 1925 and thus was unable to complete work he had done on psychotic states such as manic-depression. Of his own students and analysands, Melanie Klein kept alive Abraham's wish that the psychoanalytic understanding of the psychoses might be possible, and this was a kind of inter-generational agenda that the publishing trio of Rosenfeld, Segal and Bion took up in the 1950s (Aguayo, 2009).

However, by the mid-1950s, Bion now also began to express a need for theoretically and clinically differentiating his views from those of his colleagues. As we have seen in the cases of former Kleinian colleagues like Heimann and Winnicott, this was a somewhat hazardous undertaking! We have seen how Bion took up the psychotic's disordered thinking, specifically their misuse of language as a mode of action. Where thought was required, the psychotic took action; where action was necessary, the psychotic could remain hopelessly trapped in an internal mental web in which he attacked his own mind.

At this same time in 1955, Bion more actively took up the views of his first analyst and former supervisor (Rickman and Heimann) as he now extended the conceptual reach of analysts treating psychotic patients. He now took up the objectively and highly disturbing nature of their disordered thinking on the mind of the analyst. When the patient forcefully intruded his delusions and misperceptions *into* the analyst's mind, how did the analyst maintain his neutrality, let alone remain able to interpret the meaning of the patient's most peculiar communications? Working in a distinctive way, Bion regarded what he came to understand as the psychotic patient's 'ideo-motor activities' as a total communicational and organizing field of experience.

When the patient forcefully intruded these primitive processes *into* the mind of the analyst, the analyst had to consider their communicational impact:

how he would extricate himself from such an imprisoning literality? Bion now regarded the patient's projective identification as potentially illuminating his countertransference—as he felt literally put in the patient's shoes. Yet the analyst also carried the ego discriminating activity of being the bearer of sanity, which often also aroused envious attacks on the patient's part. Bion wrote about how the analyst survived these bits of psychic shrapnel, especially when the psychotic attacked both his own mind as well as that of the analyst. The analyst had to be mindful of how the psychotic was gripped by omnipotent destructive phantasies, which he often treated as concrete 'facts.' Massive projective identification attacks left the psychotic with 'bizarre objects,' as he attacked the links to his mind and to others. The analyst attempted to digest the psychotic's experience, so that metabolized understanding might indeed result (Aguayo, 2009).

Just as Bion had revised the psychoanalytic understanding of intra-group tensions, which led to a new view of how groups functioned, he now revised and expanded upon Freud's rudimentary ideas about psychotic patients, emphasizing their internal experience. Increasingly, through the 1950s, he revised Freud's ideas: for instance, it wasn't that psychotics hated reality and defensively altered it, they despised their *awareness* of reality. Bion dialogued with Freud's writings on psychosis, differentiating his own views as he simultaneously expanded upon the Kleinian program of analyzing psychosis. Our aim here is to trace Bion's conceptual evolution, taking particular note of how he engaged Freud's writings.

At the outset of 'Notes on the Theory of Schizophrenia,' Bion (1954) adduced some clinical material from Freud's (1915) paper on 'The Unconscious,' where a patient with an obsessive preoccupation with blackheads was regarded by Freud as working out his castration complex. Bion (1954, p. 115; 1967b, p. 29) implied that a symbolic equation was at work: to his way of thinking, when the patient picked the blackheads off his face, he imagined that he had created a deep cavity that he feared was noticed by others. Freud tied this to the patient's castration complex that was mediated by guilt feelings about masturbation; feminization thus became an internal punishment. Bion's implication however also suggested the existence of a psychotic pocket underlying a neurotic symptom.

In 'Development of Schizophrenic Thought,' Bion (1956, p. 344; 1967b, p. 36) again cited Freud's work *en passant* when he implicitly referred to 'Two Principles' without a specific citation: "Freud's description ... of the mental apparatus called into activity by the demands of the reality principle and in particular by that part of it which is concerned with the conscious awareness of sense impressions." On the other hand, Bion did cite Freud's *Civilization and Its Discontents*, claiming that it was left to Klein and her students to follow up on the importance of the conflict between the life and death instincts, crucially implicated in the understanding of schizophrenia.

It was only with 'Differentiation of Psychotic from Non-Psychotic' that Bion (1957) substantively grappled with aligning Freud's views on psychoses with both Klein's and his own. Very much in the spirit of Klein's work, which had filled in Freud's detailed map of the neurotic disorders in adults when she extended the range of analytic understanding into the actual analysis of young, pre-latency aged children, Bion now attempted to reconcile Kleinian and Freudian's views of psychotic states of mind. First and foremost, he accomplished this by a creative mis-reading of Freud's 'Two Principles' paper. Bion effected what Fisher (2009, *unpublished*) termed a 'conceptual leap' in his discussion of Freud's reality principle when he extended Freud's analysis of the capacity to acknowledge the reality of the external world to the patient's capacity to acknowledge emotional/internal reality. I agree with Fisher here that Bion now became Freud and Klein's heir in the development of the psychoanalytic understanding of psychosis.

Bion (1957) here began to define a process of thinking by means of which it became possible to incorporate emotions. So, in taking up Freud's descriptions of the 'ego functions' (attention, memory, judgement, thought and action) aspects so crucial to Freud's view of adhering to the reality principle, Bion adduced clinical examples from his work with psychotic patients to demonstrate how this adherence to the reality principle went awry. Yet the failure to adhere to the reality principle was only one aspect of the psychotic's profound dilemma: Bion also added that what was attacked was the psychotic's *awareness* of reality. So, at the heart of Bion's deployment of Freud's (1911) 'Two Principles' paper was a profound rethinking of some fundamental psychoanalytic assumptions about the relationship between the pleasure and reality principles. Bion reasoned that if analysts could understand the capacity leading to the awareness and acknowledgement of *both* external and internal reality, then we could examine how psychotic states of mind resulted from a disruption of those processes.

In 'Language and the Schizophrenic' Bion (1955a, p. 221) described how the psychotic attacks his own mind by in effect attacking the ego functions associated with it. In effect, in his most regressed states, the psychotic patient attacks his ego functions in the form of "destructive attacks on all those aspects of his personality, his ego, that are concerned with establishing external contact and internal contact." Bion (1956) augmented his phenomenological approach when he proposed a different model for the psychotic's destructive attacks. Here Bion drew upon Klein's notion of the 'splitting of the self or ego' and the projective evacuation of the ensuing fragments. Not only could the psychotic split off despised affective states, but more importantly, he could attack, split off and project the mental functions Freud associated with the institution of the reality principle. It was clear in Bion's thinking that projective identification was the defining mechanism driving the psychotic's attacks on his own mind.

To summarize Chapter 4, it seems a bit ironic that someone who was so deft in handling 'intra-group tensions' became a bit consumed by the in-fighting that occurred in the Klein group in the early 1950s. But it was also Bion, increasingly uneasy as a 'Kleinian,' who said that man was at 'war with his groupishness'—and he was no exception. While Bion along with Rosenfeld and Segal maintained a fiercely Kleinian internal line in their writings on psychosis, they all tread wearily on the slippery slope of the countertransference (as outlined by Heimann). They learned from the experience of watching long-term collaborators of Klein leave the group. Yet along with a set of ideas that Bion found attractive, he now found himself uneasily at the core of an 'all-in Kleinian' group that wrote a series of groundbreaking papers on psychosis.

When Bion drew attention to the internal experience suffered by psychotics, as when they attack their own minds—and the minds of their analysts—he began increasingly to encounter Freud's rudimentary writings on psychosis. He especially dialogued with Freud's (1911) 'Two Principles of Mental Functioning,' focusing his attention on the psychotic's enduring *internal* experience. For instance, when he took up Freud's emphasis on 'notation' and 'attention,' he did so increasingly to show the new kinds of observations that the analyst could bring to bear on what psychotic patients pervasively suffered. Previously, we have discussed this point in the group period when I termed Bion's capacity to point out what was happening in the room in real time one of being a 'facilitating indicator,' or someone who drew the group's attention to a particular phenomenon. This indicating function left the meaning of the phenomenon more open—or to use a term from a few years on in Bion's theoretical development—'unsaturated' so that the analytic dyad could explore its meaning.

Chapter 5

Further Clinical Contributions, Part I

'On Arrogance' (1958a) and 'On Hallucination' (1958b)

Introduction

I double back to Bion's work up to this point, only from a different perspective (or 'vertex' to use his term), one that an Anglo-American research group (Robert Hinshelwood, Sira Dermen, Nicola Abel-Hirsch and I) call Bion's 'Implicit Method of Clinical Inquiry.' The main question here is: can we ascertain his particular way of working in the consulting room? This is not an easy issue to understand because Bion was quite disinclined to write about analytic technique, as he wanted to avoid any specter of starting a school complete with acolytes and followers. Klein herself wrote relatively more about technique during her lifetime.[1]

Bion nonetheless did have a distinctive way of working with clinical material. For some time now, our research group (Aguayo, Hinshelwood, Dermen and Abel-Hirsch) has sifted through Bion's actual clinical work to see if we could find and describe its defining patterns. After an extensive survey of his clinical examples in all phases of his professional practice, we evolved the idea of a 'Implicit Method of Clinical Inquiry' (or IMCI). It pertains to a loosely saturated concept based on a clinically inductive method of reasoning—the analyst orients to session material with an organizing set of preconceptions and gathers clinical data, transforming it into analytic concepts, which may shed light on particular classes of patients. With enough concepts, they can form models and theories, which can be further tested. What was Bion's cast of mind like and what were the enduring features of his IMCI?

Bion's IMCI is a Janus-faced model, a set of concepts that extend to the technical interventions an analyst might make with his patients on the one side, and on the other, how these clinical concepts inform the building of theoretical revisions. One illustrative paper is Bion's (1958a) 'On Arrogance.' Given the analyst's commitment to verbal communication and understanding with severely disturbed patients, what if the patient has alternative ways, say elliptical speech and motoric/sensory gestures of making his states of mind known? The patient could experience the analyst as a projective

DOI: 10.4324/9781003364795-7

identification denying figure, in short, an obstructive object. The analyst's failure to recognize the patient's need to communicate in such a different fashion could also contribute to the analyst's actually becoming an obstructive object as well.

These clinical findings led to a fresh understanding of the Oedipus myth: if the analyst's epistemological task is to inquire and establish the psychic truth of the patient's living emotional experience, this commitment can and does elicit varying responses from patients—cooperative, conflictual and even obstructive. The analyst's epistemological task is one form of disciplined curiosity. These perspectival experiences gave Bion's IMCI additional dexterity, as there could be different aspects at play: it encompasses traditional countertransference, where the analyst might be contributing to acting like an obstructive object; it incorporates Kleinian ideas about envy, in which the patient's resentment of the analyst's sanity, particularly in making links, could render him obstructive to furthering the aims of enquiry in the analysis; and of course, situations in which both partners can contribute to obstructing the overall aims of inquiry.

In going back to the origins of IMCI in Bion's group period, Hinshelwood (2019) tells us that Bion was influenced by the Lewin/Rickman line of regarding the group analyst as existing in a social field or context in which members would projectively shape his image based on 'intra-group tensions' that would result in assigning him particular roles to play. Bion drew on his direct emotional experience with the group to ascertain what role or function he might be carrying for them. This became a part of his introspective method where accurate observations led to better or more useful formulations. So, from this 'vertex,' he carried a 'facilitating indicating' function, where he drew attention to group phenomena occurring in real time and demonstrated how to wait and see how the group would respond. He remained aware of the fundamental tension between the group's work task and the unconscious irrational forces that could obstruct or interfere with it. Most importantly, Bion's preconceptions became part of an enduring way in which he oriented and understood analytic material—and I maintain that it had an important carryover effect when he began writing about psychosis in the 1950s.

When he started analyzing individual patients, these methods were altered to accommodate a new situation. Here we posited a set of influential sources—Rickman, Klein and Heimann—who guided his work. Initially from Rickman, how the patient was unconsciously communicating with him and what role he might be playing for the adult patient. From Klein, he took up her ideas on the positions—depressive (whole-object) then paranoid/schizoid (part-object) analyses, projective identification and unconscious phantasy. Heimann encouraged the further use of his direct emotional experience, now in the form of countertransference analysis to ascertain the different kinds of unconscious communication to which he was subjected. In the case of the 'Imaginary Twin,' we saw how these ideas played out: whole-object analysis based on the analyst's direct emotional experience uncovered a patient living in an unacknowledged defensive enclave of a paranoid/schizoid type, one that allowed the Twin enough psychological leeway to appear and sound like he was emotionally engaged when in fact, he was only playing at it. Real analytic engagement commenced when direct contact with the phantasied lair was made. Rickman's idea still obtained: the analyst worked at understanding the patient's unconscious functioning while remaining its object in terms of unconscious role assignments.

Yet the Twin case had its shadowy, more pathological side, one that pointed to the patient's fear of psychotic decompensation, and in this sense, it was a meaningful prelude to Bion's turn to the study of psychosis. Its analytic study in the 1950s—still in its infancy—allowed Bion to become part of a groundbreaking publishing cohort (with Rosenfeld and Segal) that deployed part-object analysis to decipher the mysteries of psychosis. He contributed valuable ideas based on precise observations about the psychotic's enduring, internal and irrationally phantasmic experience. It led to innovations, such as the psychotic's use of language as a form of action (i.e., words-as-actions), and the psychotic's attack on his own mind.

But here a paradox occurred in the mid-1950s. Bion was also part of what I have termed an 'all-in' Kleinian group, loyal to Klein's program to analyze psychotic patients. He now also began to differentiate his work from the others in his cohort. He did this by now engaging Freud as well as Klein's work on psychosis, learning from it while critiquing it at the same time. For instance, just as Bion differed from Freud in his understanding of group psychology (as Bion came to his manhood in the crucible of total war), he now differed from Freud, who worked with neurotics, while Bion had by then had years of experience working with psychotic patients. Bion now made significant contributions on the psychotic's enduring internal experience, something else that Klein herself was not all that versed in (Aguayo and Regeczkey, 2016).

So, we now turn to Bion's (1958b) paper, 'On Hallucination,' focusing on those phenomena that Bion viewed somewhat differently from the way Freud depicted them. To boot, Bion further differentiated his views from those of other British colleagues, for instance those of D.W. Winnicott. In 1957, it seems to me that Bion also in part responded to Winnicott's entreaties, written in the form of private letters to Bion, to take up the 'environmental factor,' where the objective qualities and attributes of both mother and analyst were factored into consideration. Bion acknowledged this factor but would only slowly play it into his theoretical work over the next few years. Initially, Bion, like other Kleinians, regarded the environment as a sort of constant, i.e., when the analyst is doing their normal function of understanding and interpreting; and adhered to the Klein line that focused exclusively on the patient's internal, subjective states of mind. For practical purposes however, he did not develop this theme until 1959.

Bion (1957), for example, linked a psychotic patient's sensory experience, and here we call him 'A,' to the realm of psychological meaning. So, when 'A' talked in an elliptical way, almost as if he was talking to himself, saying things like, "I should have rung my mother today" and then breaking off the communication, Bion (1957, p. 271) hypothesized an "ideo-motoric activity, … a means of expressing an idea without naming it." The analyst thought that 'A' had attacked his mind, damaging the communicative apparatus, so that mutilated communication ensued. The links had been ruptured. Moreover, these fragmented, disconnected statements represented no connective link with the analyst. Bion here dismissed any interest in the patient's actual mother with her own attributes, past or present. He focused his interest instead with 'A's *internal* subjective experience of the analyst-as-mother in the here and now as a projection-denying object. He here marginalized what would have been the heart of the matter to Winnicott (1955). To the telephone comment, Winnicott thought it was about the patient's communication and his incapacity for making one. Winnicott here interested himself in a perspective of what was required of an *actual* external object, namely that of an attuned mother who would know from her baby's gestures what it needed.

Bion nonetheless adhered at this time to the strict focus on the patient's *internal state of mind*, the inner experience of the external object, where the analyst's task was to differentiate the 'psychotic' from 'non-psychotic' states of mind. The psychotic aspect had to be dealt with before the non-psychotic could be meaningfully analyzed. The 'rent in the ego' had to be repaired, something that made a facilitating and connecting communication possible, a move forward towards mediated verbal meaning in the depressive position; so, the disintegrative states of the paranoid/schizoid position before the potential for integrative states in the depressive position, or psychotic before non-psychotic/neurotic. The analyst existed in a dual role: as objective meaning-maker/de-coder of the patient's fragmentary, mutilated attempts at co-operation in the analytic task, while remaining its object.

Bion now deployed projective identification as explicating psychotic states of mind (e.g., the patient projected both filthy things/smells as well as his capacity for sight *into* the analyst, which the analyst then experienced as evacuated or shat out by the patient). The analyst collected these bits of fragmented communications and scanned for connecting links (e.g., the patient's reference to Bion's 'dark glasses' that he had worn some months before. It had ideographic meaning related to the non-psychotic part of his personality—and expressed an actual neurotic conflict). Yet the psychotic part exerted a pre-potent influence here, so a needed repair for an ego damaged by excessive projective identification before he could make meaning with the patient about the symbolic importance of the 'dark glasses.' Could 'A' understand that he had attacked his own mind, impairing his capacity for thought? Bion concluded with a whole host of compressed meanings in 'A' slight movement towards the depressive position.

The patient tried to achieve a capacity to see and talk with his analyst. The patient agreed that the interpretation is 'brilliant' yet convulsed, as the analyst's sanity and capacity for making thoughtful and meaningful links caused 'A' pain—he both loved and envied the analyst's sanity. 'A' hated/envied what he needed, feeling reminded of what he lacked and made him feel inadequate. Further deploying Bion's IMCI, if 'A' projected fragments into the analyst, no wonder his experience of himself was all split up and profoundly confused. The 'thin but tenacious' transference was extreme experiential vacillation and confusion, resulting in a severely constricted relationship in which there was little shared meaning or capacity to make meaning. It was still an extremely primitive form of object relationship.

The 'inchoation of verbal thought' predominated in the paranoid/schizoid position. In Bion's re-reading of Freud, he differed in the idea of the ego turning against reality by saying that the ego was never completely withdrawn from reality. Sparse though it may be, there was still a rudimentary object relationship, some reality sense left over, so that the analyst could facilitate a meaning-making contact with the sane aspect of 'A's otherwise psychotic's mind. Bion here maintained that there are neurotic islands in psychotics just as there were psychotic islands in the neurotic. Bion the Kleinian here joined his work with Segal (1957) who posited the idea of 'symbolic equations,' where 'A' equated, but did not symbolize, and Rosenfeld, who posited a notion of confusion of self and other, where 'A' profoundly confused his internal experience with that of the analyst. An attack on one's mind also represent an attack on one's links and attachments (Aguayo, 2009).

Bion (1958a) further analyzed 'A,' as he seemed like the same patient previously presented, focusing now on a clinically useful account of hallucination. Bion's IMCI now took shape: according to Sira Dermen, he started with a particular observational basis, then leapt to an intuitive image, a hypothesis on the basis of repeated patterns, a hypothesis tested in an interpretation to the patient, and eventually generalizing his understanding of one psychotic patient (or a small number of others) to a broader generalization. In particular, 'A's movements as he entered the room and lay on the couch seemingly synchronized his physical movements, as if the analyst's movements had sprung him into action. The two were part of a 'clockwork toy,' much like the 'Twin' patient, who played at being in analysis. Rote movement indicated that nothing of emotional importance would happen—quiet automaton movements culminated in 'A' saying that he had eaten nothing, was feeling empty and not able to do anything for the rest of the day.

Bion at one point reached an understanding which he put to the patient, who hallucinated that his eyes could expel as well as receive. He used his eyes to take in a part of his analyst, also using his eyes to expel it in a corner of the room visible to him when he was on the couch (in order to keep an eye on it). A first step in understanding how hallucinations were formed could now be interpreted to 'A,' who used his eyes in both an ingestive and excreting manner, all experienced concretely. 'A' then felt profoundly confused, where self and other were inextricably mixed—the analyst again existed as a mere extension of 'A's disordered thought processes. 'A' pushed out a hostile object in a seemingly unending cyclic tension of this mad dialectic, all in the service of the impossible task of keeping the hostile object at bay. Yet if these objects were pushed out, they became bizarre objects that soon threatened him; but if the analyst was forced to bear these unwanted projections, 'A' would again feel threatened by persecution from without. These cycles formed what could be seen as small circulating insanities.

Bion generalized his discoveries to other sense organs—the function of one organ could be confused with another (what Meltzer, 1967, would later term 'zonal confusion,' e.g., ejecting an object through his eyes); if 'A' said he heard something, it could mean ejecting a sound. Bion (1958b, p. 342) alerted his readers to "the double meaning that verbs of sense have for the psychotic." Awareness of this fact enabled the psychoanalyst to detect a hallucinatory process before it betrays itself by more familiar signs. But to detect signs, to even recognize them as significant, requires one to have enough under-standing and the capacity to observe closely; and a great deal of repetition for observations to fall into a pattern—thus, the inevitable back and forth between observation and clinical generalizations, and eventually theory.

Yet amidst all this solipsistic activity, small new benign aspects, something creative and collaborative—of two objects being brought together, however denuded they might be. Bion here differentiated between a part-object split-ting and a whole-object dissociative process that involves depression. 'A' became slowly a bit more integrated, becoming aware of the wish to destroy. The original splitting was much more violent and totalistic, a momentarily more benign process related to the non-psychotic part of the personality. 'A's hallucinations were earlier on, much more paranoid/persecutory, or 'zonally confused,' (e.g., "Tears are coming to my eyes") but by this he meant that tears were literally coming into his eyes from outside and were going to blind him. The patient trickled into and out of the depressive reaction—direct contact with the analyst was both needed and warded off. Since 'A' was dominated by psychotic mechanisms, he also imagined the analyst was as well. This confusional state deployed massive projective identification, so that 'A' 'saw' his analyst doing to him what in fact he had done to him upon entering the session.

Bion noticed that a good, communicative session, with integrated thought, was usually followed by a bad, fragmented, chaotic and incomprehensible ses-sion, where the patient fragmented his capacity for communication. Yet the dawning awareness of this pattern also represented something of a disagreeable loss. Subsequent work elucidated his hatred and envy of the analyst's 'successful creative achievement,' his capacity to make meaningful links. The good analytic intercourse was then disrupted and attacked by 'A,' who said: "I don't know how much I shall be able to do today. As a matter of fact, I got on quite well yesterday."

'A's budding capacity for self-understanding presented the analyst with a dilemma: did the repetition of old familiar interpretations that would tell the patient nothing new carry any value? One such interpretation proved useful when the patient said that he had placed his gramophone on the seat, i.e., Bion's interpretation was felt as both a recording and a defecation. Could he interest the patient in exploring and examining the reasons why he was having a bad session—could 'A' become interested in making meaningful links of his own?

'A' progressed when he started to report dreams, another new development. Yet there were no associations. Bion (1958b, p. 345) restricted himself to hints about what the dream might mean, "such as that he felt it was something important to tell me or that he felt I would be the kind of person who understood them." Bion's findings here harmonized with Segal's (1957) schizophrenic adolescent female, who deployed projective identification as a defense against the emergence of depressive feelings, which she found intolerable, and reversed the march towards sanity, transforming the analyst into a persecutor.

Likewise with Bion's (1957b) case, 'A's momentary contact with depressive position feelings and movement back into paranoid/schizoid fragmentation: 'A' could experience the analyst as a hallucination, a stationary thing sitting in the room rather than as an independent object; the analyst's words felt like flying projectiles, bits of feces from which the patient had to duck in order to avoid contact. 'A's horrific mangling of the analyst's interpretations also exemplified what he did to his mind.

From this vertex, 'A's dreams reflected a form of narcissistic solipsism—the analyst's mind was subjected to exactly the same kind of treatment to which 'A' subjected his own mind. 'A' anally expelled his dreams in a concretistic fashion—they were merely shat out, evacuated and not worked with. The analyst carried the meaning-making/emotionally responsive function while 'A' remained oblivious to how he impacted others.

What frightened 'A' was not the irrationality, fragmentation and incoherence associated with dreams, but the appearance of whole objects occasioning very powerful feelings of "guilt and depression ... associated with the onset of the depressive position. Their presence is felt to be evidence that real and valued objects have been destroyed" (Bion, 1958b, p. 347). Once the psychotic patient realizes how crazy his thinking appears to people around him, it can only lead to another round of immediate fragmentation.

Bion also differentiated between hysterical and psychotic hallucinations, the less disturbed varieties described by Freud earlier on and those now written about by Bion. The former relates to "whole objects and is associated with depression; the psychotic hallucination contains elements analogous to part-objects. Both types are found in the psychotic patient" (Bion, 1958b, p. 348). The main point here made by Bion vis-à-vis Freud's position: the psychotic patient *was* analyzable and his rudimentary object relatedness to the analyst could be drawn upon in the service of making therapeutic progress. Bion closed by saying that he hoped he had made his case for the possibilities of further research brought on by the "close and detailed observation of hallucinations" (p. 349).

Let me return to Bion's (1958a) 'On Arrogance' paper to further make the point of how he differentiated his views from Freud as well as Klein. Bion made a bold claim here after years of experience in working with psychotic patients: he began to be less preoccupied with 'why' certain phenomena were occurring, such as the sexually repressed contents or phantasies of his hateful attacks on the breast. Instead, he now moved towards 'what' was going on in the interactions between patient and analyst, or what can be termed 'what' type of interactions. Bion here moved in the direction of actual interactions when the analyst says: 'look at that,' 'look at what is happening in the room.' This form of notation, or 'drawing-attention-to,' which might be called a '*what* intervention' (or in Bion's terms, a 'constant conjunction'), seemed to have promoted communication, no matter how transiently. The structure of 'notation by pointing' made less of an attempt at drawing the patient's attention to causal understanding *per se*, and instead offered the patient an opportunity to describe something for their analyst to take in.

Bion later enshrined 'notation' as column 3 in the Grid, where he essentially placed Freud's Oedipus complex. These methods of group and individual inquiry form a continuity when Bion (from the group period on) took what I have called a 'facilitatively indicating' role in these two instances: neither a leader nor a participant *per se*, he pointed out phenomena in the actual interactions that he thought worthy of the group's attention and now, the individual's attention. The analyst's subjective immersion was followed by reporting back what he had discovered. Bion's increased use of 'what' interventions also led to a marginalization of 'why' interventions characteristic of the Kleinian part-object analysis as well as Freud's work with neurotically repressed patients. This methodological move furthered the move towards an explicitly interactional analysis in the 'here and now.'

To continue with the 'Arrogance' paper, Bion (1958b) further revised and fleshed out Freud's work on psychosis by delineating another aspect of the Oedipus complex by extrapolating from his experience with psychotic patients when he wrote (Bion, 1958b, p. 145; 1967b, p. 88):

> If we now turn to consider what there is in reality that makes it so hateful to the patient that he must destroy the ego which brings him into

contact with it, it would be natural to suppose that it is the sexually oriented Oedipus situation, and indeed I have found much to substantiate this view.

Yet in this instance, Bion went in a different direction, marginalizing the sexually oriented Oedipus situation as another 'why' explanation in favor of another factor, namely Oedipus' urge to know the truth, to want to face reality no matter what the cost. In another case study (in which a male patient sounded quite similar to the patient already described in the 'Differentiation' paper), the moment of truth came when the otherwise neurotic patient, who had spoken now in an unintelligible but highly fragmented way, had made it appear that it would be impossible to establish any viable or potent form of analytic relationship. Together patient and analyst formed what Bion termed a 'frustrated couple.' Then, in a moment of lucidity:

> The patient said he wondered that I could stand it. This gave me a clue: at least I now knew that there was something I was able to stand which he apparently could not. He realized already that he felt he was being obstructed in his aim to establish a creative contact with me, and that this obstructive force was sometimes in him, sometimes in me, and sometimes occupied an unknown location. Furthermore, the obstruction was effected by some means other than mutilation or verbal communications. The patient had already made it clear that the obstructing forces or object was out of his control.
>
> (Bion, 1958b, p. 146)

In Bion's distillation of Freud's notion of the reality principle and implicitly, Klein's epistemophilic instinct, he focused on the patient's internal experience; and now understood that it was one of the analyst's functions to pursue the truth. As it turns out, it was (and still is) all too frequently the case that the patient evinced difficulties in his capacity to tolerate aspects of his psychic reality, which in turn led to their projective evacuation. For his part, the analyst had to evince a capacity for containing (and this seems to be the first instance of Bion's use of this important term) the discarded, split-off aspects of the various patients who consulted with him, all while retaining a balanced outlook (Bion, 1958b, p. 145).

Putting these ideas differently, Bion assumed that the psychotic (or earliest aspect) of the personality had a pre-potent and dominating influence over the neurotic and non-psychotic aspects. And since the analyst bore the enduring interest in getting at what was truthful, it often interfered with the patient's preferred mode of defensive evasion, something that might put the patient in the position of obstructing the analyst in doing his job. In an ideal sense, the analyst who can bear their own curiosity also bears the responsibility for shouldering whatever painful and uncomfortable psychic truths emerge from the patient. This can (as it did in this case) lead the patient to experience defensively the analyst as an 'obstructive object,' someone who could clearly understand and bear something of a psychic truth that was intolerable to the patient. The patient's defensive narrow-mindedness can sometimes turn the analyst's attempt to get at the truth into something felt as primitively attacking to the patient.

Here, as Sira Dermen has pointed out, Bion made an extraordinary intuitive leap in the 'Arrogance' paper: the patient's experience of the analyst as an ingress-denying or obstructive object (to which we have referred) underscored his breathtaking re-reading of Freud's Oedipus complex. Bion regarded the analyst's role as the bearer of the 'truth-drive,' and as such, could appear obstructively to the patient's preferred mode of defensive evasion. This is not to say that Freud's version of the sexual Oedipus no longer had any purchase. Far from it: Bion was merely saying that it was secondary or existed in the neurotic layer and the psychic reality formed the 'psychotic' layer that exerted a pre-potent and dominating influence over the personality.

To conclude with a look at some recent secondary analytic literature in this area, the work of Giuseppe Civitarese, a post-Bionian Field Theorist, in his (2015) paper, 'Transformations in Hallucinosis and the Receptivity of the Analyst,' takes up a fruitful extrapolation of Bion's original views. To draw an analogy from the French political philosopher and man of letters, Baron de Montesquieu's distinction between the 'letter' and the 'spirit of the law,' my work attempts to ascertain what exactly Bion's clinical and theoretical ideas are based on a primary source reading of his work. In different words, one might say that this is the 'letter' of his work. It also gives us an orienting context for the fruitful understanding of his ideas in a new comparative context. However, merely setting out these ideas in context, while informative, does not address what makes these ideas relevant to us as contemporaries living in a new millennium. In short, we must also take into consideration the contemporary clinical 'spirit' or relevance of Bion's ideas and how the post-Bionian analysts have carried on in Bion's 'spirit,' one of truthful open inquiry.

With these considerations in mind, Civitarese's (2015) 'Hallucinosis' paper takes up an interesting point: it is clear he has Bion's (1958b) 'On Hallucination' paper in mind when he makes the point that, in contradistinction to Freud and Klein's primarily pathological view of hallucination as a profound denial of external reality, Civitarese also emphasizes the point made by Bion, namely that the psychotic patient will not feel understood unless the analyst can demonstrate his living experience of the patient's own hallucinatory experience. In other words, the analyst must convincingly suffer and experience vicariously the hallucinatory experience. From this, Civitarese (2015, p. 1092), maintains that what Bion (1963) later called a 'transformation in hallucinosis' ironically represents an "ideal state of mind towards which the analyst has to move in order to intuit the facts of the analysis."

Of course, this type of experience implies that the analyst both experiences vicariously the patient's own hallucinatory experience but maintains a sense of analytic observational separateness and distance, so that he might make use of such experiences in understanding his patient. In short, it comes down to "the subject of the analyst's receptivity" (Civitarese, 2015, p. 1091).

To conclude, there is an interesting intersection of meaning between the 'letter' and 'spirit' of these different readings. As we have seen, Bion (1958b) originally described hallucination as *solely* an aspect of the patient's functioning—and in the manner of Kleinian practice at that time, concentrated on the patient's subjective internal experience. By contrast, Civitarese (2015) emphasizes the 'intersubjective turn' made by Bion after 1962 when he formulated the notion of 'container/contained,' and subsequently wrote about the interacting subjectivities of both analyst and patient in an analytic encounter. It is by virtue of experiencing the patient's inability to suffer his own feelings, which originally underlies his hallucinations, that gives the analyst an important, and sometimes subtle and unconscious access to the patient's unmetabolized emotional self. Civitarese (2015, p. 1103) gives a charming, cinematic example of the clinical use of a hallucinatory experience: in the silent American film with Charlie Chaplin playing the role of the tramp (*The Gold Rush*), two men are starving to death in a cold barren cabin in the Yukon. Big Jim cartoonishly hallucinates the little tramp as a chicken in order to forget that he has nothing to eat. Yet this is a reminder of what he urgently needs! It is in this sense that the hallucination reminds us of the imperative need "to rediscover a true contact with reality i.e., one based on emotions and on the value system which they embody" (ibid.).

To summarize Chapter 5, we reviewed Bion's method of clinical inquiry, as a way to now set a context for his beginning to differentiate his views on psychosis from those of Freud and Klein. It was a paradox in a way insofar as Bion was a core member of the 'all-in' Kleinian group while he sought simultaneously to differentiate himself from it. He was increasingly becoming an uneasy Kleinian, feeling that he was of the group, but distant from it at the same time. In our review of Bion's two psychosis papers, we saw how Bion now focused so much attention on the patient's subjective internal experience. We concluded with a contrasting example from post-Bionian Italian Field Theory, one that fruitfully contrasts the 'letter' of the Bionian development with its contemporary elaboration, the 'spirit' of its recent evolution.

Note

1 Although Klein had disseminated her technique, these thoughts were scattered throughout her lectures and available only to students at the British Society as early as 1936 (Klein, 2017). While she intended to write a book on technique, she did not do so. The closest approximation we have to Klein's technique appeared in her posthumously published *Narrative of a Child Analysis* (Klein, 1961). However, within the London Klein group, her students were aware of her views, which she left

mainly unpublished in some 1,500 pages of notes. After her death in 1960, her students began to gather her ideas about technique once they came to realize that they had acquired a rather novel approach to the practice of psychoanalysis. Elizabeth Spillius (2007) put it well: "It is important to remember that although Klein eventually developed a new, influential and controversial theory, she was basically a clinician."

Chapter 6

Further Clinical Contributions, Part II

'Attacks on Linking' (1959)

In 'Attacks on Linking,' Bion (1959) continued his uneasy relationship to the Klein group: on the one hand, his work furthered Klein's agenda to demonstrate the viability of her ideas about the analysis of psychosis; yet on the other hand, Bion grew increasingly hesitant about his role in furthering this agenda as he had ideas and formulations that began to take him in other directions. Perhaps Winnicott had been right after all—there might be something to factoring in the active presence of a maternal figure, be it the actual mother or the mother-as-analyst. While Bion had averted any active consideration of this external figure—as it had become standard by now for the Klein group to focus interpretative attention on the patient's enduring *internal* state of mind—he now slowly began to consider the analyst-as-a-containing external figure (Aguayo, 2017).

Bion trickled into a new position, as he and Winnicott would effect what Giuseppe Civitarese has termed the 'big bang' of psychoanalysis when their work separately began to turn into what has been termed the 'intersubjectivist' direction, which among other things now meant a consideration of two analytic participants interacting with one another in real time. The active processing capacities of the analyst now could be considered, as he focused on those very same but emotionally stunted aspects of the patient. Bion (1962a) would emerge with a two-body/two-minded model within the year when he published *Learning from Experience* (Bion, 1962b). He would also recalibrate the Kleinian emphasis on pathology by also outlining a theory of normal development, all in the context of the structure and function of thinking—from the infant's initial attempts to learn from experience ('preconceptions, realizations, conceptions') to those theories deployed by the analyst in understanding his patient; from the most disturbed, thought-disordered psychotic to the most abstract scientific theories. Like Freud and Klein before him, Bion accomplished this theoretical feat from generalizations made with a small sample size: his work with primarily psychotic and near psychotic patients.

But we get ahead of ourselves. First, let's go back to the more familiar work on psychosis. Bion (1959) continued to take up the psychotic's

DOI: 10.4324/9781003364795-8

destructive attacks on meaning, now extending his findings to the attacks on linking evinced by such patients. First and foremost, and this despite the attacks on the analyst as the bearer of meaning, the maker of links, the psychotic also ultimately attacked his own mind and the associated functions (memory, notation, judgment), defined by Freud (1911) in the 'Two Principles' paper. These attacks on the mind could then be projected outwards in the form of attacks of what links one object to another. Bion also thought that these processes also reflected what less disturbed patients experienced, such as the infantile sadistic attacks on the breast, splitting and projective identification, all within the context of the early stages of Oedipus complex (Bion, 1959, p. 93). It was one thing if the patient attacked the analyst as a good, providing source—it was quite another more serious matter if he attacked his very own apparatus of perception and thought.

The analyst also stood on the receiving side of the patient's projections. In his evolving way of working, Bion regarded the analyst as carrying a linking function, the figure who stood for getting at the truthful psychic reality of the patient's life situation. His enduring stance was to be the one who puts together various aspects of the patient's conscious and unconscious communications. He stood for an emphasis on verbal communication in the present moment. Yet as we saw in Bion's (1958a) 'On Arrogance' paper, this therapeutic posture often interfered with the patient's mode of evading his internal psychic reality, resulting in his attempts to mutilate, erode or attack the figure of the analyst. The sanity-bearing aspects of the analyst could and did arouse envy; his sane thinking, and linking capacity aroused the patient's ire, but more from a sense of how much inadequacy and humiliation it stirred up in the patient. Sometimes, the better the interpretation, the more vicious the attack. The patient might sense, for the moment in which he felt unable to think meaningfully for himself, it would erode his sense of omnipotent self-sufficiency and omniscience. These aspects of the personality were felt to be under siege, hence the corresponding envious and devaluing attacks on the analyst.

From one side, Bion continued as a Kleinian loyal to her ideas. He had clearly privileged Klein's (1957) 'Envy and Gratitude' paper, one that explicated what she termed the 'infant's double relations with the breast' (i.e., the presence of the analytic pleasuring maternal breast becomes the source of frustration and deprivation in its absence). A good experience of feeling understood could often lead to violently negative reactions. One of Bion's (1959) patients reacted with violent convulsions to the experience of being understood. He had made isolated remarks that Bion (1959, p. 97) couldn't understand. They were made in the context of meeting a girl who was felt to be 'understanding.' After relaying this moment, the patient then violently convulsed, leading to a sense of a 'blue haze' that was felt to be in the room, then gone, leaving the patient depressed. In one moment, he felt understood and relieved, in the next, he turned convulsively and violently against understanding. The pleasant experience was destroyed and ejected. The analyst surmised that the 'blue' related to a violent sexual conversation. It seemed like the patient was psychologically damned either way. If the analyst understood, it was subject to the patient's enviously splitting it up and "convert[ing it] into particles of sexual abuse and ejected." Of course, if the analyst did not muster an understanding, the situation would leave the patient in a more desperate situation.

Yet attacking these links also left the patient in a bereft state of mind. Years later in 1967, Bion (2013, pp. 9–10) would provide another example of a patient attacking a needed link: when the analyst interpreted to a patient who had felt in good contact in the previous session—amidst his chronic complaint that his father had always favored his sister over him—his ensuing negative reaction was interpreted by Bion as a form of self-attack insofar as he himself had been the 'favorite' in the preceding session, but now turned against it in his more usual guise of the rivalrous brother. In effect, he turned against decent understanding and recapitulated a fruitless old rivalry.

Other psychological functions also appeared quite compromised in the psychotic. Whereas the neurotic patient could dream, differentiating a sense of self and other, inside and outside when reporting the dream to the analyst, the psychotic instead unwittingly hallucinated while awake. Bion here captured the sense of an unacknowledged waking–dreaming activity that is often evacuated, and therefore not consciously experienced, something he termed 'psychotic dreaming.' The patient might be physically present but remained emotionally absent as a result. Bion (1958b, p. 98): wrote: "My impression now is that this apparently dreamless period is a phenomenon analogous to the invisible–visual hallucination." In other words, psychotic patients dream awake, or hallucinate actively during their sessions. While dreaming awake, psychotics evince psychic material the rest of us see as visual components while asleep; and it is hallucinated into invisibility by the psychotic patient while awake.

There are other dire consequences of attacking one's links: Bion (1959, p. 101) suggested that

> there are elements that suggest a formation of a hostile, persecutory object, or agglomeration of objects, which expresses its hostility in a manner which is of great importance in producing the predominance of psychotic mechanisms in a patient; the characteristics with which I have already invested the agglomeration of persecutory objects have the quality of a primitive, and even murderous superego.

In plain language, evacuating the unwanted, despised self-elements into the other, something that in Klein's thinking produced a persecutory object—if it now included an attack on one's own mind, it could produce 'bizarre objects,' confounding both to the analyst as well as to the patient.

We can think about the origins of the patient's destructiveness in two ways: it can be regarded as primarily in-born and *secondarily, as environmentally mediated*. Klein regarded the patient's destructiveness as primarily instinctual and what varied was the quantum of aggression with which any subject is born. She enshrined this idea with a subscription to the Death Instinct. But here, Bion carefully began to augment the instinctual 'nature' views by suggesting that, at times, the patient's aggressiveness could also be maternally mediated. Think of the clinical example from the 'Arrogance' paper: since the patient felt obstructed in pursuing his usual form of evasive non-communication by the analyst, he faulted the analyst for being able to stand something that the patient couldn't tolerate. It made it possible for the patient's attacks on the analyst to be understood as a function of direct interactions in the room in real living time. Bion here now moved in a direction suggested by Winnicott, an argument about environmental 'nurture' for good or for ill.

Bion (1959, p. 106) also made an intriguing point here, however, perhaps a counter to Winnicott's ideas, when he wrote: "it can never be in the mother alone." He also altered the idea about how psychosis originated:

> These objects, whether internal or external, are in fact part-objects and predominantly, though not exclusively, what we should call functions and not morphological structures. This is obscured because the patient's thinking is conducted by means of concrete objects and therefore tends to produce, in the sophisticated mind of the analyst, an impression that the patient's concern is with the nature of the concrete object.

Too much emphasis on part-object destructiveness and not enough accent on maternal receptiveness could both lead to an overwhelming feeling of not feeling able to be contained. The patient now sought to break the link between itself and the analytic breast; therefore, no learning could occur (ibid., p. 106). The attacks on linking could also include 'connecting' type feelings themselves. By means of projective identification, one could thus evacuate one's mind and destroy the capacity for thought itself.

One can wonder here whether Bion received any criticism from his Kleinian colleagues for beginning to make these incursions into environmentally mediated experience. This was, after all, the conceptual terrain associated with Winnicott's work, which in turn had caused such a break with Klein. My conjecture is that at this time, these experiences were so subtly depicted by Bion that perhaps no one really noticed. If even sensitive observers like Winnicott did not pick it up, it is likely that no one else did either. But here, we see the beginnings of an important but subtle shift on Bion's part: he was now willing to consider the role of environmental nurture, a step away from a position he had dismissed in 1957 when he marginalized any discussion of its importance.

Another subtle shift was also occurring in the types of patients increasingly seen by psychoanalysts. For the first time, Bion (1959, p. 93) mentions how psychotic mechanisms operated in what he called 'borderline psychosis.' Again, while the Kleinian emphasis was on a descriptive phenomenology of the psychotic experience—and less on diagnosis *per se*—a new type of patient was increasingly seen in the analyst's office at that time, a sort of hybrid of neurotically psychotic or psychotically neurotic patient. Perhaps Freud and Bion's distinctions between 'psychotic and non-psychotic/neurotic' would have to be thought about afresh. The concept of borderline psychosis in effect added heft to the Kleinian idea that there is a psychotic core to the personality. In the case of the borderline, the psychotic core was actively in motion in driving extreme, yet generally not extreme enough to land the patient in a psychiatric hospital. The borderline was 'stable in their instability,' at times emitting quite destructive behavior.

The emergence of the phenomenon of the borderline patient helped in certain quarters to promote the popularity of Kleinian ideas, as it stands to reason that if Kleinian ideas had only applied to the certified psychotic patients, they would have remained the interest of a few specialists. But what would become known as the 'psychotic core,' namely a set of experiences that both psychotic and near-psychotic patients were prone to, increasingly popularized Kleinian ideas. Think back to Freud's statement in the dream book that, at some point (usually in our dreaming, sleep life), we are all psychotic. This got at the 'psychotic core,' so that Kleinians learned how to analyze psychosis before neurosis—and here, Bion's work was quite essential, especially with these new categories of patient, which would soon include Herbert Rosenfeld's (1964) description of the narcissistically disturbed.

Again, Bion provided ballast for these ideas with clinical examples. He framed these examples by now positing the analyst as a linking or meaning-making figure that was counterbalanced by a patient who was a meaning-evading or meaning-destroying subject. This established a dynamic tension in the analysis. One example was when the analyst demonstrated that the patient's mother had been able to 'cope with a refractory child,' and when he tried to express agreement, he instead wound up disruptively stammering, as if he was literally gasping for air. Both analyst and patient agreed that the patient had made peculiar sounds. In a more complicated example, another patient complained that, if he couldn't sleep, he was fearful that some catastrophe would occur, akin to insanity. The analyst interpreted that the patient feared dreaming, should he fall asleep. He denied this, saying that he could not think because he was 'wet' (1959, p. 94). (The borderline patient could be quite fearful of his dream life since his daily life was so susceptible to being irrationally and concretely governed.)

Then the analyst reminded the patient of the constant series of 'symbolic equations': sleep was equated with dreaming; dreaming equated with wetness; wetness led to contempt for the feeble sentimentality of the other. The patient disagreed at this point, and then the analyst recalibrated. Perhaps wetness was equated with hatred and envy, as in a urinary attack on the object; sleep, all of which underlies the patient's fear of an oozing away of his mind. Bion concluded here that the patient minutely split up good interpretations, turning them into 'mental urine.' Yet the patient's various urinary attacks would leave him with so much useless mental waste! Bion here reprised Klein's idea of the sadistic urinary attack on a providing object but augmented with the patient's attack on his own mind. The patient dreaded sleep because it led to a sort of irreparable mindlessness. The patient finally admitted he was 'dry' or in a precariously good state.

In expanding upon the significance and meaning of 'Attacks on Linking,' the prospect of now analyzing 'borderline psychosis' was the beginning of what would become an enduring signature in contemporary psychoanalysis in the decades following the 1960s. Think here of the work of Otto Kernberg, which was heavily influenced by Kleinian clinical experience (Kernberg, 1975), although the Kleinian experiment on the psychoanalytic treatment of psychosis would soon give way—after all, there would be a pharmacological revolution beginning in the 1970s that would have a profound impact on the treatment of psychotic disorders. Thereafter, most psychotic patients would receive a combination of medication and psychotherapy/psychoanalysis. But in the interim, the categories of neurosis and psychosis, such a staple of Freud's time, now became much more fluid, emerging now as a new middle or in-between group—borderline and narcissistic disorders. And with the Kleinian emphasis on the universality of what was termed a 'psychotic core,' the treatment of borderline (as well as narcissistic) psychotic patients expanded the usefulness of the Kleinian understanding of psychosis (Aguayo, 2009).

While we will discuss Bion's own treatment experiences with borderline and narcissistic patients in later chapters, I now turn to what succeeding generations of London Kleinians (who still count Bion among their group) have done with some of his ideas regarding psychotic and borderline states of mind. One of the most prolific of what I would term the 'first generation of London Bionian analysts' is Betty Joseph. As a seminar mate of Bion's at the British Society in the post-World War II era, she followed his work rather carefully—and since she dedicated her life's work to the study and elucidation of Kleinian technique (as heavily informed by Bion's ideas), her work is a good place to start (Aguayo, 2011).

Betty Joseph (1989), who studied alongside Bion during his post-World War II candidate years and early on took an avid interest in his ideas, came to the Klein group—and in the 1950s, started by analyzing the patient's experience of internal psychic reality. While she learned something of how to link past history with present symptoms, as taught to her by Klein (who supervised her work), she moved away (as Bion had already done) in the ensuing years from making past-to-present transference interpretations because she found them therapeutically ineffective. However correct they might have been, the patient didn't seem to feel their impact (Pick and Milton, 1994). By the early 1970s, Joseph began to take up Bion's ideas more seriously, moving now to a more 'here-and-now' approach, deploying such ideas as 'attacks on linking.' Her patient population was much like his, more in the difficult-to-treat range—the perverse, borderline and narcissistic. She attuned gradually to how defensively evasive her disturbed patients were—and she came to accentuate direct lived experience over reconstructions of an infantile past.

By the mid-1970s, Joseph would still listen to what patients had to say about their past, but she now listened in a different, more Bionian way: she drew upon the patient's report of his past as a communicative form of projective identification. She also drew upon direct emotional experience in arriving at subtle understandings of countertransference impasses with patients as well. Another Bionian modality worked with by Joseph—little mentioned by most commentators on her work—was to arrive at understandings of countertransference difficulties by evaluating how a group of colleagues (in consultation with her) listened *as a group* to clinical material. *Dealing with countertransference in a group setting allowed it to become more thoroughly informing.* One learned the difference between a narrow-subjective reaction that any one individual analyst might have to his case material and another more consensual set of reactions that revolved around feelings induced in the analyst by his patient. In some instances, difficult-to-treat borderline patients could create what Britton (2003) later termed experiences of 'dyadic exclusivity,' where the patient induced the feeling that there were only two people in the entire world—the patient and the analyst. Analysts in the Betty Joseph workshop group learned how to calibrate their own personal countertransference reactions by comparing them with those experienced by their colleagues as they themselves listened to the presented material. It provided a group method for winnowing out what was purely personal (the 'personal interference' countertransference) from what was evoked at an objective level (i.e., other members feel quite similarly to the presenting analyst).

For Betty Joseph (1989), this subtle form of countertransference analysis now replaced the old past-to-present transference work. It was focused more on the 'you and me' type of interactions over and above the more authoritative case accounts that merely tell the listener what actually happened in the analysis. In Bionian terms, the part-object language associated with Klein now gave way to the linking language associated with his own more interaction-saturated work; it was less now about the infantile relationship to the breast and more about the interpersonal experience of the psychological functions of feeding. The old Kleinian anatomical language was too abstract and experience-distant, whereas there was an immediacy to connecting to the patient's most urgent interactional anxieties in any given analytic hour. Through a Bionian lens, Betty Joseph revised classical Kleinian formulations, such as regarding the 'total situation' differently than Klein (1952) and more like Bion. It was the difference between projective identification as a communication with an organizing impact vis-à-vis projective identification as the transmission of an unconscious phantasy.

I close by taking up what a more recent second generation of British Kleinian/Bionian analysts have done with Bion's work (as explicated by Betty Joseph). Here I focus on the work of Ron Britton (2003), one of Betty Joseph's colleagues in her on-going work group that met for decades after the 1960s on a bi-weekly basis. The mandate of the Joseph group was clear: each analytic colleague took turns bringing their most 'difficult-to-treat' patients in for group consultation.

Expanding on his theoretical/clinical inheritance from Klein/Bion and Joseph, Britton (2003) has focused on the difficult-to-treat patients already mentioned. He made comparisons amongst patients in the neurotic, borderline and narcissistic spectrum, who could move with greater ease than psychotic patients between P/S and D but had special difficulties negotiating the separateness of the parental sexual relationship, one from which they were forever excluded. In other words, the emphasis on 'dyadic exclusivity' was another way the borderline screened out the analyst's separate relationship with figures outside the analysis—or in extreme cases, their relationship with their own separate mind. In theoretical terms, Britton et al. (1989) took up psychic life that traversed Klein's Depressive position into the Oedipus complex, as exemplified in papers like 'The Missing Link: Parental Sexuality in the Oedipus Complex' (Britton et al., 1989) where he borrowed the metaphor of exclusion to demonstrate how the patient would organize his analysis to appear as if it was a dyadically exclusive relationship with an analyst as parental object. Of paramount importance here was the possession of the breast, and so, the patient could only balk and become exasperated when the realization occurred that the breast had an owner—and was shared with others in ways from which the patient was forever excluded. Genuine psychic movement into the Depressive position entailed renunciation and loss, but it ultimately also led to a healthier working through of the Oedipus situation, where the patient-as-child now realized that while he had a relationship with either parent, they too had a separate relationship that did not involve him.

Britton (2003) specifically took up certain types of borderline and narcissistic patients who, in the presence of insufficient early maternal containment, had experienced painful difficulties when they approached the triangular situation represented by the parental couple. Recall here how we have discussed Bion's move towards environmentally mediated patient attacks on meaning provided by the analyst. Some patients either denied or attacked the 'link' between both parents, such as the patient who never recalled seeing his parents together as a couple in childhood—they were somehow always perceived as separate. Britton termed this an 'illusional oedipal configuration,' one in which the patient psychically denied the separate reality of the parent's relationship. These types of cases could be easily compared to more normal individuals, who could tolerate a genuine recognition of the parental sexual relationship that excluded the child. Such individuals had what Britton termed a mental capacity for 'triangular space,' where one could observe whilst being observed—the patient could participate in a relationship where he could be both the observer and observed or observe two others.

Britton here clearly implied that in lieu of the patient's lack of psychic development in these triangular capacities, it fell to the analyst to have developed these capacities from which his patients could benefit. This not only encompassed the tolerance of the usual oedipal jealousies and rivalries to which analysts were subjected, but also required the analyst to develop a capacity to commune with his own separate mind during analytic sessions, which itself formed another definitional point of 'triangular space.' For a Kleinian/Bionian analyst, Britton here put an unusual emphasis on the importance of the father as a third figure, whether in a negative (or persecutory/retaliatory) form or positive (containing and balancing, or navigational) form.

Another defining signature of Britton's work on the oedipal configuration was his emphasis on Bion's (1962) notion of 'container/contained,' an idea which we will discuss more thoroughly in Chapter 8. Following Bion's lead, Britton discussed the failure of maternal containment, a factor of nurture that could lead to the development of an 'envious destructive superego,' a pathological structure that prevented the patient from learning from experience with his objects. If the borderline patient insisted on what Britton termed 'dyadic exclusivity,' a way of pressurizing the analytic situation to create an 'it's-just-you-and-me' atmosphere, so that the analyst's external partner's need for an internal space where he could commune with his own thoughts was split off and/or denied by the patient, the analytic situation would become terrorized. The net result was an inability for the analytic dyad to generate new and fruitful psychic meaning and understanding.

In Britton's elaboration of Bion's own thinking, which didn't put much emphasis on the importance of the father in the oedipal constellation, it appears that the threat of acknowledging the analyst's separate sexual or emotional bond with either their partner or their own mind, could spell disaster. Needless to say, this type of integrated thinking presupposed a developed capacity to differentiate self from other, precisely the capacity that eluded the psychotic patient in profound confusional states of mind. Under certain circumstances, it episodically plagued the borderline patient as well.

I have surveyed this post-Bionian British secondary literature to give a flavor of how generative Bion's ideas have been, inspiring subsequent investigators to work with his rich analytic legacy in Britain from the time of Bion's death in 1979.

To summarize Chapter 6, we have seen how Bion's idea of 'attacks on linking' served as a sort of Janus-faced concept—it could appear as the patient's defensive attacks on meaning provided by the analyst or attacks on one's own mind, an experience that usually led to disorientation and instability. Yet by being able to push the experience in both directions, Bion now moved towards evolving a truly interactional psychoanalysis based in the notion of analytic containment, all calibrated in the real 'here and now' experience between patient and analyst. Attacks on one's own mind deepened the Kleinian discourse, which had anchored itself in part-object work, such as attacks on the providing breast. In balancing Klein's claims about in-born destructiveness with his own emphasis on failures of environmental 'containment,' Bion now began to calibrate the claims of nature and nurture in his conception of the infantile. Bion thought he had gained access to these core infantile experiences of psychotic patients, all of which led to new concepts and treatment strategies with both borderline and narcissistic personality disorders.

Also, since there were no publications that set out Kleinian technique in the 1950s (although Klein's technique lectures were well known by her students and candidates (Steiner, 2017), Bion merely demonstrated how he worked and understood psychotic states of mind. In transiting towards work with borderline psychosis, he altered his understanding with this new hybrid of 'psychotically neurotic' patient who displayed episodic flashes of extremely primitive, concrete and irrational behavior. He here was extremely influential insofar as he generalized what has been termed by Kleinians as the 'psychotic core' of the experiences of patients in analysis, an idea that allowed for the supple understanding of psychotic mechanisms operating in the borderline personality—and just as importantly, in lesser disturbed patients as well. We concluded by looking at the generativity of Bion's ideas when we discussed two generations of London Kleinians, Betty Joseph in the 1970s and 1980s and Ron Britton in the 1990s and in the new millennium. Kleinian work has continued to flourish with its emphasis on the 'difficult-to-treat' borderline and narcissistic patient through the use of Bionian ideas, such as attacks on linking, or other extensions, such as the patient's need for a 'dyadically exclusive' and pressurized relationship with the analyst.

Conceptualizing His
Clinical Results

Chapter 7

Bion's Incursions into Metapsychology
'The Psychoanalytic Theory of Thinking' (1962a)

Bion's Theoretical Turn

One defining event that bridges Bion's psychosis papers of the 1950s and his turn towards the more theoretically driven works of the 1960s was the death of Melanie Klein in late 1960. Single-minded in her pursuit of elucidating the child's internal phantasmic reality, she regarded her work as "finding out the truth without any concessions." To quote further from the obituary written by Bion, Rosenfeld and Segal (1961) they regarded Klein's pursuit of her ideas as steadfast enough to weather all the considerable criticism that was directed at her work during her lifetime. And in a statement that likely issued from Bion's hand (as he would have been the one of the trio of writers most familiar with English history and literature), he wrote:

> We have reason to congratulate ourselves that Melanie Klein had the equipment of heart and mind to enable her to enlarge the scope of our science and that she was able to find in our Society the conditions in which she could do so. Samuel Johnson's letter to Benet on the death of General Drury contains a passage which might epitomize Melanie Klein's attitude to her work: 'Whether to see life as it is will give us much consolation, I know not; but the consolation which is drawn from truth, if any there be, is solid and durable; that which may be derived from error must be, like its original, fallacious and fugitive.' All scientific work has as its aim to see life 'as it is'. The peculiarity of psycho-analysis lies in our belief that such an aim and its steady pursuit is restorative.
>
> (Bion, Rosenfeld and Segal, 1961)

While we know from Bion's private diaries that he had other perceptions about Klein—for instance, he privately referred to her by the nickname 'boss'—he was quite aware that she looked for ways to press her analytic and publication agendas with her star disciples and analysands. She did not for instance hesitate in conveying her belief to Bion that he would do well to set aside his group work and concentrate on psychoanalysis alone. Freud had

DOI: 10.4324/9781003364795-10

acted in a similar fashion with his analysands: with the Stracheys and Joan Riviere, he made it clear that he saw them as the English translators of his work (Gay, 1988, pp. 465–466). Next to this, however, there is another emerging truth in what Bion wrote about Klein's death—it may be quite taxing to see life as it is, but the scientific aim of psychoanalysis is precisely that—and its 'steady pursuit is restorative.' What was true for Klein was even more true for Bion. Moreover, as I maintain, the emotional price that had to be paid of being an 'all-in Kleinian,' pressing forward Klein's agenda in terms of the analyzability of psychotic patients, would now be reassessed and recalibrated by Bion. The 'boss' was dead and it made possible further acts of liberating himself from what I conjecture to have been a 'basic assumption [dependency] group.' He was now free to think his own thoughts—and publish them.

To contemporary observers, no one seemed to be struck by the stylistic differences evinced by Bion's (1962a) first paper, 'The Psychoanalytic Theory of Thinking,' written after Klein's death. Firstly, he chose a turgid and opaque way of communicating his new theories and offered very few clinical examples. There was also the curious omission of references—there were none at the end of the paper. Was this a way of saying that all the thoughts contained in the paper originated from Bion himself? Was it what Bloom (1973) has described as the 'anxiety of influence,' where Bion now sought to separate himself from past influences, almost as if he was birthing his own uniquely original thoughts? In writing in such an obscure way, was this a stylistic of concealment, something Bion was hiding from his readers? While questions abound, one thing is certain: it is important and fruitful to keep such questions at the back of our minds as we elucidate Bion's new metapsychology, one based on his work with psychotic patients.

One way to proceed—and it is only one of many—is to carefully deconstruct the 'Thinking' paper, so we can unpack its substantive argument. Such an exercise is important as it may facilitate understanding the shifts in Bion's theoretical thinking. First and most clear: postulating a new theoretical system had to be based on a palpable amount of discontent with the old one. While many fellow members of the British Society admired Klein's acumen as an analytic practitioner, some of her colleagues were less enthralled with the way she conceptualized her findings. And here, Bion was clearly having second thoughts about the Kleinian theory he had been bequeathed—and now, with Klein's death, he actively interrogated the received theory. We have seen instances where Bion insisted on his direct emotional experience in making observations, some of which did not tally with Kleinian theory. As we turn to the 'Thinking' paper, bear in mind that Bion continued in the Kleinian tradition of discussing the patient's conflicted infantile history that kept intruding itself into his present-day life. In Kleinian parlance, this would have been what Klein called 'deep' unconscious phantasy, or the conflictual infantile internal experience of the adult patient in analysis.

I assume that Bion here posited what he regarded as a more encompassing theory, one intended for use by psychoanalysts who ideally, "should restate the hypotheses of which it (psychoanalysis) is composed in terms of empirically verifiable data." In different words, the analyst must work from the ground of clinical data as a way to foot himself in theoretically robust enough propositions. This points to the inductive method, one of making detailed observations that inform hypothesis-making made during the period of Bion's psychosis papers. This is a crucial point insofar as it was Bion's clinical experience that led him to question and revise aspects of Kleinian theory, not the other way round.

To the question of the lack of references in the 'Thinking' paper, the informed reader would have understood that it was Kleinian theory that was being revised. The use of such terms as 'breast,' 'no-breast,' 'projective identification' all pertained to Klein's work. Clearly Bion had derived much benefit from engaging with Klein's work—both as an analysand as well as her avid reader. Yet the issue of the missing references left the reader guessing which analytic authorities might have influenced Bion's thinking. Perhaps there is also a *double entendre* in Bion's new phrase, 'thoughts without a thinker,' used in this paper for the first time. At the manifest level, he discussed the hypothesized infant of analysis, who feels the 'pressure of thoughts' as a demand to do some sort of psychic work; and as a result, has to develop an apparatus for thinking. Perhaps at a latent level, Bion was cultivating a bit of a mystique about himself, as 'thoughts without a thinker' could also refer to the work of other writers that Bion did not cite. We have alluded to such analysts as D.W. Winnicott, who was quite forthcoming in a series of letters written to Bion in the 1950s but was not credited in any way by Bion in any of his numerous publications during this time—or at any other time (Winnicott letter to Bion, 7 October 1955 (Winnicott 2017)). This is curious insofar as Bion would soon become President of the British Society (1962–65) and he would have had to attend all the monthly Scientific Meetings—and thus, would have had plenty of opportunities to hear and engage Winnicott's work (Aguayo, 2018a).

So, while Bion now still subscribed to Klein's ideas while he was simultaneously transforming them, this fact remained directly unstated in the 'Thinking' paper. Perhaps he thought that he had sufficiently incorporated her ideas to the point of invisibility—i.e., he no longer needed to cite Klein's specific work as a source though he mentioned her by name. By all accounts, Bion was successful in his acts of theoretical recalibration, all without being perceived as being disloyal to the Klein group. During the early 1960s, he rose to the positions of Chair of the Melanie Klein Trust as well as President of the British Society. His new theoretical work clearly dazzled and mystified its readers while remaining a bit obscure to those who read it during this time (Guntrip, 1965).

So, to a quick outline of the 'Thinking' paper: in the psychological nascency of the hypothesized infant, "thinking has to be called into existence to cope with thoughts" (Bion, 1962a, p. 111). Thinking is forced on the psyche by the pressure of thoughts and not the other way round. Psychopathology can develop either in the progression of thoughts or in the apparatus itself or both. The infant exists as a 'thought without a thinker,' while mother is the designated 'thinker.' The infant's thoughts can be classified in terms of 'preconceptions,' 'conceptions' or 'thoughts' and finally 'concepts.' Bion here gave new names to what had been formerly called 'instincts.' Recall Abraham's idea of the infant instinctually rooting for the nipple. When a 'preconception' is met with a realization (e.g., repeated successful feeds at the breast), a 'conception' occurs insofar as the infant builds up a reasonable expectation that it will be fed regularly. In Bion's (1962a, p. 111) words, when mouth is brought to nipple, a "preconception is brought into contact with a realization that approximates to it, the mental outcome is a conception." Again, this was new language and terms, but the idea associated with Klein's work remained more or less the same: the infant was born object-related, but here, Bion seamlessly added in the factor of the normally developing infant, which years before had been a factor addressed by Winnicott in his work, most especially his (1953) paper on 'Transitional Objects.'

Bion blended in the notion of the normally developing infant with the pathological version long associated with Klein's work. The question arose of what happened to the infant when there was the inevitable mating of a preconception with a frustration. When an infant rooting for the breast was met with an experience of 'no breast,' it could lead to a healthy outcome: an increased sense of frustration that became a prerequisite for thought. These developments keyed off the infant's capacity to tolerate frustration, where a situation of an 'absent' or 'no-breast' could occur because of an infant's inability to wait for a period of time. In Bion's (1962a, p. 307) words: "If the capacity for toleration of frustration is sufficient the 'no-breast' inside becomes a thought, and apparatus for 'thinking' it develops."

Doubling back to Freud's (1911) 'Two Principles' paper, the development of a capacity to think occurs when the reality principle dominates. The capacity to tolerate frustration is another way of talking about developing a meaningful experience of waiting, or in Freudian language, a well-developed secondary process thinking capacity that allows the individual to 'delay gratification' until more affects, memories can be uncovered and more fully integrated in a smoother, adaptive, reality-oriented solution. Bion here blended Klein's emphasis on the frustrated, 'no-breast' infant situation, now counterbalancing it with the infant's development of normal thinking that is attuned to the reality principle. Klein had relatively *less* to say about the psychical processes of the normal infant development.

The pathological infant, the one unable to tolerate frustration, had to decide between evasion of frustration and other forms of modification. In this instance, the Kleinian infant formed an internal 'bad object,' which was concretistically indistinguishable from the thing-in-itself and was only fit for evacuation. Put differently, this was an intolerable internal situation, one that by means of projective identification the infant sought to evade by ridding itself of the 'bad object,' which could manifest as destructive attacks on the external object perceived as frustrating or depriving. Those schooled in Kleinian ideas in the early 1960s would have not had trouble spotting the Kleinian influence in Bion's new theory here, as it seemed to be another way of alluding to what Klein (1957) had termed the infant's 'double relation' to the breast—the absence of the good providing material breast can be experienced as the presence of the bad internal persecutory one.

A predominance of bad, 'no-breast' experience went hand in hand with the infant's resorting to projective identification as a means of ridding itself of unwanted and extremely frustrating and unpleasurable emotional states. Excessive reliance on projective identification (or solipsistic styles of relating), as well as omnipotence and omniscience, left the infant trapped in an isolated and deprivational emotional world—as the perception of separateness is simultaneously snuffed out.

Bion gave a brief clinical example: a patient complained about wasting time but continued to waste it. This puzzling phenomenon was one that Freud had addressed with his idea of disavowal: one can admit something to be true in the first instance yet deny it simultaneously in the same sentence. The point here would be to explore with the patient the micro-moment when a transformation occurs—from an admitted reality to a denied one. I find it useful to express Bion's (1962a, p. 113) ideas using different language as it helps us evolve varying perspectives on the same idea. It is especially useful for those coming to read Bion for the first time, as it is quite easy to feel frustrated or distressed by his difficult and opaque writing style.

Also of importance was the further introduction by Bion of a different conception of the virtual mother. For it is mother in Bion's new model who can recognize, contain and minister to the emotionally distressed infant. If all goes well between infant and mother, then the infant, via the normal use of projective identification, makes its needs known to a mother who can both recognize and minister to them. It is when a different situation obtains, for example the fear that the infant is dying that a more pathological outcome can occur. The mother, unable to soothe her baby, would thus be subjected to increased amounts of distress from her baby—and if the need still goes by unmet or non-satisfied, a sense of 'nameless dread' can ensue.

At this point, some care must be exercised in this discussion of the virtual infant and the virtual mother. These are metaphors that reach back into Bion's Kleinian years—and while they sound like they imply a historical or developmental layer, they are analytic metaphors for how an analyst can both understand and deal with a patient in real time. Recall here that outside his home life, Bion never saw mothers and babies in his analytic practice. Again, Bion would listen to the patient discuss his early days, but all the analytic work that deployed this metaphor pertained to work done in the present moment, in the 'here-and-now.'

In effect, Bion now specified what he thought of as the listening capacities to be exercised by the analyst as a maternal figure. At the base of it, the analyst listened to verbal communications and what can be seen as deteriorated forms of communication (guttural utterances, motoric gestures, all in the realm of the non-representational), converting them via his 'alpha function' into useable elements of thought, the so-called 'alpha elements.' It was akin to the idea that mother's alpha-function served as the infant's first connection to a metabolizing other, someone who would help him deal with the pressure of thoughts. Put differently, as others, like Brown (2012) have done, Bion here also gathered a lifetime's worth of profoundly disturbing experiences—from leaving home at age 8, to witnessing and participating in the brutalizing, terrorizing and traumatizing aspects of World War I. Not that Bion ever employed such a term as 'trauma'—such a word was not to be found in his analytic lexicon, but he was still subject to experiences he couldn't metabolize. One can conjecture that Klein's analysis of Bion helped him begin to digest or at least begin to give expression to the unspoken horrors of World War I.

Throughout his efforts to evolve a new model, one point stood out very clearly: Bion now conceptualized the maternal figure as a separate psychologically processing entity, whose vital importance needed to be factored into the infant's normal and pathological development. The mother's incapacity for 'reverie' in turn imposed a psychic burden on her infant—in other words, the effect of the maternal environment of non-provision was being brought into play here. When the mother could not carry the burden of the projections emitted in her direction, all this left the infant with was what it experienced as a "willfully misunderstanding object—with which it is identified" (Bion, 1962a, p. 309). If gone unchecked, there developed what could be experienced as a vicious and pathological dialectical struggle.

Repeated experiences of obstructive refusals on the mother's part created vicious negative spirals, whereas satisfying and harmonizing attempts on the analyst's part could underlie a beneficial cycle. The subject could unite conceptions, thoughts and other conjunctions. In this instance, it added up to the patient's gradual tolerance and abiding regard for the truth.

In now turning to recent work, I have in a post-Bionian key continued to work with his ideas, deconstructing Bion's (1962a) 'Thinking' paper. I comment here on a variation of the theme of temporality, namely chronology, context and comparative theory as embedded in this paper. In the history of our discipline, one can depict the evolution of any analyst's thought as either an 'internal,' slow evolution based on the interest of the theorizing analyst; or, as a contextual evolution, where the theorist is subject to his or her own local influences. In writing about Bion's evolution as an analytic theorist, I have taken both routes (Aguayo and Regeczkey, 2016; Aguayo, 2018a). The first examined Bion's work as an 'all-in Kleinian,' a member of the Kleinian publishing cohort that worked on the psychoses project. Bion then gathered these findings, as we have seen in this chapter, both preserving them and simultaneously expanding their conceptual significance with his new theory of thinking (Bion, 1962a). In recent work, I also take the contextual tact, revising earlier views of how Bion also evolved theoretically in response to the work of *both* the London Klein group as well as the work done by D.W. Winnicott on the infant's relationship to its mother.

Thus, as a counterpoint to an internalist view, in which one can discover a hidden order of temporality within Bion's 'Thinking' paper, a theory of the patient's sense of subjectively lived time, I maintain that we mustn't overlook how Winnicott's work also may have helped Bion make what Italian Field Theory might call 'the intersubjectivist turn' or 'big bang' in the early 1960s (Civitarese, 2019). I maintain that D.W. Winnicott's own work must also figure in the theoretical mix of Bion's theoretical evolution.

To double back to Bion's striking phrase, 'thoughts without a thinker,' it also ultimately finds its origins in the early days of psychoanalysis when Freud (1911) first speculated about the origins of thinking as an evolution from primary process, pleasure principle operating in the neurotic patient, to secondary process, reality principal modes of functioning. Klein (1952) expanded upon Freud's theorizing, drawing upon Karl Abraham's somewhat divergent view of the infant as 'suckling,' born instinctually rooting for the breast (R. Steiner, 1989). This was one of the roots of British object relations theory and Klein's theory of the paranoid/schizoid position—and her own analysand, Bion, was well accustomed to discussions of a hypothetical infant governed by internal object relations. Beyond Freud's brief foray in the analysis of psychosis in the Schreber case, it was Abraham's work that turned his analysand, Klein, in the direction of the analysis of psychosis (Klein, 1946).

After Klein's death in 1960, Bion then preserved the essence of the Klein group's findings on psychosis, while simultaneously expanding their reach, by now theorizing about the evolution of normal thinking in the context of a ministering maternal figure. In having dealt with disorders of thinking for so many years, it evolved into Bion then wondering about what made ordinary thinking possible. Through a creative misreading of Freud's 'Two Principles' paper, Bion thought he could now account in a more all-encompassing way for the development of normal, neurotic and psychotic forms of thinking— and more specifically included the psychotic patient's *internal* psychic experience of the maelstrom to which he was subjected.

Bion's innovative concepts, such as 'attacks on linking' now filled out the psychotic's internal mode of psychic experience when he attacked his awareness of psychic reality and attacked his own mind, shattering it at times into micro bizarre objects and projectively expelling them into his objects. Bion also added the infant's normal thinking in the context of the alpha-function ministrations of a maternal object.

I add these considerations because Abraham and Klein's work went a bit missing in Bion's 'Thinking' paper. In various places, Bion made it clear that he had little use for Abraham's theory. In the 1978 *Paris Seminar*, he said: "and then there are these interminable, wearisome—to me—arguments about Kleinian theory, Abrahamian theory, and all sorts of theories, I cannot be interested in them because they obscure the fact that there is, as far as I am concerned, actually such a thing as a human mind or personality" (Bion, 2013; *CWB*, IX: 205). So, to the continuity of Bion's (1962a) thinking with that of Abraham and Klein, when he posits the infant's 'pre-conception' mating with the breast as a 'realization' that resulted in a 'conception,' he merely restated what Abraham and Klein had already formulated. In and of itself, it was hardly new. Any Kleinian might read preconceptions, realizations and conceptions as a restatement of the analyst's need to ascertain the psychic's enduring psychic reality, all by means of attuned interpretive work that eventuated in more inclusive meaning-making.

Then, however, there was the curiously different turn after Klein's death in 1960 that Bion made towards the development of normal thinking in the virtual infant as a 'thought without a thinker,' who now required the ministrations of an 'alpha-function' bearing mother on the road to birthing his own thoughts. Civitarese (2019, p. 185) correctly points out that Winnicott (1960) also wrestled with Freud's (1911; 1914) iconic papers and had long since arrived at the conclusion that the image of a wish-fulfilling, autoerotically centered infant was only one part of the complex story of the infant's early development. But of course, Winnicott evolved a different narrative about babies and their mothers based on thousands of direct pediatric observations.

Freud had left out the crucial and mediating role of the environmental mother of provision, a point Winnicott (1945) had made steadily in a stream of papers starting with 'Primitive Emotional Development.' Of interest here is Winnicott's own mediating theoretical role on holding—and I have argued (Aguayo, 2018a) that it is another crucial but indirect factor in Bion's seemingly sudden turn towards what had been an anathema to Kleinians for years, namely the role of the actual mother. While Winnicott initially seemed to miss Bion's (1962a) turn towards mothering and normal thinking, he would soon catch up with this development on Bion's part.

To buttress this interconnection conjectured here between Winnicott and Bion's theoretical thinking, the *Collected Works of D.W. Winnicott* (1955) have now produced a series of letters, some of which appear for the first time, that indicate that Winnicott had written to Bion a number of times suggesting that Bion was neglecting the role of the actual mother in the treatment of some of his psychotic patients (Winnicott, 2017). To my way of thinking, if we continue to look at how Winnicott pressed the claims of the importance of the maternal environment upon Bion, we might also conclude that Winnicott's quite developed ideas about developmental timelines were part of this mix. It is present in such concepts as 'primary maternal preoccupation' in the last trimester of pregnancy, 'good enough mothering,' where the mother allows the infant the initial space to believe that he omnipotently creates the world, and the gradual weaning that signals the onset of the transitional object as both a possession in itself as well as a foray into the infant's initial attempts at symbolic representation. This reflects a subtle temporal theory in itself of the varying ways in which mothers optimally attuned and provided for their infants *in utero* and in the first months of life; it is not hard to maintain that the mother plays a crucial role in the infant's transition from 'pre-reflective' states to becoming a conscious subject in his own right. It appears that Winnicott's research may have subliminally influenced Bion's new theories.

In short, in whatever way, as Civitarese (2019) maintains, that mothers figure in the birth of the infant's subjective, *lived experience together* (to use a phrase of Tom Ogden's) the 'non-reflective' experience of time might be calculated as existing in the 'paranoid/schizoid position,' or in Freud's auto-erotically, objectless state (which was also subscribed to by Winnicott). The experience of time can only therefore be a function of a human being becoming constituted as a living, conscious subject. The acceptance of this type of argument I think overcomes some of the prejudices of a bygone era, the 'anxiety of influence' or 'anxiety of originality,' where British analysts such as Bion and Winnicott were loath at times to present their work as in any way being informed by the work of other analysts. In the tense and competitive post-war tripartite training situation in London, analysts were skittish about acknowledging the work of other analysts.

This does not detract from Civitarese's subtle point about the subjective experience of temporality in a conscious, subjectively attuned patient—and what can be destroyed and go missing in concrete states of 'bad object' experiences that are merely expelled, evacuated into others. It is merely a way of saying that subtle as Bion's clinical genius was, he was not someone who lived in a purely theoretical universe of his own making.

Chapter 8

Learning from Experience, Part I (1962b)

Learning from Experience

Klein's death in 1960 liberated Bion to distill what he had learned from both her and Freud in arriving at an over-arching meta-theory to explain how the mind operates both in its irrational and rational modes. Here Bion drew upon his direct clinical experiences with groups and psychotic patients, transforming sense data into the realm of the new psychological concepts. In 'The Theory of Thinking' paper as well as his monograph, *Learning from Experience*, Bion (1962a, 1962b) attempted to encompass the thinking process from its most disordered manifestations to that of the highest functioning physical scientist. Having dealt with the problems of the chronically thought-disordered in the 1950s led him to ask: how does normal thinking unfold? Could there be a way whereby the practicing psychoanalyst might have of thinking of the actual theories he deployed in his everyday work? Could a system of notation be evolved so that the analyst might have some objective way of recording crucial developments in the work with his patients, but do so in such a way as to generate fresh hypotheses? Bion's new model adhered closely to the actual clinical situation, orienting towards the disturbed patient's infantile past that kept intruding defensively into the present.

In posing such questions, Bion's trajectory was towards the unknown, towards a way to ground as firmly as possible what the analyst could know—and communicate what he had learned to his colleagues. In taking on this massive project, he now added references that reflected a form of cross-modal, interdisciplinary thinking, where he now borrowed ideas from other disciplines—philosophy, mathematics, and literature—and pressed them at times violently into service in fashioning a meta-theory which in effect was a thinking man's guide to how to think about the psychoanalytic situation and its theoretical underpinnings.

In setting out a model that might be inclusive of Freud and Klein's most enduring findings, Bion continued to privilege Freud's (1911) 'Two Principles' and Klein's (1946) 'Notes on Some Schizoid Mechanisms.' He abstracted from these two systems of thought to both transform and learn from his

DOI: 10.4324/9781003364795-11

psychoanalytic experience to that point. Bion now also effected a discursive disjunction from previous Kleinian work on the understanding of groups and psychosis; he made a transformative break with how he had written in the past. To some of his immediate and interested colleagues in the early 1960s, they almost all admitted to bewilderment and difficulties in understanding his new work—however, these difficulties did not dissuade them from taking up its challenges.

I put into context here some ideas about what makes reading *Learning from Experience* so difficult but ultimately rewarding. First and foremost, the book was full of so many new ideas that it reads as if Bion himself had a difficult time keeping its themes properly segregated. It appears that there were two, somewhat antithetical agendas that guided Bion's thinking: an aim at thinking about how psychoanalysis could be rendered more scientific, complete with replicable experiments and testable deductive hypotheses; and a more clinical aim to deal with disturbed patients. On the latter point, generations of analysts have deconstructed Bion's *Learning*, calling attention to its brilliant and innovative psychological theorizing (Guntrip, 1965; Grinberg, Sor and Bianchedi, 1977; Grotstein, 1981; Britton, 1992; Ogden, 1994, 2004; Ferro, 2005, 2006; Civitarese, 2008, 2014; Vermote, 2019; Aguayo, 2022). On the other hand, Bion's aims at theorizing about a more scientific psychoanalysis have by and large fallen by the wayside and thus do not occupy our attention here (Malin, 2021).

In setting out his new theory of 'container/contained,' Bion drew upon Freud's (1911) depiction of the pleasure and reality principles, but distorted them in a Kleinian fashion, positing that the infant from the outset struggled with the demands of both reality and pleasure while remaining object-related. This view ran counter to that depicted by Freud: an 'objectless' infant dominated by primary narcissism, autoerotic pleasure that dominated the infant's psychic experience long before the capacity to mediate the claims of reality would set in—all in a primarily non-relational context. Yet despite Bion's textual distortion of Freud's ideas, noted by perceptive observers like Guntrip (1965), like other creative analytic theorists, he had to distort his reading of Freud to arrive at new meaning.

So implicitly building upon another one of Klein's undeveloped concepts of 'epistemophilia,' (or 'love of knowing') Bion fashioned a model of the infant that effectively birthed him into a situation where he existed as a series of 'thoughts without a thinker.' He also went beyond Klein's not factoring the mediating role of the external object: in other words, given the numerous instinctual demands for work upon his immature psyche, the infant was born in profound need of an object-relationship that could minister to those needs in a thoughtful, containing and comforting fashion. Thus, in positing the mother's 'alpha-function,' the infant's ideo-motor activities were both received, processed by means of maternal reverie and potentially returned to the infant in the form of contained and metabolized understanding. Bion as a Kleinian broke new ground here, mediating the claims of nature and nurture.

In laying out this relational matrix of how the mother ministered to her infant, Bion accepted the underlying need for maternal nurture—and at last, as Winnicott would soon note, a Kleinian was now taking seriously the claims of the external environment. Bion went about the altering of some of Klein's key concepts. While accepting the central mechanism of projective identification, which for Klein represented an omnipotent phantasy projected into the other, Bion (1955, 1959) expanded this concept by emphasizing its communicative aspect, delineating how normal development might occur within the matrix of the infant's relationship with its mother, something that complemented Klein's predominant emphasis on the infant's phantasmic relationship to the maternal body. To be clear: Bion's view both incorporated the infant's phantasmic experience of the external object, but now factored in the *separate*, emotional processing capacities of a real external object, in this case, the analyst. Communicative projective identification could also have an organizing impact on the listener in his responses to the subject, a factor that could underscore role-responsivity—for good or for ill. On the one hand, Bion transformed Klein's work by now providing additional conceptual ballast to her emphasis on the infant's pathological development in relationship to a factor she had held as an unconsidered 'constant' in her system: the mother as an end in and of herself, someone whose emotional processing capacities had to be factored into the matrix of the infant's psychic development. In Bion's creative distortion of Freud's ideas, the reality principle now operated at the intersection between a subjectively attuned mother and a subjectively receptive infant. It also included Kleinian formulations of the infantile as well. One irony, however, was that the Bionian virtual infant was fashioned directly out of work with psychotic patients, as Bion did not treat or observe infants and their mothers in his practice.

In this instance, Bion included but simultaneously expanded Klein's findings that an infant with an aggressively envious predisposition could toxify mother's best attempts at ministering to it. Thus, room was made for envy as an object-related destructive factor. Bion also, however, added how a variable infantile factor could be received by a variable mother, thus producing different admixtures of emotional matching and mismatching to produce different varieties of interactional outcome (Britton, 2008). So, Klein's pathological view of the infant could now be modulated and complemented by a different model in which the infant's nascent 'alpha-function' could be developed in relationship to a containing maternal 'alpha-function' that he assimilated through a felicitous 'learning from experience' ('pre-conception,' 'realization' and 'conception').

Through his model of 'container/contained' (Figure 8.1), the role of the external object was factored in; and as mothers are variable in their 'alpha functioning' capacities, so too are analysts. A crucial point here: the virtual infantile factor was also the patient-as-infant, while the mother was the analyst-as-maternal figure. In

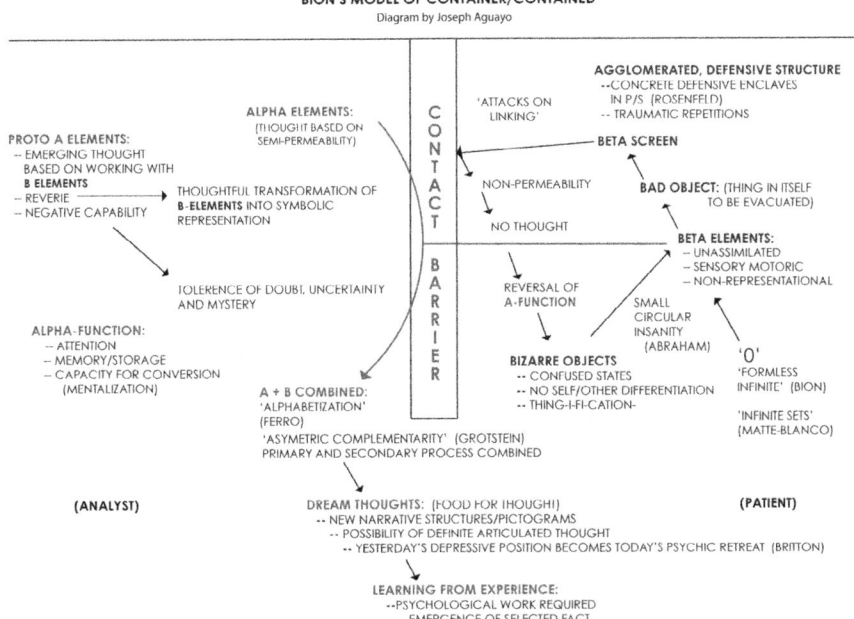

BION'S MODEL OF CONTAINER/CONTAINED
Diagram by Joseph Aguayo

Figure 8.1 Visual Diagram of Bion's Model of 'Container/Contained.'

Bion's expanding paradigm, there could be obstructions to 'learning from experience' from either side then—from the mother, who might not recognize the idiosyncratic way in which the infant was communicating, and thus prevent its communications from becoming meaningful. There were also instances of internally generated disturbances, where the infantile factor could enviously interfere with attempts made to contain and minister to it. Another unfortunate outcome occurred when the infant, who could tolerate being fed, was splitting off the capacity to feel psychically pleasured in the process. It was not an automatic given that the actual acceptance of milk would lead to the infant's feeling loved—one was a material experience, the other a psychical one. Worst of all, there could be obstructions from both sides, leading to chronic emotional misattunement between infant and mother. The infant might feel overwhelmed by β-elements (i.e., undigested thoughts, sensory experiences that could only be evacuated by means of projective identification) and couldn't think his way to a better and more effective solution. In different words, instinctual demands (or what Bion (1954) had earlier termed 'ideo-motoric' activities) forced the issue of work upon the infantile psyche. An apparatus had to be called into play, so that the infant could adapt to new tasks in meeting the demands of reality.

Put in Kleinian terms, 'in the beginning,' especially during those inevitable times where the infant must wait to be fed, the "infant is aware of a very bad breast inside it, a breast that is 'not there' and by not being there gives it painful feelings." When the real material breast was then put into the infant's mouth, it gave rise to thought; so that the sucking process is "equated with the evacuation of the bad breast." "The idea of a breast in the mind is, reciprocally, indistinguishable from the thing itself in the mouth" (Bion, 1967b, p. 57). So, there is an 'actual breast,' a 'thing-in-itself,' and the neediness and deprivation induced by its absence, i.e. the 'bad' but 'needed breast'—a compound of an emotional experience overlaid on top of a thing in itself. Here was the genesis of the 'β-element.' So, the infant, filled psychically with a bad breast experience, could evacuate it by putting the real, material breast in his mouth. The mere sight of the actual breast could make the 'bad breast' disappear.

While Bion's work was regarded as a new theory that set out the early stages of the infant's psychical development in a relational matrix to a variable mother, it was born out of a nuanced reconceptualization of the 'analyst-as-mother' and his functioning as an actively processing participant-observer in the analytic process. Borrowing here from Freud's notion that the sense organs were turned Janus-faced outward in consciousness of the sense world, and inwardly towards the world of psychic reality, Bion expanded upon 'attention' as another defining factor in the analyst's 'alpha-function.' It was the analyst's attentiveness and a capacity to tolerate frustration that focused on sense impressions and emotional experiences that led to the production of 'alpha-elements,' which were in turn suitable for storage and for the requirements of dream thoughts. When 'alpha-function' was impaired or reversed, the postulates of Klein's pathological model obtained: sense impressions remained unchanged or 'undigested,' and these 'things-in-themselves' were fit only to be evacuated by means of projective identification, something that Bion absorbed from Klein and re-packaged as 'beta-elements.'

In terms of the actual psychoanalytic work with his patients, Bion's (1950, 1954) disinclination to use in any active way the patient's early history in his interpretative work, now emphasized the analyst's capacity to remember what the patient said in alliance with "a capacity for forgetting so that the fact that any session is a new session and therefore an unknown situation that must be psychoanalytically investigated is not obscured by an already over-plentiful fund of pre- and misconception" (Bion, 1962b, p. 39). Along with a growing inclination to believe that the analytic working process could only occur in the present moment, Bion wondered if he could evolve a method of notation to deal with the cumbersome problem of recording what happened while providing material for generating fresh ideas about the material chronically encountered in analysis.

Another way of stating this idea: since the analyst's main function is to immerse himself in the subjective experience of his patient, making this in turn the object of his 'knowing' (the 'K' link) and then reporting back to the patient what he has learned, what about the possibility that the patient finds what the analyst interpretatively reports too painful to bear knowing? Here

Bion alerted the analyst to the problem of 'reversible perspective,' one that necessitated the analyst's clear explication of the patient's own 'model of mind.' To situate himself in the patient's subjective experience meant that the analyst must differentiate his own personal model of the patient's mind from that of the patient's own model of mind (Bion, ibid., pp. 82–83). If there is too much of a disjunction between the analyst and patient on which model of mind is being analyzed, then the analytic endeavor can be derailed into a therapeutic impasse because the work is conducted on parallel tracks of experience.

Another creative innovation that helped the analyst organize the mass of psychical data contained in any one hour of analysis was through the deployment of Poincaré's 'selected fact,' which Bion defined as the way the analyst attentively listened, gradually allowing a pattern to emerge that would organize a set of psychical facts in a particular way. Bion (2013) later likened it to looking at a random configuration inside a kaleidoscope; once you turn the wheel, the disorder becomes orderly; likewise, in the 'selected fact.' It unites known elements "seemingly foreign to one another, and suddenly introduce(s) order where the appearance of disorder reigned" (Bion, ibid., p. 72) Put in Klein's language of positions, the analyst tolerates waiting patiently in P/S as he allows the patient his initial associations, gradually seeing a form where only formlessness existed; from all this, a psychic pattern in the Depressive position would emerge.

Let me give a brief clinical illustration of what ideas from Bion's model of 'container/contained' look like in practice with an analyst-as-mother and patient-as-infant. A supervisee of mine, W, brought a great deal of emotionally undigested work with her five times a week analysand, B, who had suffered a great deal of early sexual trauma and projectively evacuated much of this dissociated distress into the analyst. W had to bear accounts of how B's father gradually groomed her, beginning at age 3, making her favorite breakfast foods while her mother was out shopping on the weekends. He asked his daughter to touch his penis while they ate banana bread. Father would say: "I made you feel good, now don't you want to make me feel good?" The mother was rarely home when the molestations occurred; she was absent and apparently oblivious to what was happening. To make matters worse, in the analysis, B made incessant demands for more time, more sessions and long email exchanges over the weekend, demands to which W at times acceded. W grew increasingly beleaguered and weary, beginning to phantasize that she might terminate B abruptly. The analytic situation was tempestuous and threatened to founder. At times, W feigned illness just so that she could cancel B's sessions.

As I focused on how W experienced B's raw trauma in our initial supervisory meetings, the candidate became surprisingly angry and resentful—and felt profoundly guilty for these feelings. This recognition of W's resentment towards B had the function of making for a more boundaried experience of self and other, allowing W to temporarily not feel so fused and enslaved to B's overwhelming distress and demandingness. W now phantasized openly in supervision about terminating B, getting rid of her, or firing her as a patient.

W then evolved a deeper unconscious phantasy: that somehow, B had stolen inside her, birthing her own separate phantasy that her analyst would oversee her rebirth, her starting life over again as a fetus inside a new mother. W now felt saddled with a sense of omnipotent responsibility for fixing B's broken life, privately admitting that the patient's rebirth phantasy was abhorrent and off-putting—revulsive because she also felt and acted at times as if she *was* the mother of record, someone who would bear omnipotent responsibility for a new life. W then crystallized her own phantasy—that B was an insidious Guinean parasitic worm, a deadly species that once it lodged itself in the host's intestines, could only be removed very slowly, a bit at a time lest it break off and rejuvenate itself again.

Through the patient work of symbolization in supervision—what Bion (1962) termed the evolution of alpha-function—W opened up a more psychical and emotional space for thinking under fire, realizing that B's sensory, emotional, traumatic and dissociative evacuations, a true 'beta-screen,' had rendered them both incapable of meaningful thought. B's own emotional assaults penetrated the analyst's mind, now symbolized as a phantasy of an infesting parasitic worm that rendered her incapable of thought. It also projectively reflected B's having been genitally invaded by her father, infected and possessed by the paternal penis—as a child, she felt her father's penis had a devouring mouth that bore into her. A profound bodily and emotional boundary had been broken, leaving B's mind and body violently penetrated, shattered and profoundly traumatized. The candidate's own parasitic/pregnancy image was her attempt to ingest and make emotional and symbolic meaning out of B's sexual trauma lodged within her.

W emotionally struggled with overwhelmingly violent and crazy-making experiences—at times feeling trapped in the grip of the paternal violence, a past that refused to stay past that kept intruding in a mind-numbing way into the present. Since W also felt so compassionately connected to B, she ingested the trauma, as if she too had been invaded and now possessed. The penetration of her own psychic space reflected how the analytic frame and boundaries had been trampled upon. W now realized the difference between carrying a maternal function as opposed to being identified as omnipotently responsible for the patient's emotional welfare.

During these emotional storms, W and I discussed a mutual association of our own: she and I spontaneously each recalled having seen a recent South Korean film, 'Parasite' (2019), which had as one of its main elements, a woman who had provided secret shelter for her impoverished but criminal husband in the basement of a lavishly expensive home. He lived there in hiding from the police for years, being provided food and shelter. I thought that this was our attempt to symbolize the profound unmetabolized conflicts faced by W, as I realized that B will be a long-term analysand, who desperately needs to face the horrifying truth of her past, so she can liberate herself in facing the very painful issues of endangering and unreliable internal objects with whom she has had to live.

These experiences reflected W's growing capacity to symbolize and digest her experiences of the supervision, her increasing capacity to articulate B's own parasitic states of mind. (Put differently: the candidate came to realize just how completely her mind had been overrun and filled with B's own undigested trauma and other dissociative experiences). It has made for a more differentiated and boundaried treatment frame, as the candidate can now interpret rather than merely gratify her patient's need for extra-analytic contact. Fortunately for B, the experience of having to tolerate increasing and painfully split feelings towards her analyst have been accompanied by a recent promotion at work and a sizable salary increase. Currently, rather than gratify the patient's need for contact over the weekend, the wish for daily contact has kept B from having to cope with the frustration and pain of only momentarily capturing the analyst as her own secure possession. W now provides a more containing frame and understands more clearly how she had been role-organized into accepting omnipotent, around the clock maternal responsibility for B as her daughter/friend/neighbor and lover.

B's analysis currently rests in this profoundly split transference situation: her neediness now coexists with fears of betrayal and exploitation. But that is another story. For now, a boundaried and containing space has evolved as a painful emotional journey begins towards the patient's securing a safe, sturdy and reliable object experience.

Concluding Remarks

To look at Bion's model of 'container/contained' from a different vertex, of what relevance is a model that was put forward almost 60 years ago? As a partial answer, one can submit the ordinary finding that most analytic models are related to the immediate contexts that spawn them, but do not pass the test of time. Exceptional theorists, like Freud and Klein—as well as Bion—have demonstrated a generative capacity to inspire succeeding generations of analysts with their thought, all of which leads to new innovations. I have illustrated how meaningful I have found Bion's 'container/contained' model in my own analytic practice.

In one of the many 'Introductions' written for the *Collected Works of W. R. Bion*, Chris Mawson (Bion, 2014, vol. VI: 249–257) addressed this question of clinical relevance. What have succeeding generations of contemporary London Kleinians for instance evolved from Bion's conceptual work in *Learning from Experience*? At the end of Chapter 6, I explored how Betty Joseph developed some of Bion's ideas, such as doing analytic consultations in groups, working in the here-and-now. What about succeeding generations of Kleinians in London? Has Bion's work stood the test of time? Is it still relevant today?

In engaging the contemporary clinical relevance of Bion's theoretical think-ing, Bion's mode of theory-building has continued to inspire others to evolve variations on themes discussed in his work. Certainly, the idea of 'container/contained' is very popular in contemporary psychoanalytic literature—and this model includes interrelated concepts, such as 'P/S (back and forth) with D,' 'selected fact,' 'alpha' and 'beta elements,' 'contact barrier' and of course, Bion's (1958) expansion of Klein's notion of projective identification. His move to a two-body/two-minded theory has introduced greater complexity into the question of how the analyst can think about the analytic situation.

For example, in contemporary Kleinian work, Ron Britton and John Stei-ner (1994) have expanded upon Bion's notion of the 'selected fact' by adding their observations that in the workaday clinical situation, it is often quite difficult for the analyst to differentiate a 'selected fact' from what they term an 'over-valued idea.' Sometimes the latter idea can sound like the former one, but the similarities are merely superficial. There is of course an underlying pattern in a 'selected fact,' a random set of facts that are organized by the ana-lyst. Yet there is also order in an underlying pattern that in effect is a 'crystal-lization of delusional certainty' that can appear as an overvalued idea. Perhaps it is important to bear in mind what Bion once said about interpretations: he likened it to military 'sighting shots,' where one approximated getting closer and closer to being able to actually hit the target. In other words, the analyst must always bear in mind that any interpretation is an excursion into the unknown, and that he must be careful not to impose a delusional certainty in the form of an interpretation on his patients.

One way we guard against this possibility is through the careful moment-to-moment tracking of an analytic session—all of which is associated with the work of Betty Joseph and Michael Feldman. By checking one's work with a group of colleagues, one can maintain a steady distinction between helpful and informative approximations of 'selected facts' vis-à-vis the potentially disruptive impact of an 'overvalued idea.'

Learning from Experience, Part II (1962b)

In previous chapters, we have doubled back to Bion's earlier work, having a second look at ground we have covered but always from a different vertex. In another look at Bion's (1962b) *Learning from Experience*, I further deconstruct and understand a text that has baffled, intrigued and inspired analysts for decades now.[1] One way to tackle this problem is to contextualize some of the theoretical components of the 'container/contained' model in terms of the analytic work that preceded it. To the main thesis of Chapter 9: I maintain that Bion's work with psychotic patients in the 1950s underscored both his revision of Freud and Klein on the subject, and thus led to a need to hypothesize what he considered to be a more all-encompassing model that accounted for both the disorders of thinking as well as the evolution of orderly and even at times creative thinking (Aguayo, 2022).

Conceptual and Clinical Illustrations of Bion's Model of 'Container/Contained'

In order to demonstrate the potential value of reading *Learning from Experience* as a strictly psychoanalytic text without the encumbrance of its scientific claims, very late in Chapter 27, one that I have taken the liberty of entitling, 'The K Link in the Construction of a Theory of Container/Contained,' Bion posited a new theory that in effect was based on his work with borderline and psychotic patients. He briefly reviewed his 'Theory of Thinking' paper (Bion, 1962a) with its ideas of 'pre-conception' (or 'state of expectation'), 'realization' and 'conception' (which results when a pre-conception mates with a 'realization') model. In his clinical work, Bion was paradoxically led to the problem of the origins of thinking when he repeatedly encountered disorders of thinking with severely disturbed patients. How did ordinary thinking begin at the outset of life? Theorizing about how normal infants developed their capacity for thinking by a repetitive mating of pre-conception and sense data, resulting in commensal abstraction, whereby growth was promoted in mother-as-container and infant-as-contained, Bion (1962b, p. 91) wrote: "The relationship between mother and infant described by Melanie Klein as

DOI: 10.4324/9781003364795-12

projective identification is internalized to form an apparatus for regulation of a pre-conception with the sense data of the appropriate realization."

Drawing upon his own and Klein's clinical work, he simultaneously reconceptualized and reframed her ideas, such as the infant projecting its frustration and intolerance of waiting, or a 'bad breast' feeling into a good breast, the K (or knowledge) link starting with the relationship between mouth and breast. In his reformulation, container and contained could be 'commensal,' and "are dependent on each other for mutual benefit and without harm to either" (Bion, 1962b, p. 90). He substituted the idea of a maternal container that could be projected into—and that the infant's distressed emotional and sensory states could be held as the contained. Under better circumstances, such as the infant's burgeoning capacity to tolerate the absent 'no breast' situation, the projected elements could be emotionally metabolized, the toxins removed, being returned to the infant in a more tolerable form of felicitous conjunctions permeated by emotion.

Of far greater concern to Bion was what happened when this process between infants and their mothers went psychologically awry. To get at this experience, three crucial conceptual elements were necessary and are summed up in my title for Chapter 8 in *Learning*: 'The Transformation of Beta-Elements by Alpha-Function in the Contact Barrier.' In his conceptualization of beta-elements, Bion simultaneously transformed the ideas of both Freud and Klein when he posited unassimilated emotions, sensory and motoric gestures that existed in a non-representational (or 'thing-in-itself') realm (cf. Figure 8.1, p. 89). It augmented Freud's notion of primary process that was premised on representation in the ordinary night dream when Bion called attention to his finding that psychotic patients did not dream. While he made this distinction clear in *Learning*'s Chapter 7, 'The Contrast between Psychotic and Neurotic Dreaming,' it read more like a pronouncement rather than a statement he had abundantly documented in his psychosis papers: "In this theory the ability to 'dream' preserves the personality from what is virtually a psychotic state" (Bion, 1962b, p. 16).

In his paper, 'On Arrogance,' Bion (1958) had provided clinical evidence for his theory of psychotic dreaming, yet he did not cite it in *Learning*. Recall here from our own Chapter 6 (p. 53) that he had linked a psychotic patient's daytime hallucinations and psychotic dreaming: "I felt that the 'dreams' shared so many characteristics of the hallucination that it was possible that actual experiences of hallucination in the consulting room might serve to throw light on the psychotic dream" (Bion, 1958, p. 78). Understanding hallucinations then led to a fresh understanding: that when a psychotic patient speaks of having a dream, he thinks his perceptual apparatus is expelling something, and that "a dream is an evacuation from his mind strictly analogous to an evacuation from his bowels" (p. 78). It follows that he feels he must have taken something in. "In short, to the psychotic a dream is an evacuation of material that has been taken in during waking hours" (p. 78). Hence the link between hallucination and psychotic dreaming—and Bion's conjecture that these processes precede the ordinary recall of night dreams.

In an intriguing reworking of Freud's (1895 [1950]) idea of the 'contact barrier,' Bion (1962a, p. 22) defined it as that which "separates mental phenomena into two groups one of which performs the functions of consciousness and the other the functions of unconsciousness" and related it to Freud's drive theory. Through this comparison, what Freud had described in quantitative/energetic terms as 'accretions of stimuli,' Bion now defined as 'beta-elements,' which through the function of the contact-barrier was an elaboration of Freud's notion of the binding of the drives, with the difference that beta-elements encompass unprocessed external stimuli as well as impulses arising from within. However, while Freud defined his notion of the 'contact barrier' in terms of an individual psyche, Bion refashioned and in effect 'interpersonalized' it by implying that both mother and infant each contributed disproportionately to the building up also of a contact barrier as a semi-permeable psychic membrane *between* two individuals.

In terms of 'alpha-function,' James Grotstein (1981) contextualized Bion's work and how it too was inspired by Freud's ideas while simultaneously transforming them. For instance, while describing 'alpha-functioning' (originally termed 'dream-work alpha' by Bion, 1992) Grotstein (1981, p. 7) likened it to primary process itself, calling it "a gating mechanism which receives the sensory data of emotional experience, processes it, 'alpha-betizes' it, and transforms it into alpha elements for further mental 'digestion' to be thought about or to become dream elements for postponement and storage." In place of Freud's tripartite model, where the id served as a cauldron of instincts that at times besieged the ego, Bion discussed a 'deficient alpha-function' that predisposed an individual to psychosis by not being able to mitigate the impact of sensory and emotional data.

When alpha-function operated smoothly in the contact barrier as a semi-permeable psychic membrane, neurotic analysands could report their night dreams, associating to them in a collaborative manner in analysis, where the analyst listened actively yet patiently until the scattered fragments of the patient's associations began to cohere as constantly conjoined elements. Wisdom (1964, pp. 5–6) put this point well:

> This leads to a further development of Bion's theory. It follows from what has just been said that a dream forms a barrier between two parts of the personality, namely formation by alpha-function and the use of what is formed .... The dream virtually preserves the personality from entering into a psychotic state.

This would lead to the 'selected fact,' an organizing template that gave meaning and coherence to the patient's associations. In Grotstein's (1981, p. 12) words, "The analyst's reverie is a special deployment of alpha-function which ... prepares the analytic field for those 'thoughts without a thinker' to emerge—both within the patient and within the analyst." His concluding statement positioned

Bion's theory of thinking as an elaboration of Freud's notion of dream work but transformed this notion by replacing the unconscious instinctual drives with 'inherent preconceptions.' As a result,

> the ego's defense network is counterposed, not to instinctual drives, but rather to the awareness of their significance and ultimate meaning—of a pre-conceptive marriage with their realization. In short, defenses defend against the emergence of significance (leading to) meaning rather than to instincts *per se*.
>
> (Grotstein, 1981, p. 20)

But thinking about alpha-function more carefully, Bion in effect implies that its increased sense of coherence in the contact-barrier rests on contributions from *both* mother and infant. Bion said as much when he conceptualized beta-elements as containing the infant's inherent or 'in-born' preconceptions. Depending on the fate of the beta-elements—if they failed to metabolize and in turn became the stuff of a defensive 'beta-screen,' it would by definition imply a patient deficient in alpha-function. Successful metabolization that would allow entry into the contact barrier on the other hand would implicate the patient's successful alpha-functioning, however rudimentary. The idea of analyst and patient making respective and proportional psychic contributions to the building up (or deterioration) of alpha-functioning in the contact-barrier rested on clinical experience (cf. Figure 8.1, p. 89).

As a clinical example, Bion's (1958) 'On Arrogance' paper produced an innovative rereading of the Oedipus myth, marginalizing the sexual crime in favor of portraying Oedipus as vowing to lay bare the truth at whatever cost. Translating this idea into a way of regarding the analytic relationship, Bion stressed the idea that the analyst's very commitment to psychoanalytic inquiry will make him an accessory to the crime the patient feels is perpetrated against him. He used his previous understanding of psychotic mechanisms—the mutilating attack not only on reality but on the very organs of awareness which apprehend reality—to ask: what was there in reality that made it so hateful to the patient that he must destroy the ego which brought him in contact with it? In marginalizing a sexual Oedipal interpretation, he wrote: "There is evidence that some other element is playing an important part in provoking destructive attack on the ego" (Bion, 1958, p. 88).

In effect, this meant that Bion opened up a new grid of clinical possibilities: in addressing what he felt he was missing, what he thought he wasn't understanding, it opened the door to the possibility that it might be the analyst's deficient alpha-functioning. Perhaps if the analyst insisted on the 'correctness' of his interpretation, he in effect could display deficient alpha-function to the point of relating more like an obstructive object than an understanding one. What the analyst experienced as a 'selective fact' might in fact be an over-valued idea (Britton and Steiner, 1994). If, on the other hand, the patient defensively incarcerated himself by attacking the link to his own mind, he might well remain acting like an obstructive object himself. Bion's words are quite riveting here:

> The next step forward occurred when the patient said I was the obstructing force, and that my outstanding characteristic was 'that I could not stand it.' I now worked on the assumption that the persecuting object that could not permit any creative relationship was one that 'could not stand it,' but I was still not clear what 'it' was. It was tempting to assume that 'it' was any creative relationship which was made intolerable to the persecuting object through envy and hate of the creative couple. Unfortunately this did not lead any further because it was an aspect of the material which had already been made clear without producing an advance. The problem of what 'it' was still, therefore, awaited solution.
>
> (Bion, 1958, pp. 90–91)

Then comes the creative leap:

> What it was that the object could not stand became clearer in some sessions where it appeared that in so far as I, as analyst, was insisting on verbal communication as a method of making the patient's problems explicit, I was felt to be directly attacking the patient's methods of communication. From this it became clear that when I was identified with the obstructive force, what I could not stand was the patient's method of communication.
>
> (Bion, 1958, p. 91)

Bion concludes that the patient's psychic disaster stemmed from mutilating attacks made upon this extremely primitive mode of a link, made by an object who can't stand projective identification. *The obstructive object is a projective identification denying object*—and much meaning can be derived from the patient as well as the analyst's respective and varying contributions to co-creating this particular experience.

Clinical Illustration of 'Container/Contained' Model: The Work of Ron Britton

To illustrate at a more general level some of Bion's ideas about the crucial elements comprising the theory of 'container/contained,' it is helpful to look at actual clinical material, something that by and large went missing in *Learning*. Here I cite the work of Ron Britton (1998, 2003) who as a contemporary London Kleinian, has consistently interested himself in elaborating the clinical implications of Bion's work, especially with 'difficult-to-treat' patients. Britton (1992) demonstrated the container/contained theory when he used it to discuss the analysis of a quite disturbed borderline female, Miss A. In her case, the analyst heard repetitive reports of physical rituals, such as chronic toilet flushing (to rid herself of menacing threatening thoughts), as well as going in and out of her home repeatedly before being able to leave. The emptying out of these beta-elements had dire psychic and emotional consequences, leaving the patient feeling as if she had nothing inside herself.

In her sessions, she would return to a traumatizing memory from her adolescence during World War II: in a public air-raid shelter in London, she felt overwhelmed when the bombing occurred. To make matters worse, her mother clung anxiously to her, leaving her desperate to get out, yet unable to do so. This 'claustro-agoraphobic dilemma' (Rey, 1979) was expressed as paralyzing screen memories by which she felt actively haunted. Put in Bion's new terminology, Miss A felt internally assaulted by a beta-screen comprised of elements that she could not properly metabolize, let alone understand.

Deploying the model of 'container/contained' (Figure 8.1), the analyst felt Miss A needed to have these maddening psychic experiences held in a relationship that felt like a sanctuary to her where meaning might be found. Overridden by an internally generated 'beta-screen' assault that reflected a deficient alpha-function, she needed another mind, a different alpha-function, to help her tolerate and begin to mentalize her experience. In Britton's (1992, p. 104) words: "The 'contained' gives meaning to the context which contains it. The 'container' on the other hand gives shape and secure boundaries to that which it enshrines." Analysis was thus "a bounded world (the container) where meaning could be found (the contained)" (p. 104). It was by means of projective identification that Miss A evacuated her dreaded and terrifying experiences into the analyst-as-mother, where they were modified by their sojourn there, and in turn re-introjected. In Britton's (1992, p. 106) clinical example, he posited that beta-elements went into one of three places: into the body, into the perceptual sphere, or into action. Hypochondriasis or perceptual hallucinations abounded in the case of Miss A who suffered psychosomatic ill health because, according to Britton's Bionian understanding, she had discharged unprocessed beta-elements into her body. But just as telling, the beta-screen experience could be discharged violently into the analyst himself, potentially inducing very disturbed reactions in him, all of which resulted from expulsions of 'words-as-actions,' an outgrowth of violent forms of projective identification.

Further Elaborations of 'Container/Contained'

To capture other intriguing aspects of Bion's 'container/contained' model theoretically outlined in *Learning*: in Chapters 5 and 6, he took up patient-instigated splits between psychical and material satisfaction. The operative metaphor here was the infantile analysand who could derive material sustenance from the analytic breast while experiencing emotional obstruction to genuine emotional understanding. Wisdom (1964, p. 9) put this point well:

Bion develops this line of enquiry further with the case of an infant fed but feeling unloved. Here the infant is aware of a need for the good breast, but again he equates need for a good breast to a bad breast that needs to be evacuated. Now of the experiences of the good and bad breast, the material component of milk-satiation or deprivation can be an immediate sense-impression and therefore enables us to assign chronological priority to beta-elements over alpha-elements. Intolerance of frustration, if very strong, might be dealt with by immediate evacuation of beta-elements, thus short-circuiting the formation of alpha-function. What I think Bion is suggesting is that if the beta-elements can be successfully evacuated into a suitable receptacle ..., this fact might serve ... to bring about the discrimination between the phantasy of a bad breast and the reality of there being no breast present. However this may be, in some way or other an absent breast must become recognized as an idea. In other words, absence of a thing has to be transformed into a thought.

Of course, infantile envy could be a factor when the infant regarded the breast and its emotional bounty, all to the point that it led to the destruction of alpha-function (Bion, 1962a, p. 11). The relentless pursuit of things sometimes also necessitated that the individual rid himself of "relationships with live objects" and he feels little concern or gratitude towards others. Bion wrote: "This state involves destruction of his concern for truth" (p. 11). The patient only then feels greater cravings for material comforts—"quantity must be the governing consideration, not quality" (p. 11). Yet as emotionally dissatisfying as this state of affairs might be, the patient might also persist and persist with his need for more analysis. Bion pursued this theme of the split between material from psychical or emotional comforts, concluding that the patient's potential for having emotional contact with living objects (either others or oneself) was diminished. In such a state, others feel like automatons and the universe is experienced externally and internally as being dominated by 'inanimate objects.' In a truly downward spiral, the patient cannot take in from the analyst (i.e. cannot feed from this source; the interpretations feel like flatus) and he winds up thinking that all the interpretations are 'bad.'

Again, in setting out the main theoretical ideas of 'container/contained,' Bion may have found giving clinical illustrations in *Learning* somewhat distracting. However, again there were clinical examples in his previous work that provided ballast for ideas like the psychical/material split. In the 'On Hallucination' paper, for example, Bion (1958) described how one of his psychotic patients entered the consulting room:

As he passes into the room he glances rapidly at me; such frank scrutiny has been a development of the past six months and is still a novelty .... So closely do his movements seem to be geared with mine that the inception of my movements to sit appear to release a spring in him .... As

I sit the turning movement stops as if we were both parts of the same clockwork toy.

(Bion, 1958, pp. 65–66)

These well-choreographed movements do make both participants appear like automatons—another point Wisdom (1964, p. 4) mentioned:

One consequence, Bion claims, is that if there is a destructive attack on alpha-function, this can destroy conscious contact between the person and himself or between him and others; as a result animate objects cease to be represented or are treated as inanimate.

Yet Bion also makes it clear that the emotional denuding of this particular session in the form of a dry listlessness and inability to do anything constructive was preceded by a session that was full of hostility and murderous rage—he was aware that it flowed yet was split off in the next session. Here Bion made use of Klein's ideas regarding envy—for what the patient had violently projected into the analyst, and subsequently split off in creating an emotionally denuded atmosphere that felt inhabited by inanimate objects. Putting it differently, today's patient enviously attacked the patient he was yesterday by emotionally dismantling what meaning he had made.

A Final Clinical Example

With these considerations in mind, I have offered a graph (Figure 8.1) which is a pictorial illustration of Bion's structural model of 'container/contained,' in which all the elements we have discussed in Chapters 8 and 9 now appear in pictorial form, something I think a benefit because we can now view these ideas in spatial relationship to one another.

To capture one essential idea about some of the 'disorders of thinking' we see in our therapy practices today: with borderline patients, or patients who are subject to episodes of disordered thinking, I can give the following clinical example from my analytic practice. 'S,' an analysand in her mid-30s, pregnant for the first time, complains incessantly that her mother has little sympathy or understanding of her. She comes to her session on Monday and quickly begins to yell and scream about how her mother favors her brother over her. Recently, when the mother was in the hospital with a gastro-intestinal ailment, the brother came to visit and brought his mother flowers. 'S' flew into a rage because she believed that the brother acted this way to curry favor with the mother, something that left her feeling profoundly upset because she had not brought anything for her mother. She devalued her brother as a manipulator who was trying to prove that he was a better son than his sister. As she screamed on and on in her tirade about her brother, I listened in silence. There was so much emotional noise in the room that I literally had no room to make a comment. Bion (2013) has referred to these types of emotional bombardments that can be so intense as a situation where the analyst literally cannot hear himself think.

Here now is a portion of what ensued between us in a session from her analysis: finally, after 30 minutes of non-stop screaming and crying, there was a silence, a chance for me to share an in session piece of reverie; I said: 'Well, I can imagine what it was like when your mother first gave birth to your baby brother; you were three and there she may have been in the hospital room, perhaps with flowers, all of which may have made you feel quite crowded out.'

'S' responded: 'Oh, I remember the day he was brought home from the hospital; he was all red and looked like a loaf of bread. I was told to hold the baby and pose for a photograph. I didn't want to kiss that yucky little red mess! Yes, he stole my thunder and I can recall one time, when he was just learning to walk, I tripped him as he went by—I couldn't stand him, hanging around and breathing the same air.'

In deploying the 'container/contained' model to understand the patient's emotional and sensory bombardments, the yelling and screaming represented 'S's mentally undigested 'beta-elements,' which because they could not be engaged by another person's thoughtfulness, were becoming agglomerated into a 'beta-screen.' In other words, yelling and screaming did not allow the other person a comment—in this instance, 'S' feared allowing the analyst any chance to speak because she feared that he might retaliate against her. So, the 'beta-elements' remain agglomerated and therefore no experience for the distraught patient that another person can enter into sympathetic or understanding contact with them. (The emotional connection would have been symbolized by a fruitful pairing of the patient's 'beta-elements' with the analyst's 'alpha-function' in the 'contact barrier.')

Since the patient could not allow the analyst's thoughts as a separate person in, an idea that Bion would say represents the non-penetrability of the patient's 'beta-screen,' there can be no meaningful thought, no helpful joining together of two minds in the contact barrier—and so, a vicious cycle ensues, where 'S' was left alone with her own horrific and hellish account of what feels too concretely true and enduring: her hateful rant against her brother is part of a vicious cycle of maddening thoughts and emotions that leave the patient feeling profoundly alone and in a state of almost constant emotional deprivation. Now, if this state of emotional storm was how the patient continuously experienced her life, it would represent a psychotic state of mind. In such a state, one lives in a more or less constant storm of feeling attacked from within, and being unable to sort oneself out, the patient cannot think insightfully about their emotional situation let alone regulate herself.

But, as we hear at the end of the description, 'S' eventually calmed down, allowing the analyst some space to intervene. It was characteristic of 'S' that her psychotic experiences were momentary and needed to be waited out, so that the analyst could make a potentially useful comment to convey under-standing. So, to use Bion's conceptual scheme, there was a moment where the analyst could bring his 'alpha-function' to bear on what he had been listening to—the anguish of 'S's infantile experience of sibling rivalry, where she (as a young girl of three) felt 'pushed out,' or rejected by the plain fact that her mother had given birth to another baby.

Bléandonu's (1994) work on Bion is relevant here, as he gives us still another alternative way of understanding this patient's emotional storm. The patient's disorder of thinking would represent, in Freudian terms, a person under the sway of the Pleasure principle, where she cannot tolerate waiting, or being able to delay gratification by means of thought. She lives and relives the anguish of feeling like an unwanted and rejected child, someone who feels tortured because, to her, it appears that her mother favors the younger baby brother. From 'S's point of view, there could be no other reason her mother would have a second child other than the 'fact' that the first one proved unsatisfactory. The inability to think a different thought incarcerates the patient in a prison of isolated suffering. So, as she suffers, she makes others suffer. From Freud's perspective, all the hapless patient can do is rid herself of accumulated grief, expelling it (in Klein's sense of evacuation by means of projective identification into the analyst).

In effect, as Bléandonu (1994) tells us, Klein had described how the mental apparatus rids itself of accumulated stimuli—by means of projective identifi-cation—and now, in addition to this important idea, it is significant to realize that the Reality principle in this instance works alongside the Pleasure prin-ciple. In this clinical example, the analyst is the one who bears the Reality principle, while he listens attentively as the patient screams and carries on, thinking meaningfully about what emotionally ails her, realizing that he must be patient and wait until the emotional storm dies down, so that he can make an understanding comment. In this instance, despite the emotional storm, the patient has co-operated enough to come to the analyst's office because, after all, she is in search of some understanding, an idea that links back to Klein's idea that at the core of human existence, the infant is searching for the maternal breast for some sort of emotionally connected experience. Now, referring to ideas we discussed in Chapter 8, when Bion (1962a) posited the notion of 'preconception–realization–conception,' if the patient can return over and over to analysis, and experience repeatedly the analyst's patience and capacity to understand, the potential is there for the experience of 'pre-conception.' In that state, the patient exists literally as an infant who is a 'thought without a thinker,' and if tolerated, this experience can lead to a conception that her analyst can bear being in the same room with her and help her become more capable in birthing understanding self-conceptions that would help her weather her own emotional storms.

If the patient can tolerate waiting for the emotional storm to die down (and she can tolerate frustration), the absent or unavailable internal breast becomes a thought and develops a structure for thinking. A creative spiral emerges, where a psyche develops that can tolerate frustration, and "generates thoughts which make frustration even more tolerable" (Bion, 1962b, p. 90). "The linking of preconceptions and realizations, be they negative or positive, engenders a process which leads to 'learning from experience'" (p. 91). If one cannot bring about this conjunction of sense data, there is a sense of a 'starvation of truth' that is analogous to alimentary starvation (Bion, 1962a, p. 119; Bléandonu, 1994, p. 147). In this instant, we see Bion transforming Freud's theory of instincts into a theory based on 'pre-conceptions.'

Putting these ideas differently, when thinking does not emerge, there one will find projective identification, or in Bion's (1962a, 1962b) new language, a preconception met with negative realization becomes a 'bad object' that has to be projected. In our clinical example, 'S' had a 'bad object' experience that had to be expelled or evacuated. However, it was an unsatisfying solution for her since at the root of her projective experience, she too felt like a 'rejectable sibling,' as she feared that mother favored the new baby brother over her. It is the inability to think about such situations that leads to their expulsion—in this case, this toxic brother experience was expelled *into* the analyst. For this patient's fragile psyche, expelling this 'bad object' is the same as maintaining a 'good breast' experience. In other words, by magically ridding herself of her brother—recall here that she likened him to a loaf of bread and perhaps could be eaten—she magically thought that she would remain as her mother's one and only favorite. But of course, this is magical thinking, something momentarily designed to give the patient some sort of consolation—but in the long run, this kind of experience is not terribly reassuring.

Still one other way to understand the analyst's role in this stormy clinical episode: it is the analyst who carries the maternal alpha-function in this situation—he is the one who bears curiosity and interest in knowing the psychic reality of the patient's internal condition. As such, his reverie is a 'receptor-organ,' something that helps to harvest emotionally the whole host of the patient's beta-elements, which here appear as a 'beta-screen' that forms a thick defensive wall behind which the patient is incarcerated—and the analyst meanwhile is screened out. In effect, it leaves the patient incarcerated in a vicious cycle of lacerating emotions and, ultimately, in a lowly and emotionally devalued place as the 'undesirable sibling,' the rejectable sister. However, as we saw at the conclusion of the clinical vignette, the analyst's capacity to wait out the emotional storm allowed for the experience where he could appear as a mother who could contain and metabolize her infant's distress—in effect, serving as the initial 'alpha function' for her baby—which can decrease the infant's need to use projective identification. On the other hand, an analyst-as-mother incapable of such reverie only contributes to the increased violence of the infant's projective identifications. In the latter case, one can have phantasmagorias, such as 'S's fear that if she didn't eat or devour her brother, he might retaliate and come and devour her. This after all is the experience of primitive fears of retaliation, all being filtered through the experience of omnipotence and omniscience, which are in the long run poor substitutes for learning from experience (Bléandonu, 1994, p. 148).

So, to sum up the significance of Bion's new model of psychoanalytic thinking, I have attempted to show that, with a whole host of new concepts and ideas, Bion gave us an expansive way of thinking about the analytic treatment situation. In contrast to both Freud and Klein, who concentrated most of their efforts in the very meaningful elucidation of the patient's internal (or intrapsychic) experience, Bion absorbed these models, but expanded their reach by now including the analyst as a partner in the emotional processing of primitive unconscious feelings and states of mind. In other words, where before there were the patient-as-infant's variable states of mind, complete with phantasies, projections and other forms of unwanted experience that could be projected into the analyst, Bion augmented this model by now positing the emotional variability and receptivity of the analyst-as-maternally-containing figure, the one responsible for bearing 'alpha-function' understanding of the emotional storms to which the patient was subjected.

Increasingly, a greater sense of co-operation between analyst and patient means frequent experiences of emotional and psychic life meeting at the 'contact barrier,' symbolized by the patient's increased capacity to bring dreams for analysis and express interest in uncovering what meanings they may be carrying. Ultimately, the contact barrier is a semi-permeable membrane, one that allows certain psychic elements in while screening others out. In this sense, one psychic experience that differentiates psychotic from non-psychotic is the capacity to have and report dreams. The neurotic patient has sufficient sense of a differentiated self to be able to report his dreams without undue anxiety. Indeed, in hearing the patient's own dreams, the analyst is 'subjected to' and potentially carries the redemptive and therapeutic hope that the patient can be born into becoming a subject in his own right—so that what he is 'subject-ed' to by being analyzed ultimately means the birth of the patient's own conscious sense of 'subjectivity.' The dream projected onto the dream screen of the analyst is the potential birth of a subjectively informed consciousness in the patient.

Note

1 One of first reviews of *Learning from Experience*, issued from an Irish philosopher, John O. Wisdom. In a critique of Bion's book, given at a meeting of the British Psychoanalytical Society on 17 October 1964, Wisdom's (1964) pre-circulated paper evinced an appreciation of many of the psychoanalytically innovative ideas with which later reviewers also found favor. These included refinement of core concepts in the work of Freud and Klein, such as alpha-function as a way to encompass classical dream theory while augmenting the notion of primary process with beta-elements, which also included the psychotic's experience of being unable to dream;

the expansion of Klein's notion of projective identification as omnipotent unconscious phantasy to now include its communicative function as proto-mental experience; and the augmentation of Klein's notion of 'good material breast present becoming the bad frustrating psychic breast absent' with the concept of 'no-breast' as an instigation to thinking (Wisdom, 1964, pp. 5–11; 17–24).

More distinctively however, Wisdom also critiqued *Learning from Experience*, pointing out what he thought didn't work well in Bion's argument. There were three main criticisms: (1) The structure of the book itself, where its themes appeared scattered throughout the book and in Wisdom's words, "the boundaries of chapters were not always well chosen" (Wisdom, 1964, p. 2); (2) Wisdom also took issue with Bion's penchant for notational and mathematical symbols in chapters he found somewhat incomprehensible insofar as they seemed to have no focus. Wisdom (1964, p. 11), who was an experienced logician and teacher of mathematics and physics, opined that "clear thinking is not produced by notation; a good notation is produced by clear thinking"; and (3) In another telling footnote, Wisdom (1964, p. 14, n. 1) clinched what in effect was an objection to the scientific/deductive aims of Bion's text. Again, I quote this footnote by Wisdom in full: "While on methodological matters, I do not wish to imply that Bion's methodology is wholly above reproach. There is one serious error, which has not, as it happens, led to any ill consequences. He speaks on a few occasions of 'deducing' results from observations. Nothing can be deduced or inferred from observations. Conjectures can be made and that is all. The point is crucial to scientific understanding" (Wisdom, 1964, footnote to p. 14; Aguayo, 2022).

Chapter 10

Elements of Psychoanalysis (1963), Transformations (1965), and 'Catastrophic Change' (1966)

Elements of Psychoanalysis

In the second of his epistemological monographs, Bion (1963) again started with a series of questions as he continued to explore the possibility of a meta-theory, flexible abstractions born of psychoanalytic thinking and learning from his experiences in the consulting room. This work was to be put into the service of a theoretical container for analytic theories to be drawn upon by the workaday analyst. Recall here that when Bion was President of the British Psychoanalytical Society from 1962 to 1965, it was mandatory that he attend all scientific meetings of the Society. As such, it would have meant that Bion would have heard respected colleagues presenting work in one of the three training traditions at the Society on an almost constant basis (David Bell, personal communication). It would not be hard to imagine that Bion found himself wondering if there were any commonalities between these various theories, something that might give psychoanalysis a sense of scientific respectability. If we take an analogy from the physical sciences, which were extremely ascendant in the post-World War II atomic age: there are not three different competing theories about how gravity works; so, why should that be the case in psychoanalysis?

Bion wondered: are there certain theoretical ideas that could serve as containing structures, ones that are both specific and vague at the same time? Was his criterion one where the theoretical container could be specific enough to relate to the immediate clinical situation, yet be general enough to contain an 'element' that could be compared with other theories? I think so, as Bion drew upon the analogy of the alphabet, where just a few characters could be combined in an almost infinite number of ways to make millions of words. Just as there is a 'table of the periodic elements' or Euclid's 'elements of geometry,' he conjectured that there are basic units that can be combined to produce many variations of ideas that might be applicable to the analytic situation. Bion (1963, p. 2) said it plainly: "Similarly the elements I seek are to be such that relatively few are required to express, by changes in combination, nearly all the theories essential to the working psychoanalyst."

DOI: 10.4324/9781003364795-13

Bion (1962b) had tried his hand at formulating such flexible abstractions, for instance, 'container/contained.' It could manifest as: 'female' and 'male, 'vagina and penis,' 'mother and infant,' 'projective receptacle and the patient's projection,' a 'mystic (or creative person) and the establishment.' Bion's theoretical structure was also a way of providing a dynamic container for ideas he had found useful both in Freud and Klein as his primary inspiring sources. So, for instance, Bion's 'container/contained' both included but simultaneously transformed Klein's one-body, one-mind understanding of projective identification—yes, there was a variable baby 'projecting' into a receptive and constant mother—into a two-body, two-mind understanding—a variable 'projecting' baby with a 'variably' separate and processing mother (Britton, 2008). These were two separate but not mutually exclusive models; the two-person model existed, but never to the exclusion of the one-person model. 'Container/contained' was meant to both absorb and represent projective identification, both in its pathological as well as communicative manifestations.

In taking up Bion's (1963) *Elements of Psychoanalysis*, I focus on his findings in a particular way: first and foremost, as a way of expanding upon the model of 'container/contained,' specifying those clinical ideas that were additive to the existing model; second, and this is a follow-up on the point about Bion's aim for scientific respectability in his analytic theorizing, I attend less to how he continued to delineate this kind of argument in *Elements*. Thus, rather than focus on his lingering argument about 'scientific deductive systems,' enshrined in the more abstract regions of the Grid (vertical columns G and H, Figure 10.1), I concentrate on important ways in which Bion shifted his clinical focus to generate new ways of thinking about the analytic situation. In different terms, I subdivide *Elements* and privilege the clinical/inductive over the scientific/deductive elements.

One main feature of *Elements* was to provide analysts with a clinical instrument, the Grid as he termed it, a way to categorize various forms of thought—and the uses to which they could be put. Thinking of it as a sort of 'psychoanalytic game,' an exercise after the session, allowed the analyst the opportunity to think afresh about his or her clinical experiences. Thinking in such a way might exercise the analyst's intuition and could possibly generate fresh hypotheses for further investigation. While the Grid by and large has not been taken up by succeeding generations of analysts, it still serves as a reminder of how Bion continuously shifted his perspective, all in the service of maintaining an open-minded attitude towards psychic reality, one that was non-moralistic yet empirical. Put differently, in looking at how the various vertical and horizontal categories of the Grid combined, it grounded the analyst in looking for co-concurrence, a way of looking at 'what goes with what' in an on-going fashion. To take a simple example that helps to extend our understanding of constant conjunctions: if a beta-element becomes a recurring part of a defensive beta-screen, its violent projection can be categorized as A6 on the Grid, the action part of which represents a hostile projection into the analyst.

THE GRID

	Definitory Hypotheses 1	ψ 2	Notation 3	Attention 4	Inquiry 5	Action 6	...n.
A β-elements	A1	A2				A6	
B α-elements	B1	B2	B3	B4	B5	B6	... Bn
C Dream Thoughts Dreams, Myths	C1	C2	C3	C4	C5	C6	... Cn
D Pre-conception	D1	D2	D3	D4	D5	D6	... Dn
E Conception	E1	E2	E3	E4	E5	E6	... En
F Concept	F1	F2	F3	F4	F5	F6	... Fn
G Scientific Deductive System		G2					
H Algebraic Calculus							

Figure 10.1 Bion's Grid.

While Bion throughout the remainder of his career vacillated about the clinical usefulness of the Grid, in and of itself, it represented an approximation on how speculative imagination could be cultivated, thus allowing for new thoughts to emerge. In the hands of post-Bionian analysts like Rudi Vermote (2014) the Grid becomes an intriguing way in which the patient's propensity for openness or closed-mindedness in their communications can be fruitfully tracked on a moment-to-moment basis. In Vermote's (2019) understanding of Bion's ideas, beta-elements can be conceived of as that which is 'not-yet-psychic.' Beta-elements as we have seen, are sensory experiences, affective states and other forms of non-representative or non-symbolized experiences that actively require some sort of psychic work, so that meaning can be metabolized by the alpha-function of the analyst. Since beta-elements existed in the realm of the non-representational, by the time Bion (1965, p. 13) wrote *Transformations* in 1965, he expanded the notion of beta-elements to exist as 'thing-in-itself', or that which derived from 'O' (which among other things, symbolized an infinity of possibilities).

Bion was also quite aware (and recommended) the occasional mental exercise of plotting the patient's statements on the 'Grid,' in which thoughts could be measured in terms of how crude or sophisticated they were—and to what use they were put. These categories were not merely produced for some sort of abstract 'categorization' process; they represented a statement about theories that are supposed to do a certain kind of work. We are interested in what way these thoughts can be used. For instance, along the vertical co-ordinate, we have β-*elements*, which represent the earliest matrix from which thoughts can arise. Patients with disorders of thought for instance, suffer from an excessive number of β-elements and "partly to failures in development of an apparatus for dealing with thoughts" (ibid., p. 30). On the other hand, α-*elements* are the outcome of work done by α-function on sense impressions. Recall it is the thinking apparatus that gathers sense impressions and transforms them into psychical qualities, so that at the contact barrier, these elements can co-mingle in what Grotstein (2009) calls an act of 'selective permeability.' Put differently, *dream thoughts* combine alpha and beta elements, as elaborated in the classical analytic idea of the dream as a neurotic compromise formation.

It would be far too time consuming to go into the intricacies of the Grid in an introductory text. Rather than deal with multiple numbers of categories, I will simplify the discussion by drawing upon the work of Rudi Vermote (2014), someone well versed in making use of the Grid accessible in simple English terms, which is especially useful since he relates it to how it applies to clinical material from analytic sessions.

How can we know something that is 'psychic'? We cannot know it directly; it is impossible as we generally use our senses to make inferences about psychic functioning. It is in this sense that it is improper to say that one 'sees' the 'unconscious' or the 'Oedipus complex.' These are merely organizing and invisible psychic concepts. By 1962, Bion gave the symbol α (or 'alpha') to that which is 'psychic'; and the symbol β (or 'beta) to that which is 'not yet psychic.' He kept the meaning 'unsaturated' so that the unknown remained as such. In *Learning from Experience*, Bion (1962b) discussed how what was not yet psychic changed into what is psychic. But what is the transitional link from β to α? Here Bion (1962b) deployed mathematical functions theory, or put differently: here, we can have two unknowns—and look for the link between these two (e.g. a = 2 times b is a function). In the first part of this work, Bion implicated a link between the psychic and not yet psychic. Freud never wondered how things became psychic—he accepted it as more or less a 'given' (i.e., the unconscious was always there). Bion on the other hand thought that some things always remained unknown. This was a new way to look at the problem.

But what facilitated the process of transition from unknown to known? Here Bion implicated the environmental factor of the mother; she was the facilitator involved in psychic processing from the unknown to the known. What does the maternal facilitator do? What is her function in effecting a change from β to α? The Kleinian answer was by way of projective identification as a form of communication; the infant could make its needs known to the mother. But Bion here borrowed Hume's notion of reverie, now installing in the mother. The mother's capacity for reverie is very close to the Kleinian notion of unconscious phantasy (or 'ph'); it is always continuous. They are highly related. There is a constant source of phantasy in the unconscious; it is always spontaneous and creative. He now accounted for how psychic matters became interactional between infant and mother.

The mother effected the transformation from β to α by means of her receptivity. For Bion, thinking was a spontaneous process, and was always close to phantasy. He next tried to elaborate his ideas about thinking; were there other aspects involved? Here, he relied on the theory of elements, a concept as old as the Greeks. It was used by other scientists, like Newton. From this sort of table of psychic elements, Bion continued to think that a 'science of psychoanalysis' could be created. In *Elements of Psychoanalysis*, he (1963) still maintained the belief that the Grid could prove ultimately scientific. This belief withered away by the time he wrote his next book in 1965, *Transformations*.

So, in the Grid, he posited two axes: the vertical and the horizontal; the first was the origin of thought; and the use to which thoughts were put. Then he posited all the possible categories of thought. He did not differentiate thought from emotion here; it could all be put into the Grid. Taking up the Grid in detail, we see two possibilities when there are impressions on the mind; it can become food for thought and processed; or it can be evacuated as a mere β-element. In the first vertical column, it is merely to use a category to give some sort of definition. An example: 'You are depressed.' It can be just a factual statement. Or in column 2: it can be a statement of denial, that which is false. Then the next four columns are: 'notation,' 'attention,' 'inquiry' and 'action.' These are borrowed from Freud's (1911) 'Two Principles' paper. 'Notation' is when the analyst merely notes something; the next is when he calls attention to it; the third is when there is 'inquiry' about a particular phenomenon (i.e. you ask questions about it)—which Bion had originally termed the 'Oedipus' column. The last column merely has to do with taking some sort of action (either doing or acting out). Then there are the pictorial/visual elements, such as those seen in dreams.

Then Bion moved to the idea of 'pre-conception,' or psychically, a sort of mentally wired-in 'empty box,' something that awaits something to be put into it. This is akin to the phenomenon seen in child psychology where children are pattern-seeking creatures; once a pattern is 'seen,' it tends to be remembered. In Kleinian terms, we carry around these pre-conceptualizations, say, of a breast. Once we encounter a real one, we are prepared to respond to it. There are an infinite number of neural connections, as many connections as there are stars; these links that we are (by way of evolution) prepared to make. We can never know what is there in the unknown; we have a vast number of preconceptions. We are set or programmed to realize these pre-conceptions. We are predetermined to be guided by these pre-conceptions. Our mind operates and categorizes in the conscious: by means of being able to sort out and make differentiations, we are able to control our environment. When a pre-conception meets something real, it becomes a 'conception.' It is its own peculiar thing, not nearly as abstract as a 'concept.'

In Vermote's (2014) research, there are two basic experiences a clinician can have in using the Grid: either a communication closes meaning or opens one up. The first two vertical columns are for either definition or denial; they do not lead anywhere; or to any new development. These are 'closed' columns and do not lead to psychic development. The other rows are columns of 'opening.' When you listen to material, you can attempt to differentiate whether it is psychic or non-psychic. Is there opening or closing? Bion thought that the true love or aim of the analyst lies in the experience where the analysts awaits what preconceptions might be activated within himself. This is where the analyst should be listening in terms of his patient. Bion says in a deployment of the concepts of L(ove), H(ate) and K(nowledge): you should not either love or hate your patient; you should try to understand him. What leads to closing or opening up? Bion wanted to see how movement occurs from one category to another. One uses the Grid as a kind of map, and it is most fruitful when it leads the analyst to new insights.

Again, it is an ordinary experience that those new to Bion's ideas find them difficult to understand and rather abstract. Bear in mind that at this point in his career, Bion still wanted to believe that psychoanalysis could become a more scientific pursuit, something that would transcend the incessant theoretical warfare he participated in at the British Psychoanalytical Society. It is akin to the post-World War II desire for a 'universal language,' one language that all men could speak, so that national differences could be transcended. Bion was searching for that universal language for psychoanalysis.

In expanding his model of container/contained, Bion also emphasized how generative thinking could occur in the human subject—or to put it in the language deployed in *Elements*, Bion (1963) transcended the Kleinian paradigm of pathological infant and a constant mother by invoking what he termed 'C-elements' as further elaborations of alpha-elements by the process of waking dream thought. Such manifestations might reflect an analysand's creative use of cultural myths. Invoking the model from 'The Theory of Thinking,' Bion (1962a, 1963) also implied that preconceptions existed as part of the beta-element structure, something that Ferro (2006) would term 'balpha' elements. If met with realization, these experiences could become conceptions, such as when the hungry infant repeatedly meets up with a real breast. The realization becomes a conception, or a preconception becomes saturated with meaning.

Bion also expanded upon Klein's concepts of PS and D. Yes, it still carried the significance that Klein attached to it, where one could transform fragmentation into integration, 'progression' or 'regression' from one state to another (represented by the classical Kleinian formula: PS to D to manic defense), but now Bion added a bi-directional dynamic relationship that was also a 'selected fact.' There was a dynamic back and forth between PS and D, a way of bringing things together, yet also a way of examining the degeneration of thought, what Bion (1962b) had termed 'reversal of alpha function.' It introduced order into the complexity of a psychoanalytic realization (PS↔D). Yet Bion also reiterated that he understood that all these were theoretical concepts, invisible ideas abstracted from what the analyst gathered through his or her senses; yet by maintaining a set of somewhat consistent ideas, Bion thought that such conceptual equipment could aid the workaday analyst in becoming a more objective observer of the clinical analytic situation. Bion compared these two levels of data, the sensible and invisible, un-observable elements, which are no more knowable than things-in-themselves. He (1963, p. 7) wrote: "In this respect it is not unlike Kant's concept of a thing in itself—it is not knowable though primary and secondary qualities are." So, we have an abstraction that is unknowable, but capable nonetheless of some sort of verbal representation.

Bion took a rather unusual road to specify the data of sensuous experience with which the analyst approaches his task. He defined 'common sense' in terms of what one sees, hears, smells in one's consulting room. By this, Bion means one sense that is 'common' with other senses; it is on this basis that we make inferences, say the conclusion that a patient is 'anxious' when we see him in a normally ventilated room get up from the couch pouring sweat. Bion (ibid., pp. 9–10) wrote: "I have no doubt that my impression that a man is anxious has the same validity as my impressions that a stone, say, is hard." After all, what does an analyst do when he makes an interpretation? He draws attention to something audible, visible, palpable or odoriferous. But Bion (ibid., p. 13) was also interested in specifying the dynamic relationship between our senses and our inferences and deductions: "For senses to be active only one mind is necessary: passion is evidence that two minds are linked and that there cannot possibly be fewer than two minds if passion is present."

Moving directly to the analytic situation itself, when analyst and patient meet in an 'atmosphere of deprivation,' what are the elements that make this situation distinctly 'psychoanalytic'? If the analyst is conceived as a 'scrutinizing object' and the patient is the 'object of scrutiny' (ibid., pp. 15–16), we move from a very general situation at the very outset of analysis—in which a few analytic hypotheses might apply—to a very specific situation in which (by agreement) the sense of a unique human individual would be articulated within a matter of a few sessions. But of all the possible interpretations that an analyst can give, why does he choose one as 'correct' and not another?

In practice, the analyst sees that "analytic interpretations can be seen to be theories held *by* the analyst about the models and theories the patient has *of* the analyst" Bion, 1963, p. 17). If the analyst's theories are correct in content and expressed adequately, they presumably have a therapeutic effect; something different happens when there is too much of a disjunction between the analyst's model of the patient and the patient's model of his own mind (ibid., p. 17) which Bion terms 'reversible perspective' later in the 1963 monograph. Analyst and analysand are present at the same session, yet view its emotional occurrences on parallel tracks of experience.

On the other hand, if there is too much personal interference with the analyst's observing and analyzing capacities, these danger situations, otherwise known as 'countertransference,' must be dealt with in some way outside the session. There is also the stark fact that we are all limited in the amount of analysis we can have—so we must make the best of a situation in which we may be momentarily handicapped by some personal limitation, crisis or feeling of inadequacy. We must accept that we are going to be the analysts that we are in tomorrow's session—for good or ill. Now to be clear: this does not mean that the older distinctions about countertransference still don't merit consideration. Recall here that there is the personal or subjective countertransference, where some personal conflict or complex springs up in the analyst, an obstructive factor in his ordinary analytic functioning. On the other hand, there is also the 'wider' definition associated with the work of Paula Heimann (1950) one where there can be an unconscious-to-unconscious communication between patient and analyst. It is only through the analyst's capacity to wait—by 'sustaining and subordinating' his initial emotional reactions that he is in a position to see if his emotional reactions are of an intrusive, subjective interference or a response to a subtle form of the patient's unconscious communication—or some combination of both.

Presuming that the analyst is on track with his patient, there can be a progression of observational qualities, from *notation*, to probing types of interpretations demarcated by Freud's notion of *attention*. The harmonious functioning of such capacities should yield receptivity to the 'selected fact,' by which a beam of light can be thrown on something imperfectly or obscurely known. One also notes to what uses the patient puts various interpretations, such as when he deploys it as a form of advice (in which to solve immediate problems) vis-à-vis the patient who uses interpretations to further his growth and development of his capacity to think (ibid., p. 19).

Bion's (1965) *Transformations*

In his next epistemological work, *Transformations*, Bion (1965) now further explored the search for what he termed the invariant, the truth that remains unchanged from one situation to another. What are the invariants of the analytic situation? Is there some way we can speak about truth in psychoanalysis? Since our focus remains on Bion's clinical views, he tells us that psychoanalysis belongs 'to the group of transformations.' The analyst makes a series of observations and transforms them into a psychoanalytic description. He wrote: "An interpretation is a transformation; to display the invariants, an experience, felt and described in one way, is described in another." One constant in the workaday life of the analyst is the deployment of a technique "by which the facts of an analytic experience (the realization) are transformed into an interpretation (the representation)." So, a Kleinian transformation (according to its theories) would have different invariants from a Freudian transformation. A Freudian transformation would no doubt be different than a Kleinian one, and descriptions by two analysts from the same school might also be different (just as two impressionist painters could render the same poppy field differently). Bion dedicated this work to the understanding of transformations and invariants—and how they are applied to the psychoanalytic situation.

Along the way, Bion now emphasized more clearly that the analyst needed to trust the data of his own direct sensuous experience vis-à-vis reports that he heard external to the analysis. How was he, for example, to think about a patient who comes for analysis and has an emotional breakdown during its course? We see Bion's concern with the unusual functioning of the borderline psychotic, someone who more than likely would experience some sort of episodic psychotic decompensation during their analysis. How would the analyst respond to the patient's relatives who are wondering 'what has happened'? How can the person they know appear so deteriorated in his functioning? Would the analyst be held culpable? In this crucible, the analyst centered on the only direct evidence he had, namely his direct emotional experience of the sessions themselves. There can be psychotic catastrophic events that undermine the usual order of things. All are in despair, especially since in the pre-catastrophic state, not much appeared to be happening at the surface of the patient's functioning. Was there some sort of 'theoretical violence' that the patient experienced? It is at this point that the analysts search for the invariants, ultimately the truth of what powered such a powerful emotional transformation. Perhaps he discovers that what the patient had formerly somatized quietly as pains stemming from internal objects, have now become 'externalized' in the form of external objects. "These then are the invariants or the objects in which invariance is to be detected" (Bion, 1965, p. 9). The transformation occurs in the way the analyst describes the above cited facts. Put differently: one could also say that the 'breakdown' is the invariant, as no one disputes it; what is disputed is in accounting for how the breakdown took place—and for what reasons. Naturally, the 'breakdown' will have a Rashomon quality to it—it depends on who is giving the description of the 'breakdown'—the patient, the analyst or members of the patient's family. Here, Bion acknowledges that we as separate human beings all have different perceptual vertices—the question is how we bring meaningful order to these disparate accounts. I think this was a move in the direction of radical perspectivism which also had a post-modernist feel to it: the truth was indeed quite difficult to discern.

Bion then continued his inquiry, expanding it into the ultimate unknowableness operating in the clinical situation. Take a simple example from the clinical situation: the analyst greets the patient at the beginning of the hour, but the patient feels there is something hidden in the greeting, perhaps hostility on the analyst's part. Naturally the analyst has to take up the meaning imputed by the patient lest there be further impediments to analytic understanding. And yes, while we can classify the various types of communication—say, the analyst is open and welcoming, and the patient stuck in a concrete and paranoid state of mind, or the analyst is annoyed to see the patient, we can all wonder about how such interactions originate. Of course, these are mental phenomena and as such, cannot be 'things-in-themselves' (and thus, ultimately unknowable and were originally described by the philosopher, Immanuel Kant) (Bion, 1965, p. 12).

Bion here struggled with the problem that is inherently contradictory: how does one define the 'un-definable,' or infinite? Since psychic phenomena are invisible, we can never know their true origins, and the possibilities for understanding are endless, but here, Bion provided yet another symbol, 'O,' which he took to refer to the unknowable. It was one way in which the analyst could deal with the frequent occurrence of the differences in vertices between analyst and patient as well as the differences in theoretical explanatory systems that proliferated the psychoanalytic universe. In effect, there are different systems of transformations that are operating, so how do we find a meaningful link between them all? Take the simple example of an author writing a book. It is one thing to write it, but another thing altogether different in terms of how an audience or reader transforms the meaning of the book when reading it.

So, to the ultimate truth in any given analytic moment: we can't know it directly (the Kantian noumenon), but only in its manifestations (the phenomena of everyday clinical practice), which we derive from the clinical observations we make in session (p. 15). The analyst can only describe the session as it occurred to him, as he can never know what actually happened in the situation described to him by his patient. The analyst can try as best he can to describe this experience but sees that it is "a misleading record of the experience" (Bion, 1965, p. 20).

To say this in a less complicated fashion: as analysts, we are constantly evolving models of mind deployed by our patients. We also know that the patient has his own preferred model of mind as well; it is crucial to get at what the patient's theory of causation is. As we saw in the case of the 'Imaginary Twin' in Chapter 2, Bion's model of the patient's mind did not accord for a long time with the patient's model of his own mind. That is what gave rise to the Beckettian sense of two characters traveling along parallel tracks of meaning, each in his own solipsistic universe of experience. So, in Bion's new conceptual language, the patient has his own 'O,' as does the analyst. A good connecting session would be when there was overlap between the two, a sense of at-one-ment, where meaning can be made and shared in the 'contact barrier.' Another related factor is the capacity to be resilient in making meaning, as pathology can be defined as a rigid imposition of meaning, often to the exclusion of other viable possibilities—as we saw with the borderline patient ('S') in Chapter 9 who rigidly insisted that she knew the 'truth' behind why her brother brought flowers to their mother in hospital.

Putting these ideas differently, the analyst tries to help his patient transform his experience from unconscious (i.e., the rigidly adhered to understanding) into an emotional experience of which he is conscious (where he can hear the analyst's separate perspective in a meaning enhancing way). The move here is from private, rigidly held meanings to public and thus sharable levels of experience with others. In Bion's new language, the analyst helped the patient transform his own unconscious experiences to conscious ones, where private knowledge could be attained, so that the analysand could live his or her life according to their lights and interests. It is ultimately the patient's responsibility to decide what he or she makes of the psychic experiences associated with their analysis.

So, Bion (1965, p. 33) came to a rather paradoxical conclusion about analysis: "No one can ever know what happens in the analytic session, the thing-in-itself, O; we can only speak of what the analyst or patient *feels* happens, his emotional experience, that which I denote by T (or 'Transformation.')." In this sense, Bion's theory of "transformations and its developments does not relate to the main body of psychoanalytic theory, but to the practice of psychoanalytic *observation*" (p. 34). Analysts and their patients move from experience to their representation. Bion's work helps us to understand what it is that is being represented. *Transformations* help us to understand the links between different aspects of experience and its transformation. Understanding one link helps us understand another. Perhaps drawing upon his experience as an amateur painter, Bion (1965, p. 37) likened the analyst to an artist who depicts a landscape, hoping not to run his patient's life "but to enable him to run it according to his lights and therefore to know what his lights are." It is just the analyst's perspective, not some once and forever authoritative 'truism' about the patient. In analyses that are successful, the patient discovers the potential for a wider range of meanings, or in Bion's way of putting it: the intensity of narcissism falls off as the intensity of socialism rises—and vice versa. A 'widening of the spectrum of emotions' displaces a constricted set of narrow and privileged meanings.

Bion's (1966) 'Catastrophic Change'

In a paper rarely seen in its unpublished form, Bion's (1966) 'Catastrophic Change' is both ordinary and remarkable. It is ordinary because Bion continued his epistemological thinking, e.g., couplings in the model of 'container/ contained' can be commensal, symbiotic or parasitic. Such new terms gave new meaning to familiar ideas (e.g., narcissistic and sociopathic patients seek to establish a 'parasitic relationship' inside the container). 'Container/contained' is thus a structural concept, one that can be stretched in its meaning in different directions (e.g., it is capable of being a 'constant conjunction') or conversely, it can destroy the word, theory or formulation (e.g., a man attempts to express such powerful feelings that his speech disintegrates into a stammer).

Bion also discussed the manner in which the analyst can approach any new clinical hour. He is cautioned not to approach with too much memory, as it is a 'saturated experience' and can over-dominate the analyst's capacity to be receptive. In Bion's (1966 [1970], p. 107) words: "The analyst who comes to a session with an active memory is therefore in no position to make 'observations' of mental phenomena because these are unknown and cannot be sensuously apprehended." Here, he differentiates 'memory' from 'remembering' (the latter of which is actively 'evoked' during the session itself). Bion's counsel against what he came to regard as the dangers of 'regurgitated memory' will be discussed in the next chapter.

Now I turn to what I regard as the remarkable part of 'Catastrophic Change,' where Bion (1966 [1970]) discusses 'men of genius,' or 'mystics' to use Bion's term. These rare individuals bear important 'messianic' ideas for their society— and sometimes, that society is ready to accept or at times, it can reject them. Bion here used religious terminology for his descriptions, but he was not making a religious statement, such as when he wrote: "The mystic makes direct contact with … or is at one with God" (Bion, 1966 [1970], p. 111).This contact is not available to the ordinary member of the group—and thus, his referent group, which he called the 'Establishment' makes available dogma, or "make laws or rules, by which the advantages of the mystic's communion with God or ultimate reality may, as it were, be shared at one remove by the ordinary members" (ibid.). Many examples abound here: when St. Augustine attempted to teach Catholicism to the illiterate, he devised a card that taught both religion and the

'ABCs' to the common man. For example, 'A' is for 'Anti-Christ,' 'B' is for Beelzebub, 'C' is for 'Christ.'

Yet why this intriguing sidebar in his lecture? From other clues we have, such as a book review he did in 1966, we see that Bion now felt increasingly uncomfortable in the central administrative leadership role he had assumed as both the President of the British Society and the Chairman of the Melanie Klein Trust. With so many meetings and administrative responsibilities, how would he ever find time for his creative analytic writing? We see in the book review of 1966 a statement made by Bion where he states that he often feels more comfortable with analysts who do not share his theoretical orientation than he does with members of his own group. It seemed that Bion had finally become an uneasy Kleinian leader in London.

In my view, I think that Bion here was discussing his uneasy relationship with the British Society in general and the London Klein group in particular. Perhaps his new ideas had been disruptive, whether he intended them to be or not. Yet, either way, the mystic's claims are disruptive—whether he intends them to be or not. He (1970, p. 78) wrote, "The reaction of the Establishment is to prevent the disruption and this it does as follows: It can load the mystic with such honors that he sinks without a trace." It is of interest that this sentence was struck out in the 1970 published version of this paper; and I think Bion here did not want to make any sort of public statement of his increasing disaffection with his professional life in London.

In summing up some of the main points of this chapter, we can see the increasing clinical and theoretical flexibility displayed by Bion. In thinking about what we have called Bion's 'method of clinical inquiry,' we have formed impressions of how he worked in the analytic situation (e.g. keeping a fresh mind, one that is not over-dominated by too much memory of previous sessions) and now, its theoretical complement, namely Bion's attempt to take a number of analytic theories into account, as he began his search for the 'invariant' or 'truthfulness' in the descriptions made by different analytic schools of thought. So, for example, for the 'Kleinian' analyst, who derived inspiration from P/S and D, the following aphorism occurred:

> the analyst remains mindful of 'memory and desire,' focusing instead on relating to the 'unknown' in the session. 'Any attempt to cling to what he knows must be resisted for the sake of achieving a state of mind analogous to the P/S position.'
>
> (Bion, 1970, p. 78)

In short, the analyst is 'patient' and suffers and tolerates frustration and waiting. Then, quoting Keats (1817), Bion (1970, p. 124) advocated 'patience' without 'irritable reaching after fact and reason' until a pattern evolves. Then he will attain 'security' (of the depressive position).

Part III

The Distillation of Clinical Experience and Everyday Practices

Chapter 11

Bion's (1967) Seminars and Supervision in Los Angeles

'Notes on Memory and Desire' (1967a)

Introduction: Bion at the Crossroad

By now, Bion's vigor and resiliency as an analytic theorist stood clear. While many other analysts would have been content to make a career of the kind that Bion had had—with either his group work or work as a Kleinian psychoanalyst working on the problem of understanding psychosis—and then, evolving a new metapsychology based on his findings—he now made a move in still another direction. Perhaps weary of having written so many books and papers on a new form of analytic theory and observation, and of course, we also think of the tremendous administrative burdens he shouldered as both President of the British Society (1962–65) and Chair of the Melanie Klein Trust, he put much of it aside when he decided to relocate his family and practice to faraway Los Angeles.

Once he moved there in January 1968, he would live the rest of his days there until a few months before his death in 1979. Imagine a man at age 70 suddenly deciding to uproot his life and ex-patriating to a new country; it was truly an odyssey into the unknown! He moved away from what his wife Francesca called the 'cozy domesticity' of England for the Los Angeles of the Vietnam War, the anti-war movement, hippies and the counterculture. Within the time of his relocation, there would be the gruesome murders committed by the Manson family at a home not too far from where Bion would live in west Los Angeles. It was truly a city in tremendous turmoil.

But in addition to that, Bion moved to a psychoanalytic culture that was quite tumultuous as well. American psychoanalysis in the 1960s was dominated by what was known as the Ego Psychology model, and it was quite different from what Bion was accustomed to. When he was invited to give a series of seminars and supervisions in April 1967, he had to assume that his audience of primarily Freudian-trained analysts in Los Angeles knew next to nothing of his ideas (Bion, 2013). So, he had to start from the beginning, and made a decision to present more of his clinical work and intertwine it with some theory presentation. It is fortunate for us that we have recovered this work, as it gives us a chance to appreciate more of the way in which Bion

DOI: 10.4324/9781003364795-15

(1967a) actually worked as a clinician, especially in light of the fact that he presented one of his most famous papers at these *Los Angeles Seminars*— 'Notes on Memory and Desire.' Short and written in a rather terse way, it is one of Bion's most well-known and admired papers; and it forms the core of this chapter's discussion.[1]

First, a few preliminary remarks. Bion (1965) had given this paper initially as a talk at the British Society in 1965. From the sound of it, his British colleagues were in one sense familiar with one of its main ideas, namely that all psychoanalytic work in the consulting room takes place in the present moment. Hardly a surprising idea to them. Think here of Melanie Klein's play technique with young children: the moment the child enters the playroom, it begins to play in real time, the present moment. So, at one level, Bion merely named the process that had been practiced for decades in London.

But of course, the 'Notes' paper was far more subtle than that. Actually, just months before he arrived in Los Angeles, Bion (1967b) had also published *Second Thoughts*, which was the complete collection of all his psychosis papers from the 1950s. This collection appeared with an extensive 'Commentary' section, in which Bion reviewed some of his central ideas, giving them a 'second look,' hence the title of the book. There, in scattered references, he regarded 'memory and desire' as what he called a 'constant conjunction,' a regularly recurring process that linked these two ideas. So, when he said that all psychoanalysis must occur in the present moment, he simultaneously marginalized any active efforts on the analyst's part to reconstruct the infantile conflictual history of the patient as well as not allow himself to be drawn into wishing for any particular outcome for his patient in the future. He concentrated on explicating the present moment in his work with patients (Aguayo, 2014).

Additionally, he began to question the nature of how analysts gave accounts of their session work with patients. He now thought the whole process of the clinical report was a bundle of distortions, all of which made it impossible to know what actually happened—or to put it in his new theoretical language, it was hard to know the 'thing-in-itself,' or ultimate reality, symbolized by the letter 'O.' In short, he made the reporting of cases a problematic in and of itself. How could such reports not be infused with what the analyst 'wished' might have taken place, or selectively distort what in fact might have happened? Bion (2013, p. 29) now spoke of memory and desire "in terms which are derived from a background of sensuous experience." To the extent that sensory experience was tied to the domination of the pleasure/pain principle, case reporting seemed 'rather restrictive in scope.' Using Grid terms, such reports then would represent the challenge of how to evolve one's clinical thoughts to an extent that they would be useful in communicating with one's colleagues.

Putting all this differently, the patient comes to his analytic session and reports selected vignettes from his daily life. It would be impossible to recount every single detail of his life; so, he makes a selection. From that, the analyst listens and decides to interpret the significance of the material he has heard—again, this process also involves keying in on certain themes of significance; but it too is a selection. From all that, the analyst may write a case report, another process that involves sifting through and making still more selections. Then, based on the patient's presenting and re-presenting moments of his life, the analyst re-presents this material to his colleagues based on what he or she deems important. To make matters still more complicated, once a group of colleagues listens to the clinical report, they in turn will reformulate the material they have listened to in terms that appear compelling to them. So, Bion asked: how can any clinical case report purport to be objective? It seems rife with distortions based on the selective biases of those involved.

I hope these preliminary notes set something of a context for the next period of Bion's clinical odyssey, which we will cover in this and in following chapters. Bion would spend the next 10 years of his career giving countless seminars and supervisions throughout the Americas and Europe to illustrate both his theories and the manner in which he worked as a psychoanalyst. In short, he now gave many recitations of his method of clinical inquiry.

'Notes on Memory and Desire'

When Wilfred Bion (1967a) published 'Notes on Memory and Desire' in the *Psychoanalytic Forum*, a journal little known outside of Los Angeles, no one could have foreseen what a stir this four-page paper would cause. At a personal and professional crossroad, Wilfred Bion, who had been lionized at the British Psychoanalytical Society, decided to leave it all behind when he moved his family and practice to Los Angeles. He also took a detour from years of theory-laden books, when he actually demonstrated how he analyzed difficult-to-treat patients. His innovations helped to usher in, among other developments, the contemporary Kleinian era, now complete with its own distinctive 'technique,' a lot of which was based on his work. While Klein and her adherents had published on the analysis of children and psychotics, Bion now helped in shifting their attention to also understanding and treating the near psychotic group of narcissistic and borderline patients.

The Los Angeles Psychoanalytic Society and Institute (or LAPSI) had a maverick identity among institutes affiliated with the American Psychoanalytic Association. The city of fantasy, cinema and reinvention, its Los Angeles analysts also had a penchant for what appeared to be rather unorthodox methods—at least when considered from the vantage point of the East Coast psychoanalytic Ego psychology establishment. By the early 1960s, young candidates and members alike began to show an interest in British Object Relations theory, and soon, London visitors were a yearly occurrence—D.W. Winnicott, Herbert Rosenfeld, Hanna Segal—and finally in 1967, Wilfred Bion himself. No other American institute at that time would have welcomed London Kleinian analysts—so again, this made LAPSI a bit unusual to say the least.

So, to set the stage, Bion arrived in April 1967 to give a series of clinical seminars on very disturbed patients to the LAPSI members and candidates. Two facts stand out: the medically dominated LAPSI membership, most of whom had hospitalized borderline and psychotic patients they treated, was keenly interested in the subject matter. Think here of Ralph Greenson's treatment of Marilyn Monroe in 1962. The Los Angeles analysts were anxious to hear what the London Kleinians might have to say about how to approach such trying patients. The Kleinians had been treating psychotic patients since the mid-1940s with what they regarded as classical analytic technique. The other fact is that, in this set of seminars, Bion reversed himself and gave copious case examples of how he worked with extremely disturbed patients. Bion's (2013) *Los Angeles Seminars and Supervision* are among the most accessible of his works if one hopes to understand his clinical ideas in practice. I think this is so simply because the American Freudian analysts hearing Bion speak were unfamiliar with his ideas. So, he *had* to start from the beginning if he was to stand a chance of making a communicative link with his audience.

In the First Seminar, Bion detailed his ideas about memory and desire, container/contained—and surprisingly, put his ideas across in a lucid, direct and intelligible English! Listen to Bion's own words here:

> Now the next point that I want to come to is such a simple one that I always hesitate to mention it. It is to do, if you feel so disposed, a carrying out a sort of minor experiment with your session 'tomorrow.' …. This is the attempt to allow your desires to play as small a part as possible in the analysis. *Suppress desire.* Once more, it's very easy to say but I think it's extremely difficult to do, and it may even be very difficult to know what I mean by that. So the first experiment really is this: If you catch yourself looking at your watch, and wondering when the session is going to come to an end, stop it. Try to arrange things in your consulting room in such a way that time is obvious to you, without causing you to do this kind [probably gestures at his wrist-watch], so that you don't have to worry about whether the session is coming to an end or not. Now the same thing applies to the weekend break and suchlike. Now if you'll do that, I would like you to consider what is meant by the word *desire*. I am taking a simple example, because I'm saying, 'Don't desire the end of the session,' 'Don't desire the weekend break.' If you do, it will interfere with your observations. There is something very peculiar about desire, as I'm using the term. It has a peculiarly devastating effect upon one's clinical observation.

Memory and Desire: Synopsis

So, from a clinical listening perspective, what did Bion mean by the analyst's 'abandonment of memory and desire'? Bion here was discussing a sort of ideal or optimal listening receptivity in the analyst, a mindset in which the obstructive and interfering forces were kept to a minimum. He also differentiated optimal listening receptivity from other obstructions precisely because he knew how difficult it was for the analyst to maintain an open mind—Chris Mawson (the Editor of Bion's *Complete Works*) maintained that Bion sounded so strident and exhortatory in the Memory paper because he was also talking to himself! He knew from personal experience how easy it was to become distracted and therefore obstructed in his analytic task.

Bion therefore urged analysts to clear their minds of obstacles to a relaxed yet disciplined listening receptivity, all of which made possible the emergence of a 'sudden, precipitating intuition.' He was quite fond of repeatedly citing a letter Freud wrote to Lou Andreas Salomé on 25 May 1916:

> I'm always particularly impressed when I read your remarks about one of my works. Now this is the part I want to stress. I know that I have artificially blinded myself at my work in order to concentrate all the light on one dark passage .... For my eyes are adapted to the dark, and cannot perhaps stand the strong light or a wide vision. But I have not quite become a mole, so I cannot enjoy the prospect of a lighter and wider horizon, and indeed I would not deny its existence.
>
> (Freud, 1916, pp. 312–313)

Now what is this 'artificial blindness' to which Bion referred? He suggested that, in one sense, the listening analyst keep one eye open, the other closed, so that he could clearly observe with his senses what was right in front of him while he oriented to the darkness, the unknown, the barely illuminated. In the 'Memory and Desire' paper, Bion (1967a, p. 273) made a famous statement about his new technique: "Psychoanalytic 'observation' is concerned neither with what has happened nor with what is going to happen but with what *is* happening." Bion accentuated the present moment in the analytic encounter between patient and analyst, making clear that the analyst who abandoned memory and desire could make crisp observations about his patient, all of which cleared his internal path towards operating with greater clarity in psychic darkness—the realm of the non-sensuous and ineffable. These were the necessary conditions that created an opportunity for the operation of clinical intuition, which in turn could lead to a creative evolution in analysis. For example, Bion stated that no analyst could doubt the existence of anxiety—yet it could not be directly or sensuously seen, touched or smelled; its existence was inferred. He wanted to know when he drew upon his sensuous experience as an analyst to make crisp observations—and when he, like Freud (1911, p. 213), deployed his "consciousness as the sense organ of psychical reality."

Bion thought the analyst's true trajectory was towards the unknown, that which had not yet been consciously realized, orienting towards the darkness, where more light needed to be shed. It was important to forget what one knows in the immediacy of the current session, so that some new (and here-tofore unknown) pattern might be allowed to evolve. He fleshed out how to cultivate a kind of disciplined receptivity on the analyst's part. One Los Angeles analyst wondered if this wasn't just countertransference (e.g., if one looked at one's watch, perhaps one was bored, so that it became a signal for introspection). Bion here differentiated disciplined receptivity from counter-transference—the latter was a sort of ideal state in which one has both the time, awareness and resources to handle it. The workday reality was that analysts don't often have time for such measured reflection. He pointed out the obvious in an uncommon way: the analyst will, for good or ill, enter the next session *as he or she is,* so it is better for the analyst to aspire to patience and security because he will in his workaday practice sometimes feel perse-cuted and depressed. Putting it slightly differently in 1970, Bion said that the analyst could only conduct his cases according to his own lights—all analysts were limited by their capacities, for good and for ill.

Of course, most of these ideas sound commonplace in our contemporary analytic discourse, so why did they create such a stir in Los Angeles back in 1967? Well, for one thing, it was a time when Ego psychology was in its heyday as the dominant analytic paradigm in America. It was a time when it was considered standard for an analyst to be interested in pursuing and elu-cidating the childhood history of his patients. Genetic reconstruction was standard issue, as most American analysts adhered to Freud's classical defi-nition of the transference as a displacement from past to present. To a patient who once asked Bion, 'What happened in the last session?' Bion simply said: 'I don't remember.' So, what were they to make of Bion's marginalization of the remembered past in favor of illuminating the present moment? And how did his Los Angeles listeners by and large hear this message? Well, in a word, they found themselves (for the most) feeling shocked to hear the exhortation not to remember past sessions; to resist the impulse to remember and recon-struct. Why abandon the analytic desire for memory?

Appended to Bion's 'Memory' paper were some comments by some American discussants, who were frankly bewildered. A brief example: Thomas French, the Director of Research at the Chicago Psychoanalytic Institute, wrote:

> I am completely unable to understand W.R. Bion's paper, 'Notes on Memory and Desire.' Dr. Bion starts by reminding us that memory is often distorted by desire. This is self-evident, but Dr. Bion advises us to eschew memory and desire entirely, even to the point of the analyst's not remembering the preceding session.
>
> (Bion, 1967a, p. 274)

How could the abandonment of the memory of previous sessions lead to any meaningful therapeutic evolution? Another discussant said the paper was 'illogical.' Wasn't Bion radically over-privileging intuition over what had meaningfully developed over the course of the analytic work? How could a patient's behavior in previous sessions not have tremendous bearing on his behavior in the current session?

These American critiques reflected little awareness of the Kleinian model, with its interpretations of both a deep past but also organizing present unconscious, when the patient projected unconsciously *into* the analyst. This idea of projection in the current moment was linked to another crucial Kleinian idea of projective identification, which they conceptualized as originating *within* the patient and projected *into* the analyst, all in real time. In summary words, these were projections from the patient, alive and hot, directed at the analyst, who had to field a response—all in the current moment. In this way, he served his dual function of both interpreting the patient's immediate unconscious processes while remaining their object. From this perspective, the only aspect of the patient's past that mattered was what was alive in the present moment; reconstruction was marginalized as unnecessary (and at times an encumbrance). Bion would later term this the 'past presented.' So, we can see why some of the American analysts found Bion's ideas so unacceptable. Leo Rangell would later say that if he abandoned memory and desire, he would not feel it ethical to then charge the patient a fee (Symington and Symington, 1996).

Yet a few American analysts felt illuminated by Bion's ideas, analysts like John Lindon of Los Angeles (who as the editor of the *Psychoanalytic Forum*, had commissioned Bion's paper). He admired these new ideas, finding them "logical extensions of Freud's theories and recommendations on technique" (Bion, 1967a, p. 275). He heard Bion link the patient's present with past material by means of his free-floating attention, something that required the analyst to rid himself momentarily of his memory and desire, so that he exposed himself to the full treatment. Bion's link with Freud was affirmed. Recall here Freud's (1912) own aphorism about technique: "To put it in a formula: he must turn his own unconscious like a receptive organ towards the transmitting unconscious of the patient."

Another commentator on Bion's paper in the *Forum*, Marjorie Brierley, a British Independent familiar with his work, took a more measured skeptical position. While she agreed with the image of the analyst in tranquil receptivity, she questioned Bion's underrating of the role of memory in analysis, as questions about timing and dosage of interpretations implicitly invoked the analyst's awareness and memories of previous sessions.

In response, Bion then differentiated 'an evolutionary experience' from 'regurgitated' memory, what floated into the mind unbidden *vis-à-vis* what was deliberately and consciously recalled. Perhaps some of Bion's discussants had responded too literally to the idea of abandoning memory and desire, so he differentiated what was evoked in the analyst *in* the current session from his reaching for previous formulations, which could obstruct clear observation and create stasis in analysis. Bion here agreed with Freud on the necessity of the analyst's 'artificially blinding' himself, so that new light could be thrown on an unknown pattern, something he referred to a 'selected fact.'

Clinical Examples from Bion's *Los Angeles Seminars*

Also of tremendous importance, Bion gave copious examples of his clinical work, so that a new audience of Freudian-trained analysts could be introduced to his ideas. He took up the questions put to him by analysts who were both very intrigued by the analytic treatment of psychosis yet had little familiarity with a Kleinian understanding. There was of course a practical reason for presenting his clinical work: he would soon count on these same Los Angeles analysts for referrals when he moved there within the next few months.

To Bion's clinical examples: very few in attendance at the Los Angeles seminars would have realized that Bion had been long disinclined to discuss extensive clinical case material in his writings, especially during the 1960s. Very few outside the London Klein group would have had much of an idea of how exactly Bion analyzed his patients. But in the *Los Angeles Seminars*, Bion reversed himself by giving detailed clinical accounts of how he worked with psychotic and borderline patients.

I restrict myself here to a discussion of one extensive clinical example given by Bion, one that I think reflects his recent thought about technique. It pertained to a rather angry, unruly, ranting female analysand referred to as 'borderline.' He took pains to both point out her near psychotic pathology, but also elucidated some of the emotional difficulties he personally encountered in treating her. The advantage of this case is that Bion also continued to discuss the patient's problematic analysis in the *Buenos Aires Seminars* (Bion, 2017). The young woman's analysis was in all likelihood compromised by the fact that Bion had to interrupt her treatment when he left London for Los Angeles in 1967/68. We recount his analysis of this young woman both in this and the next chapter.

Bion's work here dealt with the analyst's subjectivity and emotional processing capacities, his own abandonment of memory and desire when he exposed himself emotionally and fully to treating highly disturbed individuals. He exemplified clinically what Keats had termed 'negative capability,' "capable of being in uncertainties, mysteries, doubts without any irritable reaching after fact and reason" (Keats, cited in Bion, 1970, p. 124). This material is from Bion's (2013, pp. 81–82) Fourth Seminar in Los Angeles:

> I feel some trepidation about what I want to try to talk about this evening; I hope at the same time I will be able to explain why I feel trepidation about it. Now, I was just waiting for the session to start, I went into the waiting room and I brought the patient into my consulting room. As we were walking towards the consulting room, she had started—and

she started by expressing her doubts about analysis—about me person-ally, about the relationships with her father and much the same about her mother—what had been going on in the office, which made her doubt the efficacy of analysis—and all this between the waiting room and the couch. By the time she got to the couch, a woman of about 30, she had really warmed to the job. (laughter) To say that she seemed to be hostile was put-ting it very mildly indeed. The abuse became much more violent and in the course of this, she slithered off the end of the couch onto the floor, appeared to be frightened by the fall, which led to still further abuse and violence. She then proceeded to slap herself on the thighs, still pouring out hatred against analysis, with a parting swipe at Kleinians generally, of which she regards me as one, but made it clear that this wasn't to the exclusion of all forms of analysts—the whole lot were equally bad, but some more equal than others.

Now of course what I should tell you what she said; but it is very dif-ficult to do because the real point about this is the general impression of real hate, no nonsense about this at all. Something where I would like to use a phrase like 'psychotic hatred' to get nearer to the point, meaning by that something which one doesn't ordinarily meet with in everyday life in positions where people hate you and spite you very much. Something which one needs to qualify, one needs to say 'hate,' but something or another, to make it quite clear that you are not talking about when you ordinarily talk about when you mention 'hate.' The usual problem of psychoanalysts, the problem which crops up of course with Freud where he talked about sex, and we all know what he meant by this; it was something that wasn't accepted; it hasn't been accepted by the vast majority of people—and it is probably only understood by psychoanalysts, who have a good idea of what Freud meant by that term.

Now this business went on. The free associations, if that is what you can call them, which were conducted by a shout, turned into free asso-ciations that which conducted in a scream. I don't know if there is a fur-ther description but if so, she got there—by this time, she got off the map; she had a style of communication which isn't very easily described in ordinary English. I was a blackmailer; her father was the same. She had been given some money; she had spent it on clothes. And I thought at this point that what she was wearing might have been some of the clothes that she had spent her money on. And she was jolly well going to spend her money as she liked. I tried to get a word in and suggest that this was real hostility—what was it about? I had not got any particular confidence in making myself audible because by this stage in the proceedings, I think it was legitimate to say, not metaphorically, but literally that one began to feel that one couldn't hear oneself think.

I think that here, Bion also identified himself as an analyst who could be baffled and stumped by psychotic forms of communication. He couldn't make any immediate sense of this multi-dimensional ranting experience. Yet in a paradoxical way, he put his audience in exactly the same position in which he found himself with his patient—let's call her 'B.' I think it was a subtle means of urging his colleagues in Los Angeles to identify with him in the face of indecipherable psychotic communications. He told his Los Angeles audience that amid all of 'B's hateful screaming and ranting, when he could not get a word in edgewise, that he could not venture an interpretation. Bion again presented himself as unable to understand the immediate dynamic meaning of what had been communicated to him. Had 'B' destroyed the communicative link with her mind and her link to the analyst, so that no interpretation was possible, all to such an extreme extent that he too lost a link with his own mind? It seemed so. The analyst here appeared profoundly lost, despairing that he could make no satisfactory interpretation let alone think of an explanatory theory after 'B' left the session.

At this juncture, Bion invoked his recent ideas about memory and desire— if he approached such intensely grueling experiences, having exposed himself fully to the onslaught presented by 'B,' how was he to make sense out of such sheer cacophony? At this point, there were those in the audience, Ralph Greenson among them, who stated that such seriously disturbed patients *were* psychoanalytically 'untreatable.'

But here Bion disagreed, subtly stating that 'B' was untreatable *at that moment* and as a result, persisted with making sense out of what he had experienced as a 'climactic affair.' The analyst's task was to withstand such emotional assaults, as 'B' relied on the analyst's capacity to make sense eventually of what was bothering her. So, with 'B's loud and incessantly hostile attack in mind, Bion thought after the session about what might be the invariant here, the unalterable something that remained undetectable in a variety of different situations.

After having recovered his capacity to think, he concluded that 'B' was dominated by feelings of omnipotence and greed of the breast because she created "such a situation in that session that you proceed to bother about that patient when you're supposed to be seeing another one" (Bion, 2013, p. 94). In different words, she attempted to appropriate more than her fair share of the analyst's time and mind. When the analyst was with his next patient, he found himself instead wondering whether he should have called the police or hospital. So, another organizing fact was that he was not being fair to the rest of his practice, in effect cheating the next patient out of his full and undivided attention.

Yet the nature of psychotic bombardments was such that inevitably there would have to be moments when such dramatic enactments remained unmetabolizable and thus un-interpreted. Bion then linked this bombardment to a phantasy of omnipotence, a kind of visual 'hallucination in reverse,' when 'B' attempted to force her way into the analyst's mind through the medium of the analyst's eyes; it was an attempt at a hostile takeover of his mind. In Bion's words, 'B' in effect said: 'Well, if you won't take in what I am telling you, I will jolly well make you.'

In this example, Bion drew upon a notion of disciplined receptivity, when he exposed himself to the full onslaught of the patient's violent projective evacuations, causing him momentarily to lose his mind before he was able to recover it. In essence then, Bion deployed a wider notion of projective identification and countertransference, realizing that he needed to metabolize 'B's disparate and quite hostile communications in order to make sense of what had happened, which in turn would lead to a satisfactory and pertinent interpretation.

In this clinical example, Bion appeared to be an analyst of 'negative capability,' being momentarily able to tolerate doubt and uncertainty in his understanding of 'B.' This in turn opened the door to other colleagues joining the discussion with their own psychotic patients, who had baffled them as well. This all then led to Bion's more global point—that it was through the abandonment of memory and desire that not only exposed the analyst to the full emotional blast of the patient's communications, but also ultimately made a relevant understanding possible.

Aftermath

In hindsight, Bion's 'Notes' and its central thesis of the analyst's abandonment of memory and desire was both strikingly evocative yet also frustrating to his American audience of readers and listeners. The paper by itself was simply too short to carry much meaning to those with a preliminary understanding of Klein and Bion's ideas. For some of the analysts who however also heard Bion's clinical cases in his *Los Angeles Seminars*, they gained a more thorough understanding of Bion's expansion of Freud's notion of 'evenly suspended attention.' We now have a more complete picture of how he actually formulated interpretations as a function of how he internally processed and made sense of extremely disturbing communications.

In the immediate context of Bion's work in Los Angeles, he was pressed to explain his often difficult-to-understand theoretical ideas in a plain and direct clinical manner to a group of American Freudian colleagues, who were new to his ideas. I think Bion's *Los Angeles Seminars* also served as one informing guide to the psychoanalytic treatment of more disturbed populations, one that heretofore could only be known by the direct participants. Recall that Bion's clinical work in 1967 came precisely at the point when Otto Kernberg (1966) was just beginning to make what would become an enduring case in the United States for the psychoanalytic treatment of borderline and narcissistic patients.[2]

In all this, Bion remained focused on his primary goal of explicating by clinical example his Kleinian work with near psychotic and psychotic patients. He also evidently thought that his work had been well enough received in Los Angeles to warrant his immigration to the United States. And while Bion's decision to move to Los Angeles in January 1968 would prove momentous to the local history of psychoanalysis in Los Angeles, his London colleagues also keenly felt his loss to the British Society.

Perhaps D.W. Winnicott put it best of all when, as President of the British Society, he wrote to Bion on 10 July 1967 after learning of Bion's decision to emigrate to the United States:

> I have been told, of course, about your proposal to leave England in the New Year and to spend a few years in Los Angeles. This will be very good for Los Angeles and I think you may do a really good job there. The trouble is, however, that we shall miss you a very great deal in this country. Your position here and your personality in what you stand for in the work is of the greatest importance to us and we can ill afford to lose you.
>
> (Rodman, 2003, p. 313)

Notes

1 In what was most likely Bion's first reference to memory and desire, in *Transformations* (1965, footnote #1, 98), he mentioned a "'now' which has no past or future." A hint of the memory and desire idea—analysis can only occur in the present moment—it has no past and no future. Prior to thought, it is a β-element—or unrealized alpha-elements and dreams before they are verbalized. On the next pages, he made another allusion to memory and desire: there is a 'now' alone with a 'future' (which is now not-present) "and a past (that is, where a past used to be and is now a not-present) that are both representations of the wreckage left by splitting attacks on the present" (Bion, 1965, pp. 99–100).
2 In a book review of Bion's *Los Angeles Seminars and Supervisions* Kernberg (2017) praised Bion's interpretative stance towards borderline patients, his listening attitude and emotional receptivity. In approaching patients 'without memory or desire,' Bion helped to make possible fresh understanding of near psychotic states of mind that had heretofore been a source of intense confusion and puzzlement to psychoanalytic practitioners.

Chapter 12

Bion's (1968) Seminars and Supervisions in Buenos Aires

The Continuing Case of the Stormy Borderline Patient

Bion in the New World: From Los Angeles to Buenos Aires

Once Bion moved to Los Angeles in 1968, a new chapter began. He would henceforth continue a decade-long odyssey of clinical seminars in all three regions of the International Psychoanalytic Association. Once he carefully assessed how well versed any society was in terms of his and Klein's clinical ideas, he calibrated his seminars accordingly. Bion's (2013) *Los Angeles Clinical Seminars* for instance contrasted sharply with those he gave in Buenos Aires, where there was already a group of analysts, organized by León Grinberg, who already had some familiarity with Bion's ideas when he arrived in late July 1968. Grinberg had heard Bion at International Psychoanalytic Association Congresses and had already formed a small study group of Argentinian analysts interested in furthering their understanding of his ideas. There was also a larger group of analysts from South American countries who came to hear Bion in 1968 and they too arrived with some familiarity with Kleinian ideas, while fewer directly knew Bion's published work (Grinberg, in Bion Talamo, Borgogno and Merciai, 2000, p. xx). Within a few years of having given these seminars in Buenos Aires, the first introductory book to Bion's ideas was written by a group of Argentine analysts headed by Leon Grinberg (Grinberg, Sor and Bianchedi, 1977).

This situation in Buenos Aires was thus somewhat dissimilar from the experience Bion had had in Los Angeles, where he had come to teach and supervise—before he decided to live and work there. Bion correctly assumed that American-trained ego analysts would not be very familiar with his ideas about the treatment of near psychotic and psychotic cases, so he provided them with plenty of case illustrations. On the other hand, since Melanie Klein's ideas had been in vogue for some time after World War II in Argentina, there was more familiarity with her work, more with child than psychotic patients (Etchegoyen and Zysman, 2005). So, for example, while he barely mentioned the Grid in Los Angeles, he gave a very detailed seminar on how it functioned with his Argentine colleagues (Bion, 2018, pp. 29–46).

When Bion came to the Americas and relayed these newer views on the analyst's subjectivity as reflected in his model of 'container/contained,' where

DOI: 10.4324/9781003364795-16

the analyst oscillated to and fro from the chaotic realm of the 'paranoid/schizoid' to the 'depressive' position, from disorder to integration, there was a clash of analytic cultures. In Los Angeles, it appeared that British Kleinians like Bion understood Freud's Structural Theory in a different way from American-trained ego psychological analysts. This point was humorously brought home when one Los Angeles analyst asked Bion if he ever made 'structural considerations' (no doubt a reference to Freud's 'structural theory'). Bion replied that he considered 'container/contained' such a structural consideration (Bion, 2013, pp. 92)! This mix of analytic cultures made for a Kleinian/Freudian slight confusion of tongues, but it was not enough to dissuade Bion from moving to Los Angeles.

Let me point out some of the thematic continuities and discontinuities between the *Los Angeles* and *Buenos Aires Seminars*. To start with the obvious: after years of writing dense and opaque epistemological monographs, Bion (1962b, 1963, 1965) decided to distill his clinical thinking in the form of clinical supervisions and case presentations. Very few in attendance at the *Los Angeles* and *Buenos Aires Seminars* would have realized that Bion had been long disinclined to discuss extensive clinical case material in his writings, especially during the 1960s. There was not a lot of clinical material to be found in three theory-laden monographs, so it would have been hard except for a few close colleagues in London to have much of an idea of how exactly Bion analyzed his patients (Bion, 1962b, 1963, 1965).

In the *Los Angeles Seminars*, Bion reversed himself by spending most of the 3rd and 4th Seminars giving detailed clinical accounts of his distillation of the Kleinian method with psychotics and near-psychotics. This outstanding organizing feature of the *Los Angeles Seminars*, along with a long private supervision of an analytic case presented to him (Bion, 2013, pp. 107–131) certainly demonstrated Bion's readiness to convey how he worked with especially disturbed patients to a group of soon-to-be colleagues. Those familiar with Bion's early days in Los Angeles recall some initially worrisome months when very few came along to consult him in 1968 (James Grotstein, personal communication).

This emphasis on the presentation and supervision of clinical material now became a signature in many of the clinical seminars for the next decade. Of particular interest here is Bion's presentation in his Fourth *Los Angeles Seminar* of a stormy borderline female case, one whose analysis he continued to discuss with his Argentine colleagues. It seems that this patient was so difficult to treat that Bion made a decision to keep presenting material from this case the next year in Buenos Aires in the Fifth Seminar. I think that this case in effect forms one of the longest case presentations by Bion we have gathered thus far, one that helps us understand something of what in effect was his implicit method of clinical inquiry (Aguayo, 2018, p. xxv). We are appreciative of having this long clinical example which gives us an opportunity to understand the various elements of his unique clinical approach, one whose careful study repays the analyst ten-fold in analyzing his own difficult-to-treat patients.

If we use the terms of his 'container/contained' model Bion (1962b; Figure 8.1, p. 89) to recast our findings about 'B,' her difficulties could be understood as follows: the borderline appeared like an ordinary neurotic personality *minus* some key attributes. Freud's distinctions between primary and secondary process were of little help here since by definition, the patient was so overloaded with undigested sensory and affective states that obtrusively made having meaningful contact with one's own mind impossible. In this sense, the patient was generally reliant on the alpha-function capacity of the analyst if meaningful linking experiences were to occur. The agglomeration of the beta-elements came to form an obtrusive beta-screen, which could in turn potentially overload the analyst's alpha-function. If, as we discovered in Bion's early presentation of his case, the beta-screen attacks are so profound as to momentarily paralyze his capacity to think, then all the hapless patient could do is produce bizarre objects, feel misrelated to and begin the circular insane cycle afresh. This is a conceptualization of the stormy borderline material from the last chapter. Put differently, the patient's 'beta-screen' attack could not be transformed in alpha-elements until a few hours after the session had ended. At that point, Bion experienced a selected fact, namely that the patient had entered his mind ('hallucination in reverse') and captured the analyst's mind/breast.

In the *Buenos Aires Seminars* a year later, Bion continued the case presentation, only this time, he presented even more disturbed aspects of his experience with this patient. Right from the beginning of treatment, there had been profound difficulties: she had two previous analyses that she felt went 'so wrongly' that she was left in a profoundly demoralized state. She insisted that Bion now treat her and he asked her why she thought he would do any better. Perhaps having given analysis a try, she should just set it aside. This suggestion merely agitated 'B' and she then threatened suicide if he didn't treat her. So, the analysis began in a somewhat extorted emotional atmosphere.

Bion then confessed that perhaps another mistake was talking to a member of 'B's' family—as the patient had merely written, requesting an interview. This is an important point because as Bion mentioned in his 1977 *Tavistock Seminars* (#2) there was the matter of the potentially harmful impact of the analyst's listening to hearsay evidence about patients. This is a potential vulnerability at the outset of any patient's treatment. There is always the question of how much any analyst may want to hear what their colleagues tell them about the patient referred. But Bion here trusted his family source—and as he said that was another mistake. Another issue: while the fees were agreed upon, 'B' actually couldn't pay for her treatment; her father did.

With the atmosphere so compromised and threatened, the analysis began. It was either analysis with Bion—or death. All proceeded more or less smoothly for three months—'B' turned up, spoke and he interpreted. Then in one session, she relayed that she had a urinary tract infection, something that would cause her to leave the room to go to the bathroom during the sessions. After her return, she seemed embarrassed, anxious—the analyst thought she had to leave for 'psychological reasons.' This behavior continued—and his interpretations became more specific to her internal state of mind: was there a voice she was hearing when she left the room?' 'B' denied that, and it then seemed that Bion became somewhat insistent on what she was experiencing.

'B' then became quite upset, almost violent—how could he think she was not in touch with 'reality'? He persisted nonetheless with the interpretation of her hearing some sort of 'voice,' and she claimed to only hear her and his voice. She then accused him of not taking his work seriously; he then pointed out that she kept returning to the room even though she experienced him as an 'inadequate' analyst. He couldn't seem to say anything right, not even about the transference. 'B' then became so upset that she stood up and threatened him with her bag.

These episodes persisted—and finally the analyst concluded that her behavior was making analysis impossible. It was felt that his words were 'unimportant or insignificant.' Was he being put into a position of being just a 'bad analyst' who didn't know what he was doing—or just a mere fool? Bion went back to the 'angry voices' she was hearing in the room, the ones engaged in a 'heated argument' that she was dramatizing. From the perspective of the two participants, it might have seemed like a case of 'reversible perspective,' where the analyst's 'selected fact' was experienced by the patient as his 'overvalued idea.' The more insistent he became, the more resistive her response (Bion, 2018, pp. 60–70).

Then he was surprised when 'B' calmed down for amoment; she commented on how much better things went when he analyzed her correctly. 'B' thought he should have done it earlier. So even when he was right, he still appeared in error. Bion thought she seemed 'superior, hostile and contemptuous.' There was always something to criticize. This kind of session alternated with the more usual sessions. When Bion then voiced the feeling that these were not the conditions under which analysis could continue, she became violently angry. It seemed that Bion may have provoked 'B,' having allowed himself to be drawn into an argumentative enactment, where he was intermittently portrayed as the 'inadequate partner.' This provided fodder for still another escalation. And finally, Bion said, 'Well, enough.' And he interrupted/ended her treatment.

But after this interruption, she called him, sounding contrite and asked him to take her back—which he considered doing. The tone momentarily sounded like a sort of defensive symmetrizing when an atmosphere was created where both became equal partners rather than an analyst treating a patient. Perhaps too many promises had been made—not just by the patient, but perhaps by the analyst to her family as well. 'B' had suspected Bion had been informed about her. In either event, she felt desperate and quite uneasy while the analyst thought she suffered from 'paranoid hysteria.'

Bion offered to continue, but only if the necessary conditions to carry out the analysis remained in place—if these didn't obtain, the analysis would again be interrupted. Finally, they reached a point where she was behaving more reasonably with her family. But his pointing this out to her made her furious, as if she felt violently misrelated to. To the idea that he should act like a good analyst, Bion (2018, p. 73) retorted "that I had no obligation to be so as I was just forced to try to act like one." He tried then to get behind all the noise—on the one hand, he needed to be informed about what was happening—and yes, she was 'anxious,' but that she couldn't decide whether to help him or to deceive him. He thought she was enacting something that was playing itself out in her head, some sort of 'internal argument.'

'B' confirmed this—and said her parents were quite unhappy and that she had witnessed frequent quarrels. There was a momentary clearing, where Bion thought that such scenes occurred before she herself could speak—in other words, quite early. It all led her to omnipotently believe that she was a more trustworthy source than either her parents or her analyst. In Bion's view, that put her in an 'anxious' spot because she would have rather been the child than the parent/analyst. The patient spitefully retorted that if she had improved, it was in a space where he was a 'terrible analyst.' She went on to say that he had been angry and talked about putting an end to her analysis. Bion thought that it was difficult for her to put up with the idea that she owed anything to her analysis and her analyst. He thought that part of her improvement resulted from his insistence of some sort of discipline. This became fodder for more argumentation on 'B's part. He countered by saying that it was difficult for her to admit that she owed anything to her parents for being 'tolerant.' It was difficult for her to admit that she was indebted to some sort of discipline. How could she feel grateful for what she also despised? It was clear that the analyst had to bear an extremely trying and difficult emotional position.

As he had done in the *Los Angeles Seminars*, Bion stopped here and the audience in Buenos Aires joined the discussion. From the various questions asked, we learn that the patient's analysis was interrupted because of the analyst's move to Los Angeles.

To a question about his patient's change, Bion replied that she improved in the social sphere, dressing and behaving properly. Unfortunately, he was not able to complete this analysis. Nonetheless, it seemed that she resented the fact that she had improved—she found the idea intolerable. It seemed like the patient either had to continue analysis—and bear the misfortune of improvement—or else, suffer another collapse. Bion thought that 'B' needed to continue analysis—all in spite of the fact that she was a patient (according to Bion) that no analyst wanted. 'B' may well have been in the throes of a negative therapeutic reaction when analysis was interrupted. Yet in a very real sense, it was courageous for Bion to discuss this difficult-to-treat patient, particularly at a time when the phenomenon of the stormy borderline patient was becoming more widespread—and its treatment was still relatively new.

The question of limits and boundaries also came up for discussion. Bion ventured forth the idea that the analyst just tries to do his job; and who knows what must be done if the patient needs a 'security guard'? He also discussed what he termed 'minimum working conditions,' the ways in which the analyst sets the limits of his work situation. Is this the way he wants to live his life? What is he willing to put up with? The analyst cannot allow any one patient destroy his ability to treat another person who is in need. Nonetheless, the patient needed him to be a good analyst despite her hatred of his willingness to be experienced as an 'extorter.' Bion also thought that the patient was extremely crafty and artful at being able to exploit his vulnerabilities. Years later, in *The Italian Seminars*, Bion (1977b, p. 38) again returned to this case, referring to 'B' as a 'greedy patient' who rattled him so much that he went on thinking about her after a particularly stormy session when he should have been thinking about his own patients. For the analyst, the difficulties were not in making interpretations, but in putting up with 'B's relentless devaluation. He lamented the fact that he had had to interrupt the patient's treatment when he left for Los Angeles.

Contemporary Kleinian Treatment of Borderline Patients

In terms of how subsequent generations of Kleinian analysts have taken up some of the very difficult treatment issues posed by borderline personality disorders, the work of John Steiner (1994) is significant here. It goes without saying that there are decades of treatment experiences with scores of borderline patients that inform these later views; it is important to remember that Bion also stood at the frontier of the treatment of borderlines. Nonetheless, I offer Steiner's views as one point of comparison, all with the idea of further understanding the complex impasse in which Bion found himself with his young patient.

In addressing such difficult-to-treat patients, Steiner makes a fundamental distinction that when these patients reach an impasse or stalemate with the analyst, they are essentially barricaded within a defensive system he termed a 'psychic retreat.' In Bionian terms, we might think of this as a solid wall, a β-screen in which the patient may not have an open communication with the analyst—and the same will go the other way around—despite his efforts, the analyst cannot make a communicative link with his patient. In these circumstances, Steiner regards such primitively organized patients as momentarily incapable of seeing into themselves in any meaningful introspective manner, incapable of receiving let alone working with what he termed a 'patient-centered interpretation.' In fact, interpretations from the analyst about the patient's internal states—in 'B's case, the psychological attributions made about her need to leave the consulting room and go to the lavatory—were experienced by 'B' as hostile accusations; she told Bion that he was making it sound like she was crazy and hearing voices.

In this instance, Steiner recommends making what he terms an 'analyst-centered interpretation,' one that does not focus on the patient's internal state of mind in an explanatory sense, but instead looks at the patient's model of the analyst's mind and what is happening at the present moment. This is an extremely valuable and important idea—and complements Bion's original formulation: there is the analyst's model of the patient's mind; the patient's model of her own mind; and now, Steiner's valuably augmenting idea: the patient's model of the analyst's mind. By differentiating between 'analyst-centered' and 'patient-centered' interpretations, Steiner thinks the analyst can now attend to the subjective experience of the patient towards the analyst, and in effect, allow the analyst to address how overly preoccupied the patient becomes in his defensive articulation of his own theory of the analyst's mind. Framed in terms like, 'You seem to think I feel/think ...,' it takes up defensive projective aspects of the patient's experience of the analyst and as such, has the empathic potential of being heard by the patient.

In 'B's case, this empathic intervention might have sounded like: 'You feel me as being accusatory, as if I am casting aspersions on your sanity, all of which leads you to feel endangered in my presence.' Perhaps 'B' might have agreed with such an interpretation, as it would also signal the analyst's willingness to work with what she was making available, understanding that any form of what Steiner might call a 'patient-centered interpretation,' would have likely felt intrusive and accusatory—as if the analyst is standing in some superior position, and thus lead to more counter-accusations from the patient. Perhaps these types of 'analyst-centered interpretations' might be easier for the patient to take in because they are 'what' as opposed to 'why' type interventions. It allows the patient an opportunity to address how they perceive the workings of the analyst's mind, momentarily setting aside the issue of having their own minds as the object of the analyst's understanding.

Of course, this is a conjecture after the fact and not a way of saying that such an intervention might have made any difference in the way Bion's case turned out. It is simply a way of saying that analysts have given serious consideration to other modes of gaining access to the part of the patient's mind that might be amenable to some sort of reasonable exchange. In this instance, with a difficult-to-treat patient that perhaps was in more of an evacuative than introspective mode, the analyst's words may have felt like projective missiles being hurled at her in some sort of concrete counter-projective way. If this sense of 'words-as-actions,' felt to be things concretely hurled, then reprisals begin to feel quite in order. Of course, it is desirable that eventually the point might be reached when the patient could hazard hearing the 'patient-centered interpretation,' so that she can work more meaningfully and introspectively with what ails her.

Chapter 13

Clinical Work in Buenos Aires

Presentation of an Overly Agreeable Young Male Analysand

Introduction to Bion's Own Analytic Case Work (July, 1968)

During the initial meeting with members of the Argentine Psychoanalytic Association, Bion plunged straight in by presenting on-going work from one of his analytic cases. He was now established in Los Angeles, having just spent a summer holiday in England with his family. He flew to New York and then went on alone to Buenos Aires, where he was hosted by Léon Grinberg. Bion's letters to wife Francesca recounted how he was feted and lauded as the visiting luminary, at times having to fend off more social invitations than he could accommodate in order to preserve his stamina for work in the daily seminar meetings (Bion, 2014, vol. II: 172–177).

Bion's brief clinical presentation in the first of the *Buenos Aires Seminars* was cast in his usual manner: an existential vignette with no early childhood or family history. A 31-year-old male analysand (I call him 'C'), early in his analysis, showed signs of being 'rather co-operative and cordial.' In a typical session, Bion shared with his audience an on-going feeling of annoyance he had experienced with 'C,' who seemingly agreed with every interpretation he received. The patient recounted a dream:

> I had gone for a walk with a girlfriend, who pointed out something really noticeable, something in the sky, but I couldn't see it. She was amazed that I couldn't see it. She wasn't really my girlfriend, but someone I had known for many years and our friendship had acquired a more profound meaning in recent months.

Bion (2018, p. 3) interpreted that he was the 'girlfriend' or 'sister' that he had never had—and that the analytic relationship had become important to him. The patient was in 'complete agreement.' By this point, familiar with this characteristic response, the analyst found himself personally feeling a bit testy with 'C,' imagining himself asking: 'Well, why do you think that is correct?' Of course, he couldn't say this because 'C' had agreed with the interpretation. The patient then further elaborated the interpretation by saying his mother

DOI: 10.4324/9781003364795-17

had told him of a sister who had died before his birth. 'C' thought it might be a good idea to have his mother come to his session and talk about all this.

The analyst wondered why the patient would make such a suggestion. How would she be able to inform the analyst with more 'exact information' than he himself had, particularly about what was happening in his own mind? The patient then, as was his custom, again agreed with the analyst—he himself should be the one to give the information. Along with this, he recovered other bits of the dream: "*The objects described by the girlfriend as clouds of definite shapes were flying saucers.*" Bion remarked that this must be meaningful since the girlfriend also represented an 'aspect of his personality.' Again, the patient agreed, remarking that rain on a sunny day spoiled everything (2018, p. 4). The analyst interpreted 'C's anxiety about being attacked by 'two objects' in the dream, something that would jeopardize his relationship with the girl-friend—and this included his analyst. And again, the patient agreed with the interpretation. The analytic atmosphere seemed to be one where there was nothing but excellent interpretations enthusiastically welcomed by the patient, something the analyst had grown suspicious of. This situation seemed just as problematic as one where the patient consistently disagreed with interpreta-tions—it seemed improbable that an analyst could be consistently on point or wrong in such a fashion. It was hard to gauge what sort of emotional impact the analysis carried. The analyst remained irritated.[1]

The Analyst's Reflections on 'C's Case Material

After this brief presentation, Bion immediately took up the question of the countertransference. Much as he had done in the *Los Angeles Seminars*, he took up the idea that there could be some sort of personal interference that obstructed his attempts to maintain some sort of balanced stance with 'C.' Repeating what he had written on previous occasions, Bion (2018, p. 5) had made it clear that for an analyst to speak of 'his countertransference' is a mistaken idea because, by definition, it pertains to an 'unconscious response.' So, in the throes of the current session, the analyst does well to retain his or her awareness of a disturbing feeling, subordinating it to such time as to be able to have the resources or external help to effect its resolution. Until then, the analyst must face his patients in whatever form of emotional shape he is in. On any given day, he merely tries to do the best possible job he can.

In this instance, Bion reprised his views on countertransference that originated with his group work in the 1940s as well as with his supervision with Paula Heimann just after the war ended. Heimann's (1950) idea was that the analyst 'sustain and subordinate' disturbing feelings to such time as he has the resources to deal with them. In one important statement, it reflected his support for what has become known as the 'wider' notion of countertransference, namely that the analyst does well at times to concentrate on the unconscious-to-unconscious communication, which in turn allows him to arrive at a fresh understanding (cf.

Chapter 5). Heimann's (1950) view of countertransference—that the analyst must 'sustain and subordinate' his or her own feeling reactions to his patient, gradually discovering what their unconscious meaning is, was the source of a statement made by Bion (1955b) in his 'Group Dynamics' paper:

> Now the experience of countertransference appears to me to have quite a distinct quality that should enable the analyst to differentiate the occasion when he is the object of a projective identification from the occasion when he is not. The analyst feels he is being manipulated so as to be playing a part, no matter how difficult to recognize, in somebody else's phantasy.
>
> (IV, p. 213)

Since Bion had been keeping a vigil with his feeling of annoyance, it led to him identifying himself as the girlfriend in 'C's dream, the one who kept pointing things out to him as he remained oblivious. In short, Bion may have thought that the feeling of irritation had been induced in him by way of 'C's obliviousness. As further elaborated upon by 'C' when he recalled that the girlfriend in the dream was pointing out something more definitely menacing and dangerous, namely the flying saucers, it led to the idea that 'C' would rather remain blind by just mindlessly agreeing with the analyst—all rather than have a more authentic encounter based on difference and separateness. Bion here may have thought that his irritability emanated from something the patient was bringing, namely chronic agreeableness; it is what needed to be analyzed.

Bion then moved to the theme of free association. It is hoped that our patients speak, associate and use 'well-structured sentences and ordinary language.' At the same time, this emphasis on the semantic meaning of words, if carried to excess, tends to minimize the sensory atmosphere and the realm of undigested feelings, ones that go into making up an analytic atmosphere. These elements are also quite fundamental. It is important for the patient to engage with what the analyst has to say, all of which results from months and years of work. The analyst continues to gather up these emotional, sensory impressions that he is also not yet able to interpret since he does not yet know their meaning. He hopes that the meaning will gradually evolve—from unconscious to preconscious to conscious. In short, what has not yet been psychic will become emotionally connected understanding in the present moment. The past can then become the present; and the present in turn anticipates the future.

While 'C' came with the well-worn expectation that he would be recognized as the same agreeable patient he had been yesterday, Bion urged his colleagues to politely show *that* patient the door, as he wanted to make room to welcome a new patient—someone new that he wanted to introduce the patient to. The analyst could in the interim feel persecuted by a situation that he didn't yet understand, hence the tormenting feeling of irritation at what one did not clearly understand.

It is, however, also tempting, and sometimes makes for a complacent attitude, to remain in a situation that is comfortable and familiarly known. In this way, analyst and patient can create a comfortable and complacent stasis in the analysis. To the analyst that abandons memory and desire, however, his position is to never be at rest (Bion, 2018, p. 11). He continues to look at "the unfathomable, unrelated and incoherent situations," while focusing away from the familiar and coherent ones. But most of all, he is on the lookout for recycling old interpretations when feeling lost or tired. To work with countertransference impasses in one sense continues the unfinished work of one's analysis. It is not so much a matter of interminable analysis as it is remaining open to a psychic world of infinite possible meanings.

Another way the analyst searches for fresh new meanings is through his quest for what Henri Poincaré called the 'selected fact' (Bion, 1962b). One encounters a mass of data for which there appears to be no known pattern or coherence. Once a pattern is detected, order and coherence follow. Bion (2018, p. 10) put it well: "It brings order where there was none, meaning to where it did not exist and makes a relationship and a coherence that were previously non-existent apparent." When you see the patient today that you saw yesterday, he must not be the same patient. But herein lies the rub: it is not so easy to get rid of one's memories or well-worn habits. It is the new and emergent situation that must be appreciated. The analyst must not tarry with what he has already interpreted.

Contemporary Kleinian Extensions of Bion's Clinical and Theoretical Ideas: The Work of Betty Joseph

In my view, the 'here and now' technique work of Betty Joseph (1989) stands as a meaningful extension of Bion's own theoretical and clinical work, and her work gained traction after his death in 1979. Such meaningful 'post-Bionian' extrapolations provide further proof of how his work has endured. Betty Joseph (who incidentally was one of Bion's fellow candidate classmates) represents the initial generation that worked to distill his and other Kleinian ideas into an explicit systematic technique beginning in the 1970s. I briefly point out the ways in which her mature work took up so many of his ideas. Initially tying the patient's pathology to disturbances in early childhood, referencing them in past-to-present transference interpretations, Joseph marginalized this approach by the 1970s when she shifted her focus to the patient's direct emotional experience as lived in analysis. She continued to listen to the patient's reports of the past but deployed them to enlighten how the patient was experiencing the present moment with the analyst.

Like Bion, she took up the communicative impact of projective identification. She also took up the unconscious-to-unconscious communication enacted by the patient in analysis. She focused on both the enactments as well as discussing them in a group context with graduated analysts, so that dyadic interactions could be examined and informatively calibrated by a consensus view as it evolved in the group, still another modality that would have been familiar to Bion. Dealing with countertransference in a group setting allowed it to become more thoroughly informing. One learned the difference between narrow-subjective reactions of any individual analyst and the wider induced reactions stemming from the patient as experienced similarly by a group of colleagues (Aguayo, 2011).

Like Bion, she also marginalized the old Kleinian part-object anatomical language and interpretations. It was now a 'you and I' type of interaction over and above the 'mouth to breast.' While still subscribing to the paranoid/schizoid and depressive positions, she marginalized what appeared to be interpretative language that was too abstract and experience distant. Bion (1967a) was an important and informing source here—no memory or desire should interfere with the analyst's even hovering attentiveness. One directly observed the patient's material in plain and simple terms, allowing neither desire about the past nor wishes for the future to intrude.

Joseph's (1989) consolidation of technique also came at a time when analysts saw increasing numbers of borderline and narcissistic patients, precisely the group of near-psychotic patients that Bion had become interested in. Dubbed 'difficult-to-treat' by Betty Joseph, she now took up her understanding of Klein's (1952) definition of the 'total situation,' casting it in a 'here and now' way, where the focus was on the patient's structure of internal object relations, as they were projected into the analyst and the analytic situation. The psychic and emotional material that had remained unmetabolized and unconscious was projected in the 'here and now.' She was especially interested in how communicative projective identification was deployed by the patient to organize the analyst into a position of defensive stasis, making him role-responsive to the patient. Here, the analyst wants to know what role she is being recruited to play as it remains key to the structure of the patient's internal world and its accompanying defensive structures (Aguayo, 2011).

Betty Joseph's Case Illustration of an Overly Agreeable Patient

To illustrate just how closely aligned Betty Joseph's work on technique is with Bion's own work, I take a clinical example from a patient uncannily similar to the one described by Bion in Buenos Aires in 1968. Joseph and Bion's work are mirror reflections of each other here—and of course, she worked in complete unawareness of Bion's own work because the *Buenos Aires Seminars* was not published until 2018 (Aguayo, 2018b). It is truly a case of what the historian of science Thomas Kuhn would term 'spontaneous discovery,' where workers in two separate countries make the same discovery at the same time.

In this instance, Bion's work in 1968 remained unknown to Joseph when she published her own paper in 2000, 'Agreeableness as an Obstacle.'

In Joseph's (2000, p. 641) view, there are patients who are overly compliant in analysis—the patient agrees to all the analyst's interpretations "in such a way as to keep the treatment apparently ongoing and peaceful but actually semi-paralyzed." She goes into detail about how agreeableness is enacted in the analytic relationship and with the analyst, positing that it is a portal into the patient's defensive structure. In the analysis of an 18-year-old adolescent female, Joseph linked the agreeableness to powerful underlying anxieties about being taken over and invaded, anxieties that led to a life where she had no mind of her own.

The analyst found these deeply paranoid anxieties manifest in agreeableness to be genuine obstacles in treatment. Excessive agreement was an active and fixed way of relating, drawing the analyst into a false atmosphere of pseudo-mutual understanding. The analyst could also fear becoming intemperate or even angry themselves if they didn't go along with the agreeableness; role-recruited into a position of defensive stasis mitigated against genuine emotional understanding. A lighthearted superficiality betrayed a lack of movement in a situation in which nothing happens.

Jenny, as she was called by Joseph, fought with her parents yet remained all too agreeable with her analyst; there would be fights and violence in her dreams but not in the consulting room. The real work was in understanding the obstacles as a way into the patient's deeper anxieties. There was no interpretation to which she would not agree; however, there was very little movement in the analysis. The obstacle was the royal road towards understanding the transference problems. Jenny was immature and dependent, feeling blocked and unconfident. She accepted interpretations in an uncritical way. If shown to be agreeable, she would agree even more! Agreement piled onto agreement, a form of verbal clinging; stalemate and paralysis remained in the atmosphere. Jenny would go along with just about anything, as if she had no mind of her own.

A central incident brought these matters to the fore. After 18 months of analysis, when Jenny was accepted to a college just outside London, she initially requested that her session times be changed, but soon made it clear that she wanted to cut back a session (from 4 to 3 times a week). The analyst felt double binded by such a request: Jenny seemed to pressure the analyst to 'go along,' give in, not interrupt Jenny with any separate understanding, let alone stand firm on the issue of four times a week analysis. In effect, Jenny created a mirror image of herself in the transference, someone who would always agree with her, creating a stale 'no difference' atmosphere. The analyst was pulled in the direction of playing a role of a weak person who would just give in.

Interpretive inquiry revealed Jenny's fear of becoming too dependent on analysis—as if she would suffocate (Joseph, 2000, p. 644). Wanting the analyst's superficial approval covered over the fear of being taken over by her analyst. Hence the need to run away from the fourth session. She feared the analyst forcing her ideas on her. By placating her object in turn, she only appeared to agree, but really avoided allowing her objects to influence her. The missing fourth session now became a source of a 'difference of opinion' between the two.

The transference/countertransference situation was tricky here, while the analyst thought it preferable if Jenny kept to four sessions a week, it was easy for Jenny to project a superego attitude, as if her analyst would be angry if she didn't comply, all of which led to feeling disliked. Anxious about their differences, Jenny expected the analyst to be angry, all of which raised the compliance issue once again. While it was important for Jenny to make her own decision, the analyst interpreted that Jenny wanted her to give in. The patient too was in a double-bind: either give in and feel suffocated or come less often and feel guilty. The whole situation would have been so agreeable if only the analyst would remain an agreeable but false object that was taken in by Jenny's false agreeableness (Joseph, 2000, p. 645).

These considerations segued into Jenny's internal world, where she felt trapped between a demanding and intrusive mother and analyst, trying to be agreeable but constantly fending off the fear of the object's invasiveness and attacks. In adopting a stance of agreeableness, she could remain emotionally distant, covering over some rather significant feelings of fright and terror. In a defensive posture, she treated her dreams as if they were something to be gotten rid of, gotten out of herself—and not something for which she sought understanding. Finally, Jenny admitted to being a liar, having evolved a method where she could ward off significant others—and the fears they represented.

In being agreeable, Jenny in effect lied and hoped the other would buy it. The defensive aspect of pseudo-agreeableness came out insofar as it actually made it very difficult for her to get anything helpful because she couldn't listen to her object. She hoped others would buy the lie, all as a way of defending herself against the fear of feeling invaded and taken over. In her internal world, there were no good objects; fear was everywhere and there was no trust. Jenny tried to convey an agreeable friendliness that in effect disguised how suspicious she felt. In the interim, she remained uninfluenced. She used agreeableness to soothe herself and "protect herself from violent intrusion by the object" (Joseph, 2000, p. 648). The analytic aim was to get under the surface and recognize how the agreeableness was being enacted rather than how it was verbally expressed. Only in so doing could these serious obstacles to potential development be dealt with.

A Final Note on the Concordance between Bion and Joseph on the Agreeable Patient

The uncanny similarity between Bion and Joseph's cases merits some comment. In looking at Joseph's more clinically detailed presentation, one can make some interesting conjectures about Bion's agreeable patient. One way to understand Bion's annoyance with his young analysand was the result of feeling he himself was in a double-bind with someone who seemed more interested in maintaining a friendly and agreeable relationship rather than actually *be* in analysis. Bion may well have been in exactly the same position as Betty Joseph a few decades later: if he insisted on analyzing 'C's agreeableness, he would only agree more, thus remain oblivious to how he enacted the role of a frustrating object. So long as he remained oblivious to what was being pointed out to him—as it was in the dream with the girlfriend—he also did not have to accept any responsibility, which was also meant to exasperate the analyst.

However, there may have been a clue in 'C's further elaboration of the dream: *"The objects described by the girlfriend as clouds of definite shapes were flying saucers."* I conjecture here that very much like Jenny in the Betty Joseph case, 'C' also hid paranoid fears of persecution under the veneer of agreeableness. It seems like both patients had a terror of appearing separate or formed in their own emotional views, having learned to live in an enclave of defensive agreeableness as a way to ward off their feared persecutors. The additional defensive advantage of agreeableness was that, in effect, it organized the other in the direction of intemperateness if not downright anger.

Bion may have been aware of this bind when he presented 'C' to his colleagues in Buenos Aires in 1968. He presented the dilemma faced by the analyst in his or her everyday practice. The annoyance felt by the analyst towards his patient was to some degree a function of paranoid and persecutory anxieties being projected into the analyst by way of enactment. There was also just enough doubt on the analyst's part that his annoyance could be some personal factor of countertransference, all of which would lead to the potential for analytic stasis—the analyst here could remain worried and concerned about putting a foot wrong in analyzing the patient's agreeableness. It reprised the point made by Bion in the *Los Angeles Seminars* regarding countertransference: the workday reality is that analysts don't often have time for such measured reflection. The analyst will for good or ill, enter the next session *as he or she is*, so it is better for the analyst to aspire to patience and security because he will in his workaday practice sometimes feel persecuted and depressed.

Both Bion and Joseph's agreeable patients were cases in point.

Note

1 Bion may well have been referring to patient 'C' in the *Los Angeles Seminars* the year before in response to a question from a colleague about how he understood situations in which the patient excessively agreed with the given interpretation. Was there a difference between those analytic occasions where there was a 'clash of desires' vis-à-vis those situations in which there might be a 'communion of desires' between patient and analyst? Bion (2013, pp. 16–17) wryly commented that he was just as familiar with those occasions where there seemed to be 'extremely good

agreement' between analysand and analyst as those where "the number of mistakes I make is far beyond the law of averages ... that I am so permanently wrong you see, that there must be something odd about this situation as to why the patient comes to me (as analyst and so on), when on the evidence I get a number of misses which are far above the average—it's the same thing." Either situation, the one with the pseudo-agreeable patient or the chronically querulous one required further analytic understanding.

Chapter 14

Attention and Interpretation (1970)

Attention and Interpretation was the fourth and last of Bion's epistemological monographs, and featured chapter titles that had gone missing in his earlier monographs. In my view, since this book was primarily one of summarizing and reintegrating previous theoretical thinking, we can draw some of its chapter titles as a way of consolidating the ground we have covered thus far. *Attention and Interpretation* was also significant insofar as it also was written contemporaneously with his *Clinical Seminars*, the latter of which provided distillations of what we have termed his 'clinical method of inquiry' to colleagues in Europe, North and South America. *Attention and Interpretation* was a book that represented variations on the themes already taken up in detail in Bion's previous work—and here we follow its major chapter titles in order to distill his main findings.

Introduction

Bion made the point clear that his book was aimed at the practicing psychoanalyst who, unlike the physician who deals exclusively with sensuous experience, also takes into account the invisible, non-sensuous realm of psychical reality in treating his disturbed patients. Unlike the physician who used material objects to assess his patient's difficulties, the analyst's instrument was language. Speech could be understood as truthfully revealing as much as it could serve a concealing defensive function. Bion here focused on the various interpretive speech acts of the analyst in attempting to draw the patient's attention to some phenomena he thinks is of special importance, a point that goes back to his group period when he indicated various phenomena to which he thought the group would do well to attend (cf. Chapter 2). The analyst also rendered judgments on how the patient was receiving or making sense out of the various interpretive remarks he heard. He also invoked the Grid as a way to decide what kind of communication he was listening to—and to what purposes it was being put (cf. Figure 10.1, p. 110). Recall here Vermote's (2014) distillation of the Grid: there were opening up and closing down communications that had to be a focus of inquiry by the analyst in treating his disturbed patients (cf. Chapter 10).

DOI: 10.4324/9781003364795-18

Medicine as a Model

Freud as a physician was trained to hear complaints about physical ailments from his patients. Opining that psychoanalysis had grown beyond the medical model of searching for underlying pathogens that resulted in symptoms, Bion now thought the analyst also deployed his intuition to understand psychical reality—and that his ultimate aim was establishing the truthfulness of the patient's life situation. The Latin etymology of 'patient' is 'suffering,' and here, Bion was earnest in his claims that only genuine patients had a capacity to bear their own suffering.

Bion (1962a, p. 307) had previously differentiated those patients who had great difficulties merely suffering and those who could bear it; that is, the difference between those who were quite intolerant of pain or frustration but would not "suffer it and so cannot be said to discover it." The patient intolerant of pain merely evacuated or projected it into other, whether in the form of a β-screen, hallucinations or lies as counterfeit substitutions for being unable to bear one's own pain while finding out more about what drove it. With the intolerant patient, he would remain with non-realizable, non-verbal elements, the very thing that the 'suffering' patient would be able to turn into some sort of constant conjunction. "One man achieves the transformation; the other, who cannot tolerate restriction, does not" (Bion, 1970, p. 11) (cf. Chapter 7).

In positing the model of 'container/contained,' Bion thought it could take into account not only the relevant aspects of Freud's topographic model with neurotics but also include Klein's model for serious pathology in the near-psychotic and psychotic patients. In this conceptual expansion, he highlighted how seriously disturbed pathology threw a broader explanatory light on less serious conditions. The psychotic for instance feared infinite space because he simply could not act as a resilient container for his own thoughts. The emotion is lost in the immensity (Bion, 1970, p. 12). The more disturbed patients regularly evacuated rather than suffered their psychic experience. As such, these patients represented great challenges to the analyst—since they were so incapable of tolerating frustration, they would not allow elements to conjoin in a constant conjunction. Alternatively, he would attack the analyst who made such links; and so, the positing of a definitory hypothesis, an attempt at a binding constant conjunction, would also be problematic experiences. Substitutive activities like hallucination and acting out were preferred to thinking. The workaday analyst was constantly trying to decide what is meaningful and what is meaningless communication in the face of links that were attacked (p. 17) (cf. Chapter 6).

Bion gave a clinical example, where a female analysand hostilely depicted her mother and father's relationship as one between a panderer and whore. The analyst repeatedly was at an impasse with his patient because no matter what he said, he was made out to be wrong. While Bion encoded this as a communication-as-attack on the analyst's potency, it also represented a closed-ended dysfunctional communication. Words acted like missiles hurled at the analyst (or in Grid terms, an 'A6' category, a β-element directed in action-form at the analyst) (1970, p. 7) The aim here was to shatter and split the analyst's capacity to formulate a meaningful interpretation. A defensive enclave of meaninglessness was the aim.

Reality Sensuous and Psychic

By the time Bion (1965) published *Transformations*, he had expanded the notion of β-elements to a more encompassing notion of 'O,' or the infinite, first and foremost to signify all possibilities and potentialities—what Kant had termed the 'thing-in-itself' or the *noumenon*. However, since by definition the 'thing-in-itself' could never be known directly, the human subject had to content himself with taking up the phenomenological manifestations of or transformations in 'O' (T(O)) in the only way they could be known, which Bion now termed 'transformations in knowledge' (T(K)). Substituting terms like 'infinite' and 'finite' for what Freud had termed unconscious and conscious, led to new theoretical statements: 'O' was about 'becoming' and could not be directly known; its formlessness entered into the arena of K where it could be known, as when it became 'knowledge gained through experience.' In other words, its existence was conjectured by the analyst in a phenomenological fashion.

Bion also listed all the various psychological activities undergone by the analyst to make it possible for him to participate in the psychoanalytic experience (1970, p. 26). In the quest to establish the truthfulness of the patient's psychical reality, the analyst did well to focus on 'O,' the 'unknown and unknowable' by 'becoming' it and not merely identifying with it. The analyst attended the session and waited for the material to 'evolve.' "O becomes manifest in K through the emergence of actual events" (Bion, 1970, p. 28). A good psychoanalytic outcome was based on how much one approximated the truth. The more real the analyst could be, the more authentic he could then be with the reality of his patient. On the other hand, an overly saturated analyst, i.e., one whose mind was too full of preconceptions, could not learn because he was too satisfied; his mind was full of pleasurable memories and empty of unpleasurable components. Too many preconceptions interfered with an attitude of patient receptivity (1970, p. 29) (cf. Chapter 10).

But in order for this to work, one had to rid oneself of memory and desire in K. To get to the technical point of O and K, Bion said that the analyst must impose upon himself "a positive discipline of eschewing memory and desire." Forgetting isn't enough: "what is required is a positive act of refraining from memory and desire" (1970, p. 31). To these familiar ideas, he added faith or F, a sense that there was an ultimate reality and the truthfulness of one's psychical reality could be known. An 'act of faith' did not represent a religious sentiment for Bion, but a sustained belief in the knowability, however derivative, of O (1970, p. 31). It was also hard to think of a successful analysis not involving the element of the "analysand's becoming reconciled to, or at one with, himself" (1970, p. 34) (cf. Chapter 11).

Opacity of Memory and Desire

To come back around to these ideas, there is a paradox involved in Bion's injunction to abandon memory and desire. It is at one level a disciplinary ideal state of active receptivity, yet at the same time must contain a minimum number of preconceptions. Since it is impossible to eliminate all preconceptions when doing analytic work, the analyst aspires to keep such saturated notions at bay. Put in the form of a question, how does the analyst enter the session unsaturated, and allow himself to be open to a spontaneous evolution from the formless infinite? (1970, p. 41).

Some of the aphorisms deployed here by Bion had already appeared in his *Los Angeles Seminars*: "Memory is the past tense, whereas desire is reflective of the future" (Bion, 1970, p. 45). Clearing one's mind of such obstructive factors opened the analyst up to what Bion had termed the 'full blast' of the patient's total communications. We saw a graphic example when Bion faced the emotional and sensory bombardment of his borderline female analysand ('B') when he despaired for hours after she left his office (cf. Chapter 11). In this analytic endeavor, his faith was central, and needed to remain unsaturated by any element of memory or desire. Neither memory nor desire were essential to making new formulations, but paradoxically, these elements had to be stripped away in order to approximate O. Discarding these elements was a necessary preparation for an evolution in O (Bion, 1970, pp. 32–33).

Theories: Particular Instance or General Configuration

The idea of abandoning memory and desire can certainly be an unsettling one for the beginning practitioner. The urge to take notes and recall material from previous sessions is all too great a temptation. In going against analytic 'training' of memory or mechanical recordings of sessions, how do we observe the patient's state of mind? Bion's variation on Freud's notion of free-floating attention posited the importance of footing oneself in the sensuous observations of one's patients through the deployment of the common senses on the one hand, but never to the exclusion of a capacity to turn inwardly towards the invisible realm of psychic reality. This Bion claimed was the *discipline* required by a practice of such 'artificial blindness' (or turning away from sensuous reality) that could lead to intuitions about the patient's psychic reality (1970, p. 67). Put differently, the analyst's aim here is to "diminish sensuous contact to bring psychic reality into focus" (1970, p. 69) (cf. Chapter 11).

The Mystic and the Group

Reprised from his 'Catastrophic Change' paper of 1966, Bion here revisited his group work of the 1940s, but now from the vertex of an innovative individual (the mystic) and his or her relationship to the Establishment (his referent group). There could be either a harmonious or discordant relationship between the mystic and the group; for instance, the felicitous reception of Faraday's discovery of electricity vis-à-vis the antagonistic reception of the Jewish rabbinate to Jesus. Would the mystic's 'new idea' be received well or pose a disruptive consequence for the group? Perhaps Bion was a bit self-referential when he wrote that there was always a potential for the mystic to stand (or appear) in some sort of antagonistic relationship to the group's rules/customs/conventions. He reprised the same phrase in 1970 previously used in the 'Catastrophic Change' paper—that one could be "loaded up with honors to the point where one sank without a trace" (Bion, 1970, p. 78). I conjecture that this was a veiled reference to Bion's problematic relationship to the London Klein group, whose work he would rarely cite once he left London in 1968 (cf. Chapter 10).

Returning again to his group work of the 1940s, Bion again emphasized the 'bestial' or 'animal' nature of man's 'herd instinct,' an idea of William Trotter, his surgeon mentor at University College London Medical School. Basic human emotions (in a group sense) correspond to birth, dependence, pairing and warfare, a restatement of Bion's three main Basic Assumptions (cf. Chapter 1).

'Container and Contained'

Never tiring of shifting his sightlines—or vertices—Bion returned to the model of 'container/contained' first posited in *Learning from Experience*. Deploying a pictorialization of what one would find in anyone's analysis, the analyst's mind was depicted as a 'container,' and that which the patient brings was not initially 'containable' within the analytic container. From this vertex, it serves as a model for certain patients who act out and overburden the containing capacities of the analyst in certain characteristic ways.

Recall also that 'container/contained' was what Bion termed a 'loosely saturated idea,' where it could signify mother and infant, breast and mouth, male and female, penis and vagina—and finally in the 1970 context, another variation on the mystic and the establishment, only in this context, the 'institutional' training of psychoanalysts. Likening the ruling caste in analytic institutes to religious cults, complete with rules and dogmas, Bion clearly thought his work stood outside of and in certain ways, antagonistic to entrenched training systems. It is hard to avoid the conjecture that he was referring to the training situations in both London and Los Angeles. As he wrote in his private diary, *Cogitations,* after having left London he was sad to say that he wouldn't miss being there—and yet within a few years, he made the same statement about his colleagues in Los Angeles (Bion, 1992, p. 334) (cf. Chapters 8 and 9).

Bion also included here psychoanalytic theories that cannot sufficiently 'hold' the available psychoanalytic facts—in this turn towards the theoretical side of his method of clinical inquiry, he focused attention on the 'institutional' training of psychoanalysts. He would in future years make ironic statements about the value of institute training for those aspiring to become psychoanalysts: despite its at times dubious claims to knowledge, psychoanalysts had to see to it that psychoanalysis survived (Bion, 1990, 2014, p. 66). Well-known psychoanalysts, such as Otto Kernberg (1996) have followed suit here, discussing the numerous ways in which institute training can tend to kill off a candidate's capacity for creative psychoanalytic thinking. In *Attention and Interpretation*, Bion took up psychoanalytic institutes as a form of 'Establishment' thinking in which there exists a

> ruling caste not unlike a theological group complete with 'rules' or 'dogmas' for those who are by nature not fitted to have direct experience of being psychoanalytic ... so that they may, as it were by proxy, have and impart knowledge of psychoanalysis.
>
> (Bion, 1970, p. 73)

Again, Bion did not name specific groups here, but one can wonder to what extent he was referring to 'ruling castes' in either his old or new institutes in London or Los Angeles.

Concluding Remarks: Rudi Vermote's Work on Transformations in K and O

Again, as further evidence of the durability of Bion's ideas, I now take up the work of Rudi Vermote (2019), who dedicated a considerable portion of his recent book, *Reading Bion*, to a consideration of what he considers *the* major theoretical innovation of Bion's work, namely the caesura between transformations in knowledge and 'O.' He detailed how Bion continued to move from T(K) to T(O), that is, from representations in thinking to experience that has not yet been represented. Unlike British Kleinians (e.g., O'Shaughnessy, 2006) who tend to polarize Bion's work by either preferring the London Bion (T (K)) or emphasizing the exclusive importance of T(O), Vermote *seeks to integrate both sides now*. For instance, he is dexterous in elucidating T(K) in his understanding of how Bion deployed the Grid to understand the evolution and/or the deterioration of thinking—and the defensive uses to which it was put. Alongside T(K), he also elaborates the manifold ways in which the practicing analyst can approximate states of being and momentary becoming in O, all of which serve to facilitate the patient's contact with his or her own essence, the invariant or characterological core. So, whereas reverie helps the analyst's alpha function to make sense of the patient's evacuations and communications, a letting go to a thorough free-floating attention opens up to the awareness of a non-representative, undifferentiated zone of experience. Vermote makes his integrative thinking quite clear in trenchant statements like: "Seen from O, all Bion's concepts and the attitude he advocated acquired another sense" (2019, pp. 130–131).

In his gloss on *Attention and Interpretation* (1970) Vermote (2019, pp. 140–168) continues to develop Bion's O position initially broached in *Transformations*: he now elaborates what happens at the undifferentiated, not-yet-psychic level. Bion took up the limitations of T(K), thinking that the "sensuous could be overcome by focusing on the patterns of invariants throughout the transformations rather than trying to understand and looking for causal and narrative relations and meaning." Now in T(O) he eschewed understanding and coherence, preferring to be in touch with the psychic zone of the infinite. Older concepts take on fresh meaning, e.g., the hallucinatory layer of experience is now an 'infinite zone' and derived from O, meaning something helpful to the analyst while still retaining its pathological definition evolved with Bion's work with psychotic patients. In his new language, analyst and patient could have divergent hallucinatory experiences on different vertices for better or for ill. Here, Vermote's views very much accord with those of Civitarese (2015) who also sees the beneficial effects of the analyst's occasional transformations in hallucinosis (cf. Chapter 5).

In further elaborating O, the analyst's domain was now one of "emotional-psychic reality [which] is observed by intuition and is not bound to space, time and causation" (Vermote, 2019, p. 142). Bion now defined truth as contact with O: "Real truth finds itself from O, without verbal and categorizing thoughts, where one may see intuitively what is" (ibid.). Vermote adroitly traces psychic life beyond three-dimensional space throughout Bion's work, starting with the group period (proto-mental states) early epistemology (beta-elements) and finally with his theory of O, which could also be referred to as the 'layer of hallucinosis.' Put differently, beta-elements acquired a new meaning in light of T(O). They are the elements that are closest to O, "but not yet appropriated by the psyche with its categories of time and space" (Vermote, 2019, p. 143).

In parsing out separate quadrants of meaning for T(K) and T(O), Vermote emphasizes the origin and necessity of a finite space for T(K). In other words, from the infinite to the finite, the latter is required as a space in which thinking can occur. Vermote (2019) writes: "We created a representation of three-dimensional space in order to make the thinking of emotional experiences possible, although mental space remains unknowable" (p. 144). Psychotics lacks such a containing space, scattering their psychic fragments and debris far and wide, all reflective of their mental disturbance and fear of infinite space. There is a black-hole, greedy space with psychotics who lack representation in a three-dimensional world. They can feel pain but will not suffer it. Grotstein (1983) took up these subjects papers he collected in a volume commemorating Bion's work.

In listening and analyzing from the O-Vertex, the analyst's attitude and openness to O can either assist or hinder its evolution in the patient's psychic development. While Bion certainly thought that having one's own training analysis helped, it could also be a source of obstruction, particularly if one is overly identified with the method of one's training analyst. The analyst waits for contact in O, and its phenomenological emanation in the form of T(K). As it is with T(K), a T(O) presupposes frustration tolerance, a secure waiting for coherence or the selected fact.

At the level of psychoanalytic technique, Bion, aside from the short paper on 'Memory and Desire,' was generally disinclined to write about technique. He regarded the abandonment of memory and desire as a further distillation of Freud's notion of 'even-hovering attention.' Bion balanced sensuous observation—and its ultimate release towards the zone of psychic reality, where the operation of intuition became paramount. It is the freedom from memory and desire that opens the analyst up to intuiting O, the ultimate psychic reality; there is a sort of 'blindness' that is required that is a "prerequisite for 'seeing' the evolved elements of O" (Bion, 1970, p. 59). Here, Vermote's views are much like those of Thomas Ogden (2015) who regards psychic reality as opening up once the obstructive aspects of memory and desire are marginalized (cf. Chapter 11).

Towards that end, Bion (1967a) differentiated between evoked and regurgitated memory—it is more important for the analyst to privilege the dream that floats unbidden into his or her mind than to recycle bits of analytic theory let alone what the patient is already aware of. Blinding oneself to sensuous experience opens one up to dream-like states. Put simply, Bion privileged the importance of dreams for both the patient as well as the analyst—"the dream is the *evolution* of O" (1970, p. 70). Put differently—and in Bion's terms, the essence of his technique remains "to detect a pattern that remains unaltered in apparently widely different contexts" (1970, p. 92). One works towards remaining open to O, so an evolution from it can become apprehended (p. 160). Vermote gives a clinical vignette—of a patient who discussed how a small sailboat crossed with a big one; he was also interested in World War II. The constant conjunction was a "fascination with danger and the presence of a catastrophe." It emerged repeatedly in different forms.

Vermote also reminds us that Bion reworked his ideas about memory and desire in *Attention and Interpretation*. If one is eschewing memory and desire, then the analyst gets in contact with 'Faith,' a belief that ultimate reality and truth exists, all in spite of the fact that it does not seem so at the moment (1970, p. 30). The term 'Faith' is actually part of Bion's scientific stance: in the midst of chaotic, disturbing and not-yet-understood psychic phenomena lies a not-yet-realized selected fact. This kind of anticipatory belief sustains us in our daily analytic practices. In Bion's words, "Faith is a scientific state of mind and should be recognized as such. But it must be 'faith' unstained by any elements of memory or desire" (Bion, 1970, p. 32; Vermote, 2019, p. 155). Faith in O can open the analyst up—if he or she is in awe of mystery—to the analysand's projections and his own analytic objects. Too much focus on helping the patient can often result in a Grid column 2 experience of shut down. "This psychic reality is found when O evolves to a point where it can be discerned through sense-impressions." The intersection between infinite and finite can sometimes be captured in words, but here, we remind ourselves of Grotstein's notion of the contact barrier as one of 'selective permeability,' remaining open to O but not being overwhelmed by it to the point of senselessness at the same time.

In my view, Vermote's text particularly shines when, like Bion, he demonstrates what he has learned by reading outside of the field of psychoanalysis. We know of course that Bion invoked Kant, Plato and the Christian mystics as an experiential underpinning to the theory of O as a-sensuous and unknowable. If we try to grasp O by perception or understanding, we lose contact with it, like a camera which becomes useless when light leaks in. Here, Vermote (2019, p. 150) brings in material from Nicolas of Cusa, a neo-Platonic thinker from the 15th century. Following Eckhart, he advocated a 'doctrine of ignorance,' where speculation is needed, a mixture of science and imagination to "apprehend the unknowable God and infinity." One focuses one's analytic attention on psychoanalytic objects that evolve from the hallucinatory layer—one can attain illumination by a beam of darkness. The analyst maintains a meditative stance, tolerating the dark and un-knowing, being patient enough to allow for something to arise from the infinite layer. One may be taken by strong visual images, as the undifferentiated becomes differentiated and experienced. Bion is not here advocating mystical experience so much as he is looking for "a psychic change within the well-defined psychoanalytic frame, which is different from a religious experience" (ibid.).

Bion reminded us in the 1967 *Los Angeles Seminars* that, in states hovering just above sleep, the analyst sometimes slips into an actual state of sleep during a session. The margin between the two can be quite narrow, this capacity for dreaming along and not actually falling into an actual sleep state. Putting the patient's thoughts into 'verbo-visual' terms involves putting other elements out of focus. It takes a lot of discipline to "de-focus—peripheralize the irrelevant without falling into the opposite error of permanent insensibility" (Bion, 1991, p. 232). It is why Bion talked about the opacity of memory, desire and understanding This is what Bion had in mind when he said that every time we see a patient, it must feel like it is for the first time. Remaining in uncertainty and unknowingness can help us get a glimpse of O.

And yet, what wonders await us if we can take into account but overcome sensuous experience—Vermote's (2019, p. 157) writing is quite vibrant here: "Our mind defends itself against the Medusan, petrifying qualities of our not-knowing and not-being-able to know. It is difficult to imagine that we originate from and are surrounded by nothingness." We are ordinarily bound by our minds as prisons when we aim at mastery over the physical world. We tend to close off our intuitions behind a 'veil of illusions' that we create to feel secure. When we come into contact with O, which is like the sublime, we momentarily are horrified, then delight in being "confronted with overwhelming, awe-inspiring natural phenomena, like seeing a star-spangled sky" (ibid.).

In his concluding remarks to *Attention and Interpretation*, Vermote regards Bion's last epistemological work culminating with T(O) as a radical new way of understanding psychic change. In so doing, he continues to also emphasize both T(K) and T(O) as a "dual track of psychic functioning and change" (Vermote, 2019, p. 166). After completing *Attention and Interpretation*, Bion did not develop any new concepts. He subsequently experimented with "style, form and clinical practice" (ibid.)

Chapter 15

Bion's *Clinical Seminars*

An Implicit Method of Clinical Inquiry
(1967–78)—A New Wave of Bion Studies?

Introduction

After 1967 when he presented, lectured and supervised at so many analytic societies, such as those in Los Angeles, Buenos Aires, São Paulo, Brasilia, London, Rome, New York City and Paris, Bion had reached a point where his clinical theorizing days were by and large behind him—and he now moved to distill what he had learned from so many years of professional practice as a psychoanalyst and consultant. Since much of the clinical and supervisorial work Bion did in these later years has been published in the last decade, one new organizing question can be asked: how did Bion go about distilling what was essential to his mature clinical style? How did Bion go about disseminating some of his centrally important ideas for the practicing analyst in the *Clinical Seminars* (1967–1978)? I maintain that this now available clinical work represents a potential 'new wave' of Bion studies, a way in which we can further our understanding of the practical ways in which he understood and articulated the clinical and supervisorial situations. As such, this clinical work represents a new frontier for creative exploration and fresh research, some of the results of which I have discussed in previous chapters (cf. Chapters 11, 12 and 13).

With the exception of Bion's 'Notes on Memory and Desire,' a paper that he wrote and rewrote a number of times (Bion, 1965, 1967a, 1967b, 1970) he was disinclined to write much about psychoanalytic technique. Without offering some sort of systematic approach to technique, as some of his colleagues like Betty Joseph (1989) would make a point of doing, he had no interest in heading up a school or interpretive approach that others could follow (Aguayo, 2011). Although many colleagues would have been interested in studying with him, he formed no school of the kind that Mrs. Klein had done. For those who are interested in learning from Bion's practical work, studying some of his many cases and supervisorial examples has been meaningful.

The Anglo-American research group described in Chapter 5 posited that Bion had a particular way of thinking about clinical material that can be

DOI: 10.4324/9781003364795-19

abstracted from the plentiful examples we now have from the late *Clinical Seminars* period (Aguayo, Hinshelwood, Dermen and Abel-Hirsch, in press). I focus here on two examples from the *Clinical Seminars*, so we can chart a bit of Bion's late distillation of his clinical methods. Our group has for some time now sifted through Bion's actual clinical work from all periods of his published work to see if we could find and describe its defining patterns. After an extensive survey of many of his clinical examples, we evolved the idea of an 'Implicit Method of Clinical Inquiry' (or IMCI). It pertains to a loosely saturated concept based on a clinically inductive method of reasoning—the analyst orients to session material with an organizing set of preconceptions and gathers clinical data, transforming it into analytic concepts, which may shed light on particular classes of patients. With enough concepts, they can form models and theories, which can be further tested. Our research group asked: what was Bion's cast of mind like and what were the enduring features of his IMCI?

Bion's IMCI is a Janus-faced model, a set of concepts that extend to the technical interventions an analyst might make with his patients on the one side, and on the other, how these clinical concepts inform the building of theoretical revisions. One illustrative paper is Bion's (1958a) 'On Arrogance' (cf. Chapter 5). Given the analyst's commitment to verbal communication and understanding with severely disturbed patients, what if the patient has alternative ways, say elliptical speech and motoric/sensory gestures of making his states of mind known? The patient could experience the analyst as a projective identification denying figure, in short, an obstructive object. The analyst's failure to recognize the patient's need to communicate in such a different fashion could also contribute to the analyst's actually becoming an obstructive object as well. These clinical findings led to a fresh theoretical understanding of the Oedipus myth: if the analyst's epistemological task is to inquire and establish the psychic truth of the patient's living emotional experience, this commitment can and does elicit varying responses from patients—cooperative, conflictual and even obstructive. The analyst's epistemological task is one form of disciplined curiosity. These perspectival experiences give Bion's IMCI additional dexterity, as there can be different aspects at play: it encompasses traditional countertransference, where the analyst might be contributing to acting like an obstructive object; it incorporates Kleinian ideas about envy, in which the patient's resentment of the analyst's sanity (especially when making links) can render him obstructive to furthering the aims of enquiry in the analysis; and of course, situations in which both partners can contribute to obstructing the overall aims of inquiry.

There is of course an important caveat here: I maintain that Bion's method is implicit because he never clearly set out more than a bare outline of his psychoanalytic technique (Bion, 1965, 1967a, 1967b, 1970). To further complicate matters, we simply haven't had sufficient clinical examples until these past few years in order to make a thorough investigation of how his method of inquiry might be described. After years of theorizing, and along with his move to the United States, where his ideas were barely known, Bion had to start from the beginning, especially with analysts new to his ideas. As we have seen in the *Clinical Seminars* in Los Angeles of 1967, he lectured to an audience of primarily Freudian analysts who by and large had little familiarity with his ideas (cf. Chapter 12). So, he proceeded from how he oriented to the clinical hour, which he also likened to how he proceeded with initial supervision consultations—without memory and desire. He treated each hour, whether clinical or supervisorial, as if it was a first session. He eschewed getting the patient's background or early history, preferring instead the foreground of recent work, all cast in a rather existential manner. As he memorably stated: "Psychoanalytic observation isn't concerned with what has happened or what will happen, but with what *is* happening" (Bion, 1967a, p. 273). His focus was on the analyst's ideal receiving set of tranquil receptivity, a maximum openness based on the capacity to tolerate mystery and doubt, something he also realized that it was easier said than done.

In the ensuing years, Bion was then afforded the opportunity to work through his innovations in theory and technique through his visits to different analytic cultures throughout the world, all with their own distinctive local cultures and assumptions about the analytic process. Since our focus lies in outlining what we have learned about Bion's IMCI, we concentrate on those late *Clinical Seminars* that shine a light on how Bion worked in the clinical and supervisorial situation. We thus do not focus here on those *Clinical Seminars* that primarily consisted of lectures on psychoanalysis and culture, philosophical and literary concerns (e.g., the *Italian Seminars*, 1977; the *New York Seminars*, 1977; the *Tavistock Seminars*, 1978 as well as the *Paris Seminars*, 1978).

Bion's Implicit Method of Clinical Inquiry: Technical Aspects

I start by looking at how Bion's IMCI maps out in examining a detailed example of his work as a supervisor. Here I draw upon the work of my colleague, Nicola Abel-Hirsch. Since Bion noted that he treated all first sessions, whether they were for patients seeking analysis or colleagues seeking supervision, as essentially the same, we take an example now from Bion's work as a supervisor. We are fortunate to now have extensive examples of his work as a supervisor (e.g., the *Los Angeles Seminars* of 1967; and *Bion in Brazil* in the 1970s). One way to conceptualize how Bion did such work: he deployed one of four modalities as a consultant to presented material.

Modality 1: He both talked with the presenter and audience in discussing general principles of technique. These ideas were general and meant to be taken as orienting principles for the workaday analyst (e.g., the analyst generally did well to not ask questions of his patient).

Modality 2: He spoke with the presenter about his specific case, as an attempt to expand the current meaning of the material discussed in the supervision. This dyadic discussion could entail exchanges between the presenting supervisee and his patient and/or the supervisee and questions posed by Bion himself. Here, Bion was case-specific, taking up the details of the session presented for comment.

Modality 3: He could make conjectures that went beyond the clinical material presented, positing deep, unconscious themes in the material under discussion. Here, Bion deployed clinical intuition, venturing something about the patient's deeply unconscious or enduring underlying sense of himself—or addressing what may appeared in plain sight, such as conscious everyday misperceptions.

Modality 4: Bion at times addressed the small or large groups he was working with. What were their sharable impressions of the material? Were they a sort of active/listening group whose views could shed important light on the material discussed?

Of course, while Bion could also mix these various modalities, he generally established one of the above-mentioned modalities as the key to the session. He varied his comments according to circumstance and how he heard the material.

Bion's *Supervision in Los Angeles* (1967)

We have an extensive supervision that Bion conducted with a small group of Los Angeles analysts in April, 1967. The patient, Mr. X, was married and in his thirties, a businessman and manager, who presented with depressive symptoms and difficulties functioning effectively at work. He seemed lost as to how to explain why things went badly for him, resorting at times to sexually provocative behavior and drug usage. Relatively successful at his work, he was also interested in psychoanalysis and had been in analysis for some time when he reported the following dream at a Monday session:

> I was parked in a slum in an alley, where there was criminal activity. I struck up an acquaintance with a man who lived in the area. I felt threatened and thought I could eliminate the danger by leaving the area; yet I stayed. I wandered down the alley and watched this suspicious activity. There was an acquaintance, who I guessed had been and was a politician—and I asked him about this; and as it turned out, the man was running for two offices, Lt. Governor and Governor; yet I couldn't follow this man's explanation of why he was running for two offices at the same time. A third suspicious character appears outside the house; and I was told that he is 'always messing around here.' As my wife and I walked down the alley, some Black boys appeared on a roof walkway, a

connection between two buildings, and they checked out my wife, a 'babe' that they were going to get. My wife and I ran away down the alley into an all-night liquor store run by Black girls. When we relayed the threat to them, they were told that the police had already been called; it was quite customary. I wondered if I should wait for the police or run to his car. How would I proceed with my wife? I was confused as to what to do …. The police were there supervising some demolition of a structure, or doing construction work rather than police work. The patient enjoyed the 'unusual character' of the slum area.

(Bion, 2013, pp. 108–110)

In his associations, Mr. X regarded the politician as a 'confident person,' who was laying plans for things that would come about. The third character looked like a 'trashy Southerner,' reminiscent of the character Popeye in William Falkner's novel, *Sanctuary*. Mr. X wondered if the politician was a 'grandiose part' of himself, someone who sought spurious methods for writing off expenses (e.g., building lobster traps for a business he did not intend to start, but simply as a way to write off his sea diving expenses). He recalled meeting a down and out Southerner, someone convicted of second-degree burglary, a person he felt indifferent towards.

In examining how Bion (2013, p. 113) oriented to this clinical material, he deployed modality 1 at the outset: he asked his colleagues how they wanted to proceed, mentioning that he was in the position of some advantage—he was only in the position of hearing the material for the first time, whereas the presenter and his colleagues had the extra burden of previous discussions and experiences with the patient. He emphasized the general point of hearing the material fresh for the first time. In a very practical way, he was not hampered by either memory or desire, but simply listening to the material as it was presented. He quoted (as he did on other occasions) Freud's famous 1916 letter to Lou Andreas-Salomé, where he discussed his analytic work as one where he threw a 'beam of intense darkness' onto an obscure and unilluminated spot—the point of any analytic interpretation was to shed light on what is unknown and not clearly understood.

While Bion conveyed a sense of listening to the group's associations to the material (Modality 4), his primary interest remained with what he himself made of the material, and in this instance, the enduring psychic reality of Mr. X's underlying sense of himself, his enduring state of mind. Generally in these sorts of one-off supervision sessions, Bion moved quickly to establish a general hypothesis of how he assessed the patient's invariant style of relating, something of a pattern that the analyst might be able to see across a variety of different situations. It also provided the group with a stimulus for further discussion.

To Bion's summary clinical conclusions, mainly cast in Modalities 2 and 3, Mr. X was perpetually doubtful—and while he physically attended his analysis, he had yet to decide whether he wanted to 'be' in analysis. The new analytic week offered him another opportunity to wrestle with this question—in one respect, while he was there to be seen, he effected a number of various defensive maneuvers to escape psychic and emotional detection. On the one hand, he accorded tremendous emotional legitimacy to attending an analysis with a respectable and well-regarded analyst. Yet on the other hand, as his dream seemed to indicate, he psychically preferred the company of seedy people in suspicious circumstances, evincing interest in forbidden and secretive anal activities (e.g., lurking around in dirty alleys, asking questions about the secret rat torture and anal punishments in Freud's Rat Man case) all the while fearing being caught doing so. In assessing this patient for analysis, Bion (2013, p. 115) felt he would be in "for trouble," "plenty of difficulty," but that he would take the patient in for psychoanalytic treatment, in a full-term, open-ended five times a week format that would last for a long time.

Bion's working hypothesis here was that Mr. X had effected what he termed a 'bogus cure,' an ever-shifting (and shifty) set of maneuvers where he kept himself and his objects in perpetual doubt. Since he simply couldn't make up his mind who and what he wanted to be, Mr. X suffered a profound split: he disavowed his intense interest in his seedy pursuits yet felt stigmatized and sullied by them in his attempts to wear the veneer of social respectability. Simply put: Mr. X could not decide who he wanted to be, both inside and outside his analysis. He appeared more narcissistically self-adhered than bonded emotionally to the analyst, drawn on the one hand towards illicit and illegal activities, yet quite apprehensive about this, which led to the desire to pass in polite society as legitimate and respectable.

When asked by a group member what interpretative intervention Bion might make, he responded by focusing what he termed (from Freud's (1916, pp. 312–313) letter to Lou Andreas Salomé) a "shaft of darkness on the covered activity." Mr. X hid in plain sight looking for company where his complaints and his *modus operandi* wouldn't be detected. The 'bogus cure' was realized "by wearing a disguise to fit in with his peers" (Bion, 2013, p. 116). He needed to get away (inside and outside his analysis) with delinquent activity while passing as respectable. Yet this profound split with his external objects also appeared inside the analysis as well. In other words, his self-description as 'grandiose' also reflected a suspicious and negative transference view of the analyst. Was the analyst like the police in the dream, associated with doing constructive work, or would Mr. X himself be caught as one of the suspicious characters and arrested? His compromise solution seemed to be to camouflage himself as a member of a criminal class but hiding at the same time as respectable. Bion was struck by how Mr. X looked for the right crowd so he wouldn't be noticed as being a delinquent person.

In coming to such summary statements, Bion's aim was to provide an incisive yet clinically useful working clinical hypothesis for the group's further consideration. I submit that this is a representative example of how Bion supervised: assessing only the material presented in an existential, one-off way, so that the experiential invariants of the patient's enduring way of experiencing himself might be approximated and thus provide further material for exploration and discussion.

Bion's *Supervision in Brasilia* (1975)

To another example: in 1975, both Bion and his wife were invited to spend the month of April in Brasilia, during which time he worked with groups and individuals, lectured at the university and took part in panel discussions. The occasion of this clinical supervision was a gathering of a small group of analysts. I designate the presenting analyst as 'P' and the patient as 'Y.'

'P' presented a session from his practice today—a woman who has consistently refused to lie down on the couch instead sat, complaining of feeling agitated and dizzy. 'P' linked her runaway thoughts with a fear of a runaway body over which she had no control. 'Y' responded concretely, as if 'P' could prevent her from moving about. Bion called attention to the fact that 'Y' was with 'P' voluntarily; 'P' could not make her attend or leave his office. Further inquiry revealed that the patient seemed to think that the analyst *was* controlling her mind and her movement.

Bion then clarified further questions and addressed his colleagues: how would any analyst feel with this patient? Would he want to know more, or not see her at all? In response to the questions asked by 'P' of 'Y,' Bion raised the general technique issue of not asking questions, preferring instead to sit with the patient in her distress (Modality 1). Bion realized that while he could stand sitting in silence, perhaps the patient would feel unduly agitated—and thus walk out. There was the separate question of what the patient feels they can actually stand.

He then addressed the case-specific aspects of the material presented. He questioned why it was that she experienced being in the analytic space as one that was binding her freedom of movement. Bion nonetheless went on to suggest what he thought about saying to the patient. He pointed out the various options as to how she could occupy space in the room—and more than that, her psychic freedom to shape her environment in whatever way she felt most conducive to her needs. The interest was in watching what use 'Y' made of the analytic space. The couch has been there all along—what was occurring that made her discover it (again) today, all to the point that she would consider leaving the session?

Bion then came to another general point: every session is really a first session. Although the patient and analyst come to know each other in some sort of regular way, that was no reason to keep the situation in analysis static. "One is really putting pressure on the patient to grow up, not remain a baby or a patient or a neurotic or a psychotic forever" (Bion, 1975, p. 3). Besides expecting fees and punctuality, the analyst expected some improvement

(Modality 1). But he made the point that we also expect that the analyst would keep improving as well, all of which is made more possible when a space was left open to learn something new. This was one the practical reasons that the analyst interpreted the patient's need to make him or her appear omniscient, as it fosters passivity and idealization.

In concluding with these final vignettes, I hope that I have captured some of the spirit that this 'new wave' in Bion studies represents. In another sense, it is one of a set of waves that have continued to crest since he originated his groundbreaking work after World War II.

References

Aguayo, J. (2009). 'On Understanding Projective Identification in the Treatment of Psychotic States of Mind: The Publishing Cohort of H. Rosenfeld, H. Segal and W. Bion (1946–1957).' *International Journal of Psychoanalysis*, 90: 69–90.

Aguayo, J. (2011). 'The Role of the Patient's Remembered History and Unconscious Past in the Evolution of Betty Joseph's "Here and Now" Clinical Technique (1959–1989).' *International Journal of Psychoanalysis*, 92: 1117–1136.

Aguayo, J. (2014). 'Bion's "Notes on Memory and Desire"—Its Initial Clinical Reception in the United States: A Note on Archival Material.' *International Journal of Psychoanalysis*, 95: 889–910.

Aguayo, J. (2015). 'Filling in Freud and Klein's Maps of Psychotic States of Mind: Wilfred Bion's Reading of Freud's "Formulations Regarding Two Principles in Mental Functioning".' In G. Legoretta and L. Brown (eds.), *Freud's Formulations Regarding Two Principles in Mental Functioning*. IPA Freud Series.

Aguayo, J. (2017). 'The Complete Works of W.R. Bion.' *International Journal of Psychoanalysis*, 98: 221–243.

Aguayo, J. (2018a). 'D.W. Winnicott, Melanie Klein and W.R. Bion: The Controversy over the Nature of the External Object—Holding and Container/Contained (1951–1967).' *Psychoanalytic Quarterly*, October, 2018.

Aguayo, J. (2018b). 'Introduction.' In *Bion in Buenos Aires*, ed. J. Aguayo, L. Pistener de Cortinas and A. Regeczkey. London: Routledge, pp. xxi–xxv.

Aguayo, J. (2022). 'Reappraising John O. Wisdom's Critique of W.R. Bion's Learning from Experience at a Meeting of the British Psychoanalytical Society—17 October 1964.' *International Journal of Psychoanalysis*, 103: 350–367.

Aguayo, J. and Regeczkey, A. (2016). 'Rethinking the role of small-group collaborators and adversaries in the London Kleinian development (1914–1968).' *Psychoanalytic Quarterly*, 85: 695–725.

Aguayo, J., Hinshelwood, R.D., Dermen, S. and Abel-Hirsch, N. (in press). *Bion in the Consulting Room: A Method of Clinical Enquiry*. London: Routledge.

Anzieu, D. (1989). 'Beckett and Bion.' *International Review of Psychoanalysis*, 16: 163–169.

Beckett, S. (2009). *The Letters of Samuel Beckett*. Vol. 1: 1929–1940. Cambridge: Cambridge University Press.

Bion, W.R. (1948). 'Group Methods of Treatment.' In W.R. Bion, *The Complete Works of W.R. Bion* (or *CWB*), IV. London: Karnac, pp. 61–70.

Bion, W.R. (1950[1967]). 'The Imaginary Twin.' In W.R. Bion, *Second Thoughts: Selected Papers on Psycho-Analysis*. New York: Basic Books.

Bion, W.R. (1951). 'Letter to Francesca Bion.' In *The Complete Works of W.R. Bion*, Vol. II. London: Karnac, pp. 93–94.

Bion, W.R. (1952). 'Group Dynamics: A Review.' *International Journal of Psychoanalysis*, 33: 235–247.

Bion, W.R. (1954). 'Notes on a Theory of Schizophrenia.' *International Journal of Psychoanalysis*, 35: 113–118. Also in: *Second Thoughts*, pp. 23–35.

Bion, W.R. (1955a). 'Language and the Schizophrenic.' In M. Klein, P. Heimann and R. Money-Kyrle (eds.), *New Directions in Psycho-Analysis*. London: Tavistock Publications, pp. 220–239.

Bion, W.R. (1955b). 'On Group Dynamics: A Re-View.' In M. Klein, *et al.* (eds.), *New Developments in Psychoanalysis*. London: Tavistock Publications, reprinted in: W.R. Bion (1961). *Experiences in Groups*. New York: Basic Books, pp. 141–191.

Bion, W.R. (1956). 'Development of Schizophrenic Thought.' *International Journal of Psychoanalysis*, 37: 339–343. Also in: *Second Thoughts*, pp. 36–42.

Bion, W.R. (1957). 'Differentiation of the Psychotic from Non-Psychotic Personalities.' *International Journal of Psychoanalysis*, 38: 266–275. Also in: *Second Thoughts*, pp. 43–64.

Bion, W.R. (1958a). 'On Arrogance.' *International Journal of Psychoanalysis*, 39. Also in: *Second Thoughts*, pp. 86–92.

Bion, W.R. (1958b). 'On Hallucination.' *International Journal of Psychoanalysis*, 39. Also in: *Second Thoughts*, pp. 65–85.

Bion, W.R. (1959). 'Attacks on Linking.' *International Journal of Psychoanalysis*, 40: 308–315.

Bion, W.R. (1961). *Experiences in Groups and Other Papers*. New York: Basic Books.

Bion, W.R. (1962a). 'The Psychoanalytic Theory of Thinking.' *International Journal of Psychoanalysis*, 43: 306–310.

Bion, W.R. (1962b). *Learning from Experience*. London: Heinemann. Reprinted in paperback, London: Maresfield Reprints, H. Karnac Books (1984).

Bion, W.R. (1963). *Elements of Psycho-Analysis*. London: William Heinemann Medical Books.

Bion, W.R. (1965). *Transformations*. London: William Heinemann Medical Books.

Bion, W.R. (1966). 'Catastrophic Change.' *Bulletin of the British Psychoanalytical Society*, 5: 13–25. It also appears as 'Container and Contained Transformed,' Chapter 12 in: W.R Bion (1970), *Attention and Interpretation*.

Bion, W.R. (1967a). 'Notes on Memory and Desire.' *The Psychoanalytic Forum*, 2: 272–273;279–290.

Bion, W.R. (1967b). *Second Thoughts: Selected Papers on Psycho-Analysis*. London: Heinemann.

Bion, W.R. (1970). *Attention and Interpretation*. London: Karnac.

Bion, W.R. (1975). Brasilia Seminars. In *Clinical Seminars and Other Works*. London: Karnac.

Bion, W.R.(1977a). *A Memoir of the Future*. London:Karnac.

Bion, W.R.(1977b). *The Italian Seminars*. London:Karnac.

Bion, W.R. (1990). *Brazilian Lectures: 1973, Sao Paulo; 1974, Rio de Janeiro/Sao Paulo*. London: Karnac. The *1973 Sao Paulo Lectures* also appear in Bion (2014a), Vol. VII.

Bion, W.R. (1992). *Cogitations*. London: Karnac.

Bion, W.R. (2013). *The Los Angeles Seminars and Supervision*, eds. J. Aguayo and B. Malin. London: Karnac.

Bion, W.R. (2014). *The Complete Works of W.R. Bion*. London: Karnac, 16 Volumes.

Bion, W.R. (2017). *Bion in Brazil: Supervisions and Commentaries*, eds. J.A. Juanquiera de Mattos, G. de Mattos Brito and H. Levine. London: Routledge.

Bion, W.R. (2018). *Bion in Buenos Aires*, eds. J. Aguayo, L. Pistener de Cortinas and A. Regeczkey. London: Routledge.

Bion, W.R., Rosenfeld, H. and Segal, H. (1961). 'Melanie Klein.' *International Journal of Psychoanalysis*, 42: 4–8.

Bion Talamo, P.Borgogno, F. and Merciai, S.A. (eds.) (2000). *W.R. Bion: Between Past and Future*. London: Karnac.

Bléandonu, G. (1994). *Wilfred Bion, His Life and Works, 1897–1979*. London: Free Association Books.

Bloom, H. (1973). *The Anxiety of Influence: A Theory of Poetry*. Oxford: Oxford University Press.

Britton, R. (1989). 'The Missing Link: Parental Sexuality in the Oedipus Complex.' In R. Britton, E. O'Shaughnessy, M. Feldman and J. Steiner, J. (eds.), *The Oedipus Complex Today*. London: Routledge.

Britton, R. (1992). 'Keeping Things in Mind.' In R. Anderson (ed.), *Lectures on Klein and Bion*. London: Routledge, pp. 102–113.

Britton, R. (1998). *Belief and Imagination: Explorations in Psychoanalysis*. London: Routledge.

Britton, R. (2003). *Sex, Death and the Superego*. London: Karnac.

Britton, R. (2008). 'The Baby and the Bathwater.' Unpublished paper given at James Grotstein Annual Lecture, Los Angeles, California, 9 February 2008.

Britton, R. (2013). 'Commentary on Three Papers by W.R. Bion.' *Psychoanalysis Quarterly*, 311–321.

Britton, R. and Steiner, J. (1994). 'Interpretation: Selected Fact or Overvalued Idea?' *International Journal of Psychoanalysis*, 75: 1069–1078.

Brown, L. (2012). 'Bion's Discovery of Alpha Function: Thinking under Fire on the Battlefield and in the Consulting Room.' *International Journal of Psychoanalysis*, 93: 1191–1214.

Civitarese, G. (2008). 'Immersion versus Interactivity and the Analytic Field.' *International Journal of Psychoanalysis*, 89: 279–298.

Civitarese, G. (2014). *The Necessary Dream: New Theories of Technique and Interpretation in Psychoanalysis*. London: Karnac.

Civitarese, G. (2015). 'Transformations in Hallucinosis and the Receptivity of the Analyst.' *International Journal of Psychoanalysis*, 96: 1091–1116.

Civitarese, G. (2019). 'The Concept of Time in Bion's "A Theory of Thinking".' *International Journal of Psychoanalysis*, 100: 182–205.

Etchegoyen, H. (1982). 'The Relevance of Here and Now Transference Interpretation for the Reconstruction of Early Psychic Development.' *International Journal of Psychoanalysis*, 63: 65–75.

Etchegoyen, H. and Zysman, S. (2005). 'Melanie Klein in Argentina: Beginnings and Development.' *International Journal of Psychoanalysis*, 86: 869–894.

Ferro, A. (2005). 'Analyst at Work.' *International Journal of Psychoanalysis*, 86: 1247–1256.

Ferro, A. (2006). 'Clinical Implications of Bion's Thought.' *International Journal of Psychoanalysis*, 87: 989–1003.

Fisher, J. (2009, *unpublished*). '*The Emotional Experience of Container-in-K.*' Unpublished paper given at the Bion in Boston Conference, July, 2009.

Freud, S. (1895[1950]). Project for a Scientific Psychology. *Standard Edition (S.E.)*: 1: 283–397.

Freud, S. (1900). The Interpretation of Dreams. *S.E.*: 5.

Freud, S. (1905). 'Fragment of an Analysis of a Case of Hysteria.' *S.E.* 7: 3–122.

Freud, S. (1911). 'Formulations on the Two Principles of Mental Functioning.' *S.E.* 12: 213–226.

Freud, S. (1912). 'The Dynamics of Transference.' *S.E.* 12: 97–108.

Freud, S. (1914). 'On Narcissism: An Introduction.' *S.E.* 14: 67–102.

Freud, S. (1915). 'The Unconscious.' *S.E.* 14: 159–215.

Freud, S. (1916). 'Letter to Lou Andreas Salomé, 25 May 1916.' In *Letters of Sigmund Freud*, ed. E. Freud. New York: Dover, pp. 312–313.

Freud, S. (1921). 'Group Psychology and the Analysis of the Ego.' *S.E.* 18: 65–144.

Gay, P. (1988). *Freud: A Life for Our Time*. New York: Norton.

Glover, E. (1927). 'The Technique of Psychoanalysis.' *International Journal of Psychoanalysis*, supplement, 3: 1–141.

Grinberg, L. 'Foreword.' In P. Bion Talamo, F. Borgogno and S.A. Merciai (eds.), *W. R. Bion: Between Past and Future*. London: Karnac, p. xx.

Grinberg, L., Sor, D. and Bianchedi, E. (1977). *Introduction to the Work of Bion*. New York: Aronson.

Grosskurth, P. (1986). *Melanie Klein: Her World and Her Work*. New York: Knopf.

Grotstein, J. (1981). *Splitting and Projective Identification*. New York: Aronson.

Grotstein, J. (1983). *Do I Dare Disturb the Universe? A Memorial to W.R. Bion*. London: Karnac.

Guntrip, H. (1965). 'Book Review: "Learning from Experience" by W. Bion.' *International Journal of Psychoanalysis*, 46: 381–385.

Heimann, P. (1950). 'On Countertransference.' *International Journal of Psychoanalysis*, 31: 81–84.

Heimann, P. (1952). 'Certain Functions of Introjection and Projection in Early Infancy.' In M. Klein *et al.*, *Developments in Psychoanalysis*. London: Hogarth.

Hinshelwood, R.D. (2008). 'Melanie Klein and Counter-transference: A Note on Some Archival Material.' *Psychoanalysis and History*, 10: 95–113.

Hinshelwood, R.D. (2019). 'John Rickman Behind the Scenes: The Influence of Lewin's Field Theory on Practice, Countertransference, and W.R. Bion.' *International Journal of Psychoanalysis*, 99: 1409–1423.

Jackson, P. (director) (2018). *They Shall Not Grow Old*. Documentary. Wellington, New Zealand: WingNut Films.

Joseph, B. (1989). *Psychic Equilibrium and Psychic Change: Selected Papers of Betty Joseph*, ed. by M. Feldman and E. Spillius. London: Routledge.

Joseph, B. (2000). 'Agreeableness as an Obstacle.' *International Journal of Psychoanalysis*, 81: 641–649.

Jung, C.G. (1935[1968]). *Analytic Psychology: Its Theory and Practice – The Tavistock Lectures*. New York: Vintage Books.

Keats, J. (1817). 'Letter to George and Thomas Keats, 21 December 1817.' In H.G. Rollins (ed.), *The Letters of John Keats*, Vol. 1. Boston, MA: Harvard University Press, 1958.

Kernberg, O. (1966). 'Structural Derivatives of Object Relations.' *International Journal of Psychoanalysis*, 47: 236–253.

Kernberg, O. (1975). *Borderline Conditions and Pathological Narcissism*. New York: Aronson.

Kernberg, O. (1996). 'Thirty Methods to Destroy the Creativity of Psychoanalytic Candidates.' *International Journal of Psychoanalysis*, 77: 1031–1040.

Klein, M. (1929). 'Personification in the Play of Children.' *International Journal of Psychoanalysis*, 10: 193–204.

Klein, M. (1930). 'The Importance of Symbol Formation in the Development of the Ego.' *International Journal of Psychoanalysis*, 11: 24–39.

Klein, M. (1932). 'The Psychoanalysis of Children.' In *The Writings of Melanie Klein*. Vol. 2. New York: Free Press.

Klein, M. (1946). 'Notes on Some Schizoid Mechanisms.' *International Journal of Psychoanalysis*, 27: 99–110.

Klein, M. (1952). 'Notes on Some Schizoid Mechanisms.' In M. Klein *et al.* (eds.), *Developments in Psychoanalysis*. London: Hogarth.

Klein, M. (1957). 'Envy and Gratitude.' In *The Writings of Melanie Klein*. Vol. 3. New York: Free Press, 1975.

Klein, M. (1961). 'Narrative of a Child Analysis.' In *The Writings of Melanie Klein*. Vol. 4. New York: Free Press, 1975.

Klein, M. (2017). *Lectures on Technique by Melanie Klein*, ed. J. Steiner. London: Routledge.

Klein, M., Heimann, P. and Money-Kyrle, R. (1955). *New Directions in Psychoanalysis: The Significance of Infant Conflicts in Pattern of Adult Behavior*. London: Tavistock.

Makari, G. (2008). *Revolution in Mind: The Creation of Psychoanalysis*. New York: Harper.

Malin, M. (2021). 'R.B. Braithwaite's Influence on Bion's Epistemological Contributions.' *International Journal of Psychoanalysis*, 102: 653–670.

Mawson, C. (2014). 'Introduction.' In W.R. Bion, *Learning from Experience*, in *The Complete Works of W.R. Bion*, IV. London: Karnac, pp. 249–257.

Meltzer, D. (1967). *The Psychoanalytic Process*. London: Heineman. Reproduced in 2008 by Karnac. The Harris-Meltzer Trust Series.

Miller, I. (2013). *Beckett and Bion: The (Im)patient Voice in Psychotherapy and Literature*. London:Routledge.

Ogden, T.H. (1994). 'The Analytic Third: Working with Intersubjective Clinical Facts.' *International Journal of Psychoanalysis*, 75: 3–19.

Ogden, T.H. (2004). 'On Holding and Containing, Being and Dreaming.' *International Journal of Psychoanalysis*, 85: 1349–1364.

Ogden, T.H. (2015). 'Intuiting the Truth of What's Happening: On Bion's "Notes on Memory and Desire".' *Psychoanalysis Quarterly*, 84: 285–306.

O'Shaughnessy, E.(2005). 'Whose Bion?' *International Journal of Psychoanalysis*, 86: 1523–1528.

Pick, D. and Milton, J. (1994). 'Interview with Betty Joseph.' Melanie Klein Trust website.

Rey, J.H.(1979). 'Schizoid Phenomena in the Borderline.' In E.Spillius (ed.), *Melanie Klein Today: Development in Theory and Practice*, Vol. I. London:Routledge, pp. 203–229.

Rickman, J. (2003). *No Ordinary Psychoanalyst: The Exceptional Contributions of John Rickman*. London: Routledge.

Rodman, F.R. (2003). *Winnicott: His Life and Work.* Cambridge: DeCapo Press.

Roper, M. (2012). 'Beyond Containing: World War I and the Psychoanalytic Theories of Wilfred Bion.' In S. Alexander and B. Taylor (eds.), *History and Psyche: Culture, Psychoanalysis and the Past.* Basingstoke: Palgrave Macmillan, pp. 129–147.

Rosenfeld, H. (1952). 'Notes on the Psycho-Analysis of the Superego Conflict in an Acute Schizophrenic Patient.' *International Journal of Psychanalysis*, 33: 111–131.

Rosenfeld, H. (1964). 'On the Psychopathology of Narcissism: A Clinical Approach.' *International Journal of Psychoanalysis*, 45: 332–337.

Rosenfeld, H. (1965). *Psychotic States: A Psycho-Analytical Approach.* London: International Universities Press.

Sanfuentes, M. (2003). 'Group Dynamics: A Re-view.' In R. Lipgar and M. Pines (eds.), *Building on Bion: Roots: Origins and Context of Bion's Contributions to Theory and Practic.* Philadelphia, PA: Jessica Kingsley Publishers, pp. 118–131.

Segal, H. (1957). 'Notes on Symbolic Formation.' *International Journal of Psychoanalysis*, 38: 391–397.

Segal, H. (1964). *Introduction to the Work of Melanie Klein.* London: Heinemann Medical Books.

Showalter, E. (1985). *The Female Malady: Women, Madness and English Culture, 1830–1980.* New York: Pantheon Books.

Spillius, E. (2007). *Encounters with Melanie Klein: Selected Papers of Elizabeth Spillius.* London: Routledge.

Steiner, J. (1994). 'Patient-Centered and Analyst-Centered Interpretations: Some Implications of Containment and Countertransference.' *Psychoanalytic Inquiry*, 14: 406–422.

Steiner, J. (2017). 'Introduction.' In J. Steiner (ed.), *Lectures on Technique by Melanie Klein.* London: Routledge, pp. 1–23.

Steiner, R. (1989). 'On Narcissism: The Kleinian Approach.' *Psychiatric Clinics of N. America*, 12: 741–770.

Strachey, J. (1934). 'The Nature of the Therapeutic Action of Psychoanalysis.' *International. Journal of Psychoanalysis*, 15: 117–146.

Symington, J. and Symington, N. (1996). *The Clinical Thinking of Wilfred Bion.* London: Routledge.

Tennyson, A., Lord. (1854[1969]). 'The Charge of The Light Brigade.' In *The Poems of Tennyson.* London: Longmans.

Vermote, R. (2014). 'On Bion's Grid.' A Pre-Conference Workshop Presentation at the Bion International Conference, Los Angeles, California, October 23, 2014. Notes compiled from a recording by J. Aguayo and edited by C. Harrang.

Vermote, R. (2019). *Reading Bion.* London: Routledge.

Willoughby, R. (2006). 'W.R. Bion.' In R. Skelton (ed.), *Encyclopedia of Psychoanalysis.* Edinburgh: Edinburgh University Press.

Winnicott, D.W. (1945). 'Primitive Emotional Development.' In *Through Pediatrics to Psycho-Analysis.* New York: Basic Books, pp. 145–156.

Winnicott, D.W. (1953). 'Transitional Objects and transitional phenomena: A study of the first not-me possession.' *Internatinal Journal of Psychoanalysis*, 34: 89–97.

Winnicott, D.W. (1955). 'Winnicott Letter to W.R. Bion, 7 October 1955.' In *The Collected Works of D.W. Winnicott*, Vol. 5 (2016). Oxford: Oxford University Press, pp. 83–87.

Winnicott, D.W. (1960). 'The Theory of the Parent Infant Relationship.' *International Journal of Psychoanalysis*, 41: 585–595.

Winnicott, D.W. (2017). *The Collected Works of D.W. Winnicott.* L. Caldwell and H. T. Robinson, eds. Oxford: Oxford University Press.

Wisdom, J.O. (1964). 'Dr. Bion's Theories of Function and Thinking.' Paper presented at a meeting of the Imago Group on 14 April 1964; and at the British Psycho-analytical Society, 17 October 1964. This paper appeared slightly revised as: 'Forty Years of Metapsychology.' In J.S. Grotstein (1981) *Do I Dare Disturb the Universe? A Memorial to Wilfred R. Bion.* Beverly Hills, CA: Caesura Press, pp. 601–624.

Index

Printed in Great Britain
by Amazon

Printed in Great Britain
by Amazon

62589414R00107